DOING ACCESSIBLE
SOCIAL RESEARCH
A Practical Guide

Daniela Aidley and Kriss Fearon

D1612659

First published in Great Britain in 2021 by

Policy Press, an imprint of
Bristol University Press
University of Bristol
1-9 Old Park Hill
Bristol
BS2 8BB
UK
t: +44 (0)117 954 5940
e: bup-info@bristol.ac.uk

Details of international sales and distribution partners are available at
policy.bristoluniversitypress.co.uk

British Library Cataloguing in Publication Data
A catalogue record for this book is available from the British Library

ISBN 978-1-4473-5108-5 hardcover
ISBN 978-1-4473-5109-2 paperback
ISBN 978-1-4473-5112-2 ePub
ISBN 978-1-4473-5111-5 ePdf

Cover design: Qube Design Associates, Bristol
Front cover image: shutterstock 1563808432

Bristol University Press and Policy Press use environmentally responsible
print partners.

Printed in Great Britain by CMP, Poole

In loving memory of Gisela Erika Heide

Contents

Contents

List of checklists and tables

Checklists

Chapter 7

Chapter 8

Chapter 9

Tables

Glossary

Ableist, ableism Discrimination or prejudice against disabled people.

Academic beneficiaries Groups of researchers and academics within the field and in other disciplines that will benefit as a result of new research findings, outcomes or methodology.

Academic impact The contribution that research makes to advancing knowledge in the field, and measurement of how well the research is received.

Access fatigue Emotional exhaustion and frustration associated with constantly having to check on or ask for access provisions, taking into account the possibility (based on previous experience) that the information is incorrect, and the resulting barriers this places in the way of participation.

Accountability An ethical approach to conducting research that takes into account both its impact on the research participants and their access to the research findings.

Active accessibility Proactively identifying and then removing barriers to participation, and responding positively when participants disclose their access requirements.

Advisory group A panel formed to give knowledgeable guidance and a degree of oversight to a research project, to ensure it remains on topic, and to give reflections and a steer on research issues as they arise. It is made up of people with relevant experience in the field who can give an informed view.

Aversive ableism Describes how people who would not verbalise ableist prejudice nevertheless may still hold uninformed or stereotyped attitudes about disability, or feel uncomfortable around disabled people, meaning that they treat disabled people differently.

Braiding A methodology for combining different qualitative and arts-based research methods.

Cluster sampling Sampling on the level of item clusters rather than items, for example teams rather than employees, or households rather than residents.

Confirmability Refers to the researcher having recognised and (where possible) limited the extent to which their own personal views and life experience have affected the way that the research has been conducted and ultimately the findings that are presented.

Credibility Describes how well the research reflects participants' experiences.

Debriefing Refers to the researcher informing participants of any deception that was part of the study, outlining why the deception was necessary and what the true nature or research question of the study was.

Dependability The ease with which a researcher outside the study can establish the procedures and processes used to conduct the research, which enable them to evaluate how well it has been conducted.

Economic beneficiaries The groups that will receive economic benefit directly from the research, for example through improved economic performance or increasing efficiency.

Economic impact The benefits of research in terms of economic growth, which could cover skills, innovation, strategy, product development or productivity.

Emancipatory research Research with the explicit aim of campaigning for greater equality for its participants (in this case, disabled people), creating social change and facilitating personal change for everyone taking part.

Exclusion criteria Describe features that mean people do not form part of the research sample.

Homophily The tendency for people to form social groups based on shared characteristics, needs or interests.

Inclusion criteria Describe features the participants must have in order to take part in the research.

Intersectionality 'A lens, a prism, for seeing the way in which various forms of inequality often operate together and exacerbate each other' (Crenshaw, quoted in Steinmetz, K. [2020] 'She coined the term "intersectionality" over 30 years ago. Here's what it means to her today', *Time Magazine*, 20 February. Available at: https://time.com/5786710/kimberle-crenshaw-intersectionality).

Medical model of disability Focuses on a person's impairment rather than on the environment that makes access difficult; sees disability as something that is a medical issue and should be viewed and treated medically.

Microaggressions Brief comments, behaviour and language that convey ignorance, and negative expectations of or negative views about an oppressed group – in this case, disabled people.

Mixed media In the context of this book, a research method comprising similar instruments in different media, such as paper/phone/online.

Non-probability sampling Does not use reliably random selection methods and does not allow for the calculation of an item's probability of inclusion in the sample.

Participatory research Co-designed and co-conducted in collaboration with the research participants, where the intended outcome is to make positive changes to an existing process or setting.

Population The whole group of people that could potentially form part of a social research sample.

Probability sampling The method of sampling is chosen in a way that every item has the same chance of being included in the sample, and that probability can (theoretically) be calculated.

Reflexivity The process of acknowledging and documenting the influence of the researcher on the research data collection and outcomes.

Reliability A strategy for ensuring research quality, evaluated differently in quantitative and qualitative studies. In quantitative methods, it refers to instruments giving accurate readings without making a statement on whether the measurement is appropriate given the circumstances.

Representativeness The extent to which findings from a quantitative study's sample can be applied to the population as a whole.

Research advisors People who have expertise in an area because of their personal life experience, and who can therefore provide a view to a research team on how to conduct and share research, sometimes referred to as 'experts by experience'.

Research impact 'The demonstrable contribution that excellent research makes to society and the economy' (ESRC [Economic and Social Research Council]/UKRI [UK Research and Innovation] [2021] 'What is impact?' Available at: https://esrc.ukri.org/research/impact-toolkit/what-is-impact/).

Respondent validation After the research has been completed, the researcher provides participants with a summary of the research outcomes and asks for their views, to see whether and how far participants corroborate the research findings.

Semantic coding Coding each piece of content according to its function within the document, for example, whether it is a heading, image, paragraph or list.

Simple random sampling Simple selection of participants or sample items by randomisation techniques without regards for strata, clusters, etc.

Snowball sampling   Asking existing/already recruited research participants to recommend subsequent participants, thus quickly extending the potential participant group.

Social beneficiaries   Communities or organisations whose circumstances or practices are improved through changes made as an outcome of research.

Social model of disability   It is the environment, both physical and social, that disables the individual by preventing their full participation in society.

Societal impact   The impact of research on society, for example by changing attitudes, policy or practice in ways that effect people's lives.

Stratified sampling   Drawing from defined strata (subgroups) of the population to make sure all relevant strata are represented in the sample.

Transferability   The extent to which the research findings or the analytic concepts developed within the research can be applied to other research contexts; similar to generalisability in quantitative research.

Triangulation   Using different methods to approach the same research question or variable and to confirm/validate respective findings.

Validity   In quantitative research this refers to the extent to which the way of measuring is appropriate for the variable of interest.

Vignettes   Descriptions of one or more fictional characters who may be using a service, who interact with an organisation, use a product or participate in research.

Acknowledgements and thanks

We would like to thank Catherine Gray, Philippa Grand, Dawn Rushen and Amelia Watts-Jones at Policy Press for their sterling support during the publication process and their patience in dealing with our enquiries and delays. We also want to extend our thanks to the anonymous (to us) readers and reviewers of the book proposal and earlier versions of the manuscript for their kind and helpful feedback. We are very grateful to Kitt Boulton, whose insight was invaluable and whose feedback was poignant and incredibly helpful. Finally, we would like to thank Kate Wood for supporting us in developing the initial book proposal.

Daniela extends her love and gratitude to Dr Jack Aidley for being an amazing husband and partner. Jack's unwavering love and support sustained her in a period of time that saw the two buying and moving into a three-centuries-old farmhouse shortly before Daniela's mum's cancer returned and she passed away in the middle of 2020 – all against the background of the COVID-19 pandemic.

Kriss would like to thank Dr Sally Ruane for her support in developing the idea of mainstreaming accessible research practice, and also to Jennifer Coughlan and SimpleUsability for the opportunity to put some of this guidance into practice, and for sharing reflections on how well it worked.

Introduction

Aim and audience of the book

The starting point for this book is the observation that current research methods and methodologies constitute potential barriers for disabled people to participate in research. It is our experience that, outside research explicitly focusing on disability, accessibility is rarely, if ever, seen as a concern in the research planning stage (see also Berghs et al, 2016). We both feel strongly that, as researchers, it is our responsibility to make research more accessible, both for ethical and methodological reasons, and we want to use our joint expertise to offer practical advice on steps researchers can take to ensure more people can participate, and more voices are heard.

In doing so, we want to make sure that this book is clear and accessible to researchers, particularly those not yet familiar with the current debates surrounding the definitions of and perspectives on disability. Thus, for readers with a background in disability-focused or adjacent research, most of the theoretical considerations in this book will be very familiar. Generally, however, our focus is explicitly on practical advice, and, while we will provide some introduction to key concepts, this will be kept brief. Instead, we will recommend additional sources where key concepts can be explored in the 'Further reading' sections at the end of each chapter.

This book comprises nine chapters. In this chapter, we give a brief overview of disability prevalence globally, and set out the ethical and methodological case for accessibility, particularly in relation to validity and research quality, and the benefits of conducting research in an accessible way. We also introduce the concept of intersectionality and discuss its implications, and we talk about using vignettes in the process of developing research methods.

In Chapter 2 we discuss the distinction between research *on* (disabled) people and research *with* (disabled) people, and the wider implications of this distinction. We discuss the politics and ethics of conducting research with disabled people,[1] and provide an overview of research methods developed specifically for disadvantaged groups, such as, for example, participatory, emancipatory or partnership-led. We look at the importance of using inclusive language and terminology such as the debate between the use of 'disabled people' or 'people with disabilities', and we introduce the concept of active accessibility.

Chapter 3 discusses accessibility as an overall consideration in research design. We start by examining how a research question might touch on questions of accessibility, and how accessibility can be built into the research design through suitable choices of method. We outline which factors may affect participation generally as well as in specific forms of research, such as case studies and longitudinal research, and we talk about sources of support and advice at this stage.

In Chapter 4 we look at developing a sampling approach that allows for recruiting a diverse pool of participants, both in qualitative and quantitative research. We discuss how different types of sampling might pose particular barriers to participation, and how these barriers might be mitigated.

This is followed by Chapter 5, which examines how the recruitment process and communication with (potential) participants can be made more accessible. We provide recommendations on how to reach out to a diverse group of participants. We discuss advertising and recruitment strategies, and deal with the question of how to access a population with specific needs that does not define itself as 'disabled'. As part of the participant recruitment process we explore the issue of emotional labour provided by participants, and how this relates to issues of compensation for participation.

Building on this, Chapter 6 moves on to discuss accessibility in the context of research involving face-to-face interactions with participants, focusing on qualitative research, but not exclusively so. We outline how to select an accessible venue and improve the accessibility of existing venues. We examine a range of face-to-face research methods, such as interviews and focus groups, and discuss how these methods can be adjusted to make participation more accessible.

Following Chapter 6's focus on face-to-face research methods, Chapter 7 focuses on research methods involving no direct face-to-face interaction with participants, such as methods that are conducted via email, the web, video conferencing, phone or messaging services. This includes an overview of accessibility issues related to online survey software as well as a comprehensive discussion of designing and planning accessible surveys (paper-based and digital), and how to test and pilot research before it is launched.

In Chapter 8 we explore how to maximise accessibility when using more than one research method, whether through triangulation or by using mixed methods. The chapter also discusses some of the accessibility issues related to less established research methods, for example photo research, and their advantages and disadvantages.

Last, and following through with the chronological approach, Chapter 9 outlines how to write up and communicate research findings and research resources. In this chapter we discuss how to develop and disseminate information such as research data or student resources in a more accessible format, whether through books or journals or through case studies.

Before we begin, however, we are going to clarify both the concepts we used and also the argument underlying this book.

Disability and impairments: definitions and prevalence

What do we usually think of when reading the term 'disability'? How do we define it? It is quite likely that one of the first images that comes to mind is a person using a wheelchair, or perhaps someone using a cane or being accompanied by a guide dog. Similarly, definitions often make reference to the absence of particular abilities, to a lack of abilities or senses, to an inability to perform certain tasks, a lack of functioning that is either congenital or acquired through illness or accident. All of this is by no means implausible (we will get to the caveats in a moment), and, in fact, we find that most official definitions make reference to these and similar terms. For example, the United Nations (UN) Convention on the Rights of Persons with Disabilities (CRPD) states:

> Persons with disabilities include those who have long-term physical, mental, intellectual or sensory impairments which in interaction with various barriers may hinder their full and effective participation in society on an equal basis with others. (UN, 2006, p 3)

The EU has ratified the CRPD, and thus member states are slowly following. In Germany, for example, people are considered disabled if 'they have physical, mental, cognitive or sensory impairments which in combination with attitude- or environment-based barriers keep them from equal participation in society with a high probability for more than six months' (Sozialgesetzbuch, §2 SGB IX).[2] Outside the EU, individual countries are adjusting their individual definitions. For example, in the UK, '[y]ou're disabled under the Equality Act 2010 if you have a physical or mental impairment that has a "substantial" and "long-term" negative effect on your ability to do normal daily activities'. Here, 'substantial' is defined as 'more than minor or trivial, eg it takes much longer than it usually would to complete a daily task like getting dressed' and 'long-term' 'means 12 months or more'.[3] In the US, relevant legislation is covered by the Americans with Disabilities Act (ADA) 2000: '[U]nder the ADA, you have a disability if you have a physical or mental impairment that substantially limits a major life activity such as hearing, seeing, speaking, thinking, walking, breathing, or performing manual tasks.'[4]

Although these definitions look quite similar, there are some very important differences. Notably, the first two definitions make references to 'impairments which in interaction with [various] barriers may hinder ... participation', whereas the other two definitions refer to impairments having an effect on the individual's life or limiting their activities. This expresses an important distinction, namely whether it is the impairment itself (whether related to, for example, mobility, cognition, mental health or sensory processing) that constitutes the disability, or whether it is encountering barriers *because of* the impairment from which the disability is derived. We see this difference reflected in two of the models used to talk about disability: the medical model and the social model of disability.

Broadly speaking, the **medical model of disability** considers the impairment itself to be the disability. In this model, paraplegia (an impairment of the motor function in the lower extremities) is a disability which, in turn, requires a person to use a wheelchair. In the **social model of disability**, however, it is the environment, such as the lack of wheelchair ramps, doors that are too narrow or a lack of wheelchair spaces on public transport, that disables the individual by preventing their full participation in society. In this model, physical or psychological impairments are not inherently disabling, but are made so by a lack of consideration within society, resulting in lack of accommodation in the environment. That said, these two models are not the only models used in the literature, and Chapter 2 discusses this in more detail.

It is in the spirit of the social model that this book is written as it is precisely those disabling barriers in the research environment that we are trying to help reduce for our participants. We are concerned with barriers to people with a wide range of conditions, including, but not limited to:

- *Cognitive:* impairments of the processing or retaining of information, such as, for example, dyslexia or dyscalculia, attention deficit disorder, autism, learning disabilities (though note the caveat on p 11) or dementia.

- *Motor:* impairments restricting the individual's range of movements, including, but not limited to, the ability to walk or lift or grab things. These may derive from congenital disorders or be acquired through accidents or progressive diseases such as arthritis or motor neurone disease.
- *Other health conditions:* respiratory issues, cardiovascular conditions, auto-immune diseases, etc. This also includes physical impairments leading to fatigue, etc.
- *Sensory:* impairments concerning one or more senses, such as, for example, loss of hearing or Deafness, sensory processing disorder, congenital blindness, autism spectrum disorder, etc.
- *Mental health:* conditions such as anxiety, obsessive-compulsive disorder, eating disorders and bipolar disorder.

This list shows that the range of disabilities is wide, and suitable accommodations can vary widely, too. At the same time, the sheer variety of impairments and potential disabling environments means solutions need to be complex and flexible. It also suggests that familiarity with one type of disability will not necessarily translate into suitable knowledge for a different type of disability – a point made by Barnes and Mercer (2005).

The prevalence of impairments is, perhaps surprisingly, quite high. Globally, the World Health Organization (WHO) estimates that 15.3 per cent of the population have a disability, of which 2.9 per cent 'experience significant difficulties in functioning' (WHO and The World Bank, 2011). Looking at the latter group, rates vary widely across age: the *World Report* finds a prevalence of 0.7 per cent of those aged 14 or under, 2.7 for those aged 15–59, and 10.2 per cent for those aged 60 or over. They also vary across WHO regions: from 2.6 per cent for the Americas to 3.1 per cent for African countries (WHO and The World Bank, 2011). And, of course, they vary between countries. For example, the US Census Bureau (2014) estimates that 27.2 per cent of the American population were living with a disability in 2013/14. In the UK, official figures (from the Office for National Statistics [ONS], 2018) estimate an overall prevalence of 22 per cent of the population in 2018,[5] although these figures are likely to under-report the prevalence, as people living in care or retirement homes were not included.

Statistics only provide a momentary snapshot of disability prevalence, not least because whether disability forms part of an individual's identity can fluctuate because impairments and abilities can fluctuate and shift. An illness can flare up (for example, multiple sclerosis or fibromyalgia), or be well controlled with medication (for example, asthma or diabetes). Some impairments can be compensated or mitigated to various extents (wearing glasses, using an inhaler or insulin, using a wheelchair, using a sign language interpreter). Impairments can be congenital or acquired through accident or illness, and may subsequently be permanent (for example, incurable and/or progressive illnesses) or temporary. A person may have a broken leg and thus be temporarily motor-impaired; an ear infection may lead to temporary hearing loss. Not being disabled is therefore always provisional. Everyone can become temporarily impaired – spraining an ankle, breaking an arm, getting an ear infection. Far from impairments being an isolated issue and one that is only relevant to researchers who explicitly look at research questions relating to the impairment, making research accessible is therefore important for everyone.

Because disability can be temporary and because its effects can substantially fluctuate in severity and impact, getting reliable data on its prevalence is challenging. At the same time, how people perceive themselves and to what extent disability forms a part of their identity can also fluctuate. Not everyone who would formally be categorised as disabled identifies themselves as disabled, and people who may not be formally categorised as being disabled nevertheless may identify as disabled. Therefore, it is important to know the context in which disability figures were collected, that is, whether they are based on self-reporting, or by applying external criteria, such as a formal definition, or by virtue of having used a specific recruitment channel, such as a disability service organisation.

Last, not all disabilities are visible. While using a wheelchair communicates the impairment immediately to the outside observer, other impairments such as, for example, hearing loss and chronic fatigue, and many chronic illnesses such as asthma, diabetes or fibromyalgia, are not immediately visible or obvious and neither are mental health conditions. This frequently adds considerable stress to the individual since they now have to navigate decisions about whether to disclose their impairment (see, for example, Wilton, 2006), and often face additional problems such as others not believing the existence or extent of their illness or doubting the need for accommodations (Stone, 2005; Kattari et al, 2018). Visible impairments, on the other hand, mean that the act or decision of disclosing is not under the individual's control. Sometimes this can mean that the impairment takes front and centre of the interaction (see, for example, Mader et al, 1989; Low, 1996).

The case for accessible research

Participation in society is a human right. In their CRPD, the UN states that 'everyone is entitled to all the rights and freedoms set forth therein, without distinction of any kind', furthermore 'reaffirming the universality, indivisibility, interdependence and interrelatedness of all human rights and fundamental freedoms and the need for persons with disabilities to be guaranteed their full enjoyment without discrimination' (UN, 2006). In fact, the UN defines exclusion as a type of discrimination:

> "Discrimination on the basis of disability" means any distinction, exclusion or restriction on the basis of disability which has the purpose or effect of impairing or nullifying the recognition, enjoyment or exercise, on an equal basis with others, of all human rights and fundamental freedoms in the political, economic, social, cultural, civil or any other field. It includes all forms of discrimination, including denial of reasonable accommodation. (UN, 2006)

Science is a social and political endeavour, and so is participation in research. It follows that, where individuals encounter barriers to participation – such as online surveys that are not screen reader-friendly, phone interviews that exclude participants with auditory impairments, focus groups on premises that are not wheelchair-accessible or paper surveys only conducted with one fixed layout and format – and where these barriers exclude them entirely from participation, they are restricted in exercising their rights and participating in society.

Having said that, let us clarify that by 'exclusion from research' we specifically mean exclusion from *research that is not explicitly focused on disability*. We are not saying that there is no research on disability, impairment or accessibility! There has been much research on these topics – for example, on accessible city planning, or on disability in education or work, such as Baumberg (2015) looking at 'employment latitude', that is, the extent to which education and qualifications affect whether disabled people can respond to changes in the workplace or labour market, or Barnes and Mercer (2005) looking at the social exclusion of people with disabilities. Instead, what we are saying is there is little consideration of accessibility in research where disability or impairment is *not* part of the research question, and, with that, little consideration of the implications for research participation. Such exclusion is rarely intentional:

> Social exclusion in research can be the result of investigators not being "aware" or not choosing to look into the direction of the excluded (Kroll, 2007). Participants are thought of as being "too difficult" or "too hard to find". Investigators may cite tight study budgets, resource and time scarcity that do not allow for extensive accommodations. (Kroll, 2011, p 66)

The prevalence of impairments in the general population is quite high. From a quantitative, methodological perspective this would mean that, where barriers to research participation exclude participants with impairments, a sample can, by definition, no longer be representative.

Preparing with vignettes

While we will begin to discuss specific ways to make research more accessible in Chapter 3, there is one method of helping us plan and design our research methodology that we would like to introduce now, because we will be using it frequently throughout the book, and that is the use of **vignettes**.[6] Vignettes are descriptions of one or more fictional characters who may be using our service, interact with our organisation, use our product or participate in our research. Vignettes represent the kind of people who may be using our services, interact with our organisation, use our product or participate in our research. They are a way of translating theoretical requirements into specific, practical criteria. We use vignettes here and in subsequent chapters to illustrate some of the barriers people might encounter while participating in our research – and to show how to identify and mitigate those barriers in advance.

VIGNETTE

Linden is a market researcher testing a campaign for a high-end touring bike. The client wants to test consumers' reactions to the new print ad, and so Linden has put out a call for participants on a runners' online forum, asking for people who exercise at least three hours a week, who have spent at least €4,000 on their last bike, and who would like to participate in an eye-tracking study. Linden briefly thought about accessibility, but decided

> that this wouldn't be an issue for this study since all participants should be reasonably fit. Today Linden is welcoming the first batch of participants and is confronted with a problem: one of them has his foot in a cast – he broke his foot (in a cycling accident, fittingly). Unfortunately, the office building doesn't have an elevator, and the eye-tracking lab is on the third floor, so Linden is faced with the choice of asking his participant to make his painful way up to the third floor – or to send him away.

Returning to the research and its findings, where a sample is not representative, its validity – and, here, its ecological validity in particular – is at risk, as the findings cannot necessarily be applied to the population the sample purports to represent. There are arguments that representativeness is not always necessary and occasionally even a hindrance, but these arguments are usually either made in a context of research in the natural sciences (see, for example, Rothman et al, 2013), where the focus is on the observation and analysis of physical, biological or chemical processes, or in the context of qualitative research (Polit and Beck, 2010). In quantitative research in the social sciences we should ensure that the findings and any policy decisions based on them are applicable and useful to as many from the underlying population as possible.

VIGNETTE

> Pavati is a senior lecturer at a US university in the Mid West. She is particularly interested in the impact mentoring in the workplace can make on graduate students' transition from university into the workplace. As part of her teaching experience, she has had contact with the accessibility services several times, and is therefore aware that students sometimes require accommodations for their studies – often, this is done in the form of extra time for exams, or, for example, for students with dyslexia, a cover sheet informing the marker not to mark for spelling. Since Pavati would like to interview the graduates several times, both before and during their new roles, neither of those accommodations is suitable for the form of research she is planning. She is therefore unsure which accommodations she might be able to offer to research participants – and whether they are even necessary.

Voices that are not heard cannot inform research or policy – in the words of Kroll (2011, p 66), 'exclusion skews the "evidence-base".

This in turn may affect resource allocation in health and social care systems and wider social policies.' For example, participation in local politics can be nigh on impossible if, as a recent survey found, 40 per cent of local council websites are inaccessible (Digital Leaders, 2018). And the consequences are tangible, and potentially life-threatening. A recent example may well be the implementation of plastic straw bans in a number of larger US cities, for example in Seattle (see, for example, Garrand, 2018) and New York (see, for example, Espinal, 2018), and one that has been effective in the UK from 1 October 2020 (DEFRA and Eustice, 2020). In all of these cases, the suggestions for the ban are rooted in a laudable attempt to cut down on plastic waste, but failed to take into account the needs of disabled people. For many disabled people, there is (as yet) no alternative to plastic straws: paper straws dissolve too fast and constitute a potential choking hazard; metal straws are too inflexible and can cause severe injuries (see, for example, Sharman, 2019); bamboo or glass straws pose a risk of injury to users with little motor control; other reusable straws cannot be sterilised properly or cannot be used for hot drinks (Pepper, 2018; Vallely, nd). Banning plastic straws therefore results in substantial problems for disabled people who need them, and makes it more difficult for them to take part in public life without incurring physical harm. A failure to consult all members of the population and to collect a wide enough range of voices can thus have real, tangible and harmful consequences caused not by malice but by lack of information.

But making research accessible is not just a matter of research quality; it is also a matter of ethical behaviour. In this context we, the authors, acknowledge our privilege as white, well-educated and non-disabled researchers affording us a voice not afforded to others; we acknowledge that this in itself can be an issue (Humphrey, 2000). The oppression of marginalised groups is often perpetuated by putting the burden of educating others onto members of the marginalised group, requiring additional emotional and physical labour, which is usually unpaid. With this book, we want to start meeting the responsibility given to us by our relative privilege by taking on some of that work.

CHECKLIST 1: DO YOU NEED TO CONSIDER ACCESSIBILITY IN YOUR RESEARCH?

☐ Do you send out links to online questionnaires?

☐ Do you use paper questionnaires?

☐ Do you conduct research over the phone or contact participants by phone?

☐ Do you require participants to attend interviews in public places or premises of your choosing?

☐ Do you conduct interviews via video conferencing, phone or face-to-face?

☐ Do you design information material for participant recruitment purposes?

☐ Are you conducting group discussions?

☐ Does your study require participants to participate via several modes (eg, online, paper, face-to-face)?

☐ Does participation in your study entail time commitments over multiple sessions or a longer period of time?

If you answered 'yes' to any of these questions, accessibility is something you need to consider for your research.

Before we proceed, we want to make explicit two aspects of accessibility in research that we are *not* covering in this book. First, this book does not discuss research methods involving children of any age. This is not because we think accessibility is not an issue with children – as the statistics show quite clearly, disability is present at any age. Rather, we think that the ethics of conducting research with children adds a layer of complexity that we cannot do justice to in the scope of this book.

Another omission is research methods with people with intellectual disabilities. This does not imply that people with intellectual disabilities aren't part of the general population or will not be found in a mainstream research setting. While we have cited some research designed to include people with intellectual disabilities, and the checklists contain some recommendations that could make research more inclusive, this aspect of research methods is beyond our expertise. If you are looking at inclusive research, we recommend using focused resources such as the excellent guidance in Nind (2008).

Making research more accessible takes work

Taking accessibility into account at every stage, from conceiving the research question and developing the methodology and the sampling process to disseminating the findings, takes more preparation, more resources, more attention to detail and more effort than continuing with research as usual. Sometimes this might feel exhausting and frustrating, and cause resentment at having to put in more work, the impact of which may not be immediately apparent. We want to acknowledge the frustration that may arise from this. At the same time, we suggest it directly reflects just how much everyday research and work environment still constitute barriers. Any resentment felt therefore needs to be directed at those barriers, not at the people excluded from participation.

We might decide that there is a limit to the time and effort that we can commit into making our research more accessible. Several countries have equality laws that contain the concept of 'reasonable adjustments' or 'reasonable accommodations', aiming to encourage employers to think positively about the changes they can make to make their workplace more disability-friendly. We want to emphasise that decisions about what we can or can't do are an active choice, and this has a number of implications for our research. Part of the purpose of this book is to help make those decisions about what is possible by giving practical guidelines on how to put accessibility into practice.

Why it is not only about disability

While the focus of our book is on making research participation more accessible to participants with disabilities and impairments, we are very much aware that accessibility requires a broader view, also taking into consideration participants' gender, age, class, ethnicity and so on: a woman's experience as a wheelchair user may differ from a man's experience, and a non-binary white person's experience of vision impairment may again differ from a vision-impaired Black man. Crenshaw (1989) used the term **intersectionality** to describe how different axes of oppression, such as, for example, race and gender, can intersect and amplify the experienced oppression. The experience of Black[7] women is different from the experience of white women, and different again from the experience of Black men or Black non-binary people. Quinlan, Bowleg and Ritz's (2014) discussion of how poor women are treated in psychological research is another example of applying the lens of intersectionality, as is Mik-Meyer's (2015) observation that the behaviour of male employees with cerebral palsy was perceived in a feminised way by their colleagues. In a study looking at the socioeconomic disadvantages of disabled people, Kavanagh et al concluded:

> Overall, women with disabilities had slightly elevated odds of living on a low income, not being in paid work and experiencing multiple disadvantage compared to men with disabilities, but experienced similar levels of low education and housing vulnerability.... However, the magnitude of these relative differences was much lower than the same comparisons between women and men. This suggests that gender may be operating in different ways when disability is present. (2015, p 196)

In the context of accessible research, intersectionality also means that making research more accessible for one specific group may at the same time make it more accessible for other groups. For example, offering more than one mode of communication and research participation might make it easier to participate for someone working full-time who cannot take time off for a focus group meeting to participate; ensuring the premises are accessible with lifts available and wide enough door frames also means the premises can be navigated by a parent and their child in a pram; spacing participation sessions out over a longer period of time and offering plenty of breaks means it is easier not only for participants who fatigue more easily but also for those with caring responsibilities and/or very busy working lives. Yet sometimes accommodations are mutually exclusive: lowering the brightness of a document background to reduce glare can make it more difficult for others to read it; for some, making a document accessible means increasing the font size, while for others it means decreasing the font size; and a brightly lit room that provides good visibility can be extremely uncomfortable for participants with sensory processing disorders.

CHECKLIST 2: HOW TO APPROACH ACCESSIBILITY

☐ Keep in mind that impairments are not always visible.

☐ Do not make assumptions as to whether your participants may or may not have impairments because they are of a certain age or work in a particular profession.

☐ Do not assume participants will tell you whether they have an impairment and whether they have any accessibility needs.

☐ Make thinking about accessibility your default setting.

Summary

In this chapter we outlined the overall structure of this book. We then showed how prevalent disability is, across geographical regions as well as across age groups. We introduced different types of disability and the different ways in which disabilities might be categorised. We then argued that accessibility needs to be a key consideration in our research process for both ethical and methodological reasons – and that we need to take a broader view towards accessibility and its intersection with other characteristics.

In Chapter 2, we move on to discuss issues that frequently arise when including disabled people in research. We describe methodological approaches originally designed for researching with disabled people, and we explain what the Universal Design (UD) approach is, and why we have taken this approach in this book.

Notes

[1] We use 'disabled people' rather than 'people with disabilities' as our writing is informed by the British context, where the identity-first approach is more accepted. We acknowledge that in other countries and cultures there are different preferences. For a brief discussion of identity-first vs people-first language, see Chapter 2.

[2] See www.sozialgesetzbuch-sgb.de/sgbix/2.html

[3] www.legislation.gov.uk/ukpga/2010/15/enacted

[4] www.ada.gov/workta.htm

[5] Interestingly, and perhaps poignantly, if anyone tries to access the disability statistics from the 2016/17 Family Resources Survey on the ONS website, they are advised that the document may not be suitable for users of assistive technology. They can, however, request that this be made available to them by emailing a given email address and asking for a copy in a suitable format, thus requiring an extra step

of work for users of assistive technology. In contrast, the UN's documents are immediately available in an accessible format.

6 These are similar to the concept of 'personas' used in marketing, but are used here for a different purpose.

7 The usage of 'Black' person rather than 'person of colour' reflects the preferred usage in the context of the UK; we acknowledge that this does not reflect preferred usage in other countries and cultures.

Further reading

Crenshaw, K. (1989) 'Demarginalizing the intersection of race and sex: A black feminist critique of antidiscrimination doctrine, feminist theory and antiracist politics', *The University of Chicago Legal Forum*, 1989(1), Article 8. Available at: https://chicagounbound.uchicago.edu/uclf/vol1989/iss1/8/?
Kimberlé Crenshaw's seminal text on the intersection of gender and race is a good starting point into the concept of intersectionality.

Goodley, D. (2016) *Disability Studies: An Interdisciplinary Introduction* (2nd edn), London: SAGE Publications Ltd.
This book provides a much more detailed and nuanced introduction into the discussion of disability and related theoretical concepts.

References

Barnes, C. and Mercer, G. (2005) 'Disability, work, and welfare: Challenging the social exclusion of disabled people', *Work, Employment & Society*, 19(3), 527–45. Available at: https://doi.org/10.1177/0950017005055669

Baumberg, B. (2015) 'From impairment to incapacity – Educational inequalities in disabled people's ability to work', *Social Policy & Administration*, 49(2), 182–98. Available at: https://doi.org/10.1111/spol.12118

Berghs, M., Atkin, K., Graham, H., Hatton, C. and Thomas, C. (2016) 'Implications for public health research of models and theories of disability: A scoping study and evidence synthesis', *Public Health Research*, No 4.8, Chapter 2: Methods. Available at: www.ncbi.nlm.nih.gov/books/NBK378950

Crenshaw, K. (1989) 'Demarginalizing the intersection of race and sex: A black feminist critique of antidiscrimination doctrine, feminist theory and antiracist politics', *The University of Chicago Legal Forum*, 1989(1), Article 8. Available at: https://chicagounbound.uchicago.edu/uclf/vol1989/iss1/8/?

DEFRA (Department for Environment, Food & Rural Affairs) and the Rt Hon George Eustice MP (2020) 'Start of ban on plastic straws, stirrers and cotton buds', Press release, 1 October. Available at: www.gov.uk/government/news/start-of-ban-on-plastic-straws-stirrers-and-cotton-buds

Digital Leaders (2018) '4 in 10 UK council websites are inaccessible.' Available at: https://digileaders.com/4-in-10-uk-council-websites-inaccessible

Espinal, R. (2018) 'Why I introduced a ban on plastic straws for NYC', *USA Today*, 16 August. Available at: https://eu.usatoday.com/story/opinion/2018/08/16/plastic-straws-why-introduced-ban-new-york-city-editorials-debates/1014374002

Garrand, D. (2018) 'Seattle ban on plastic straws to go into effect July', *CBS News*, 20 June. Available at: www.cbsnews.com/news/seattle-ban-on-plastic-straws-goes-into-effect-july-1

Humphrey, J.C. (2000) 'Researching disability politics, or, some problems with the social model in practice', *Disability & Society*, 15(1), 63–86.

Kattari, S.K., Olzman, M. and Hanna, M.D. (2018) '"You look fine!" Ableist experiences by people with invisible disabilities', *Affilia – Journal of Women and Social Work*, 33(4). Available at: https://doi.org/10.1177/0886109918778073

Kavanagh, A.M., Krnjacki, L., Aitken, Z., Lamontagne, A.D., et al (2015) 'Intersections between disability, type of impairment, gender and socio-economic disadvantage in a nationally representative sample of 33,101 working-aged Australians', *Disability and Health Journal*, 8(2), 191–9. Available at: https://doi.org/10.1016/j.dhjo.2014.08.008

Kroll, T. (2011) 'Designing mixed methods studies in health-related research with people with disabilities', *International Journal of Multiple Research Approaches*, 5(1), 64–75. Available at: https://doi.org/10.5172/mra.2011.5.1.64

Low, J. (1996) 'Negotiating identities, negotiating environments: An interpretation of the experiences of students with disabilities', *Disability & Society*, 11(2), 235–48. Available at: https://doi.org/10.1080/09687599650023254

Mader, B., Hart, L.A. and Bergin, B. (1989) 'Social acknowledgments for children with disabilities: Effects of service dogs', *Child Development*, 60(6), 1529–34. Available at: https://doi.org/10.2307/1130941

Mik-Meyer, N. (2015) 'Gender and disability: Feminizing male employees with visible impairments in Danish work organizations', *Gender, Work & Organization*, 22(6), 579–95. Available at: https://doi.org/10.1111/gwao.12107

Nind, M. (2008) *Conducting Qualitative Research with People with Learning, Communication and Other Disabilities: Methodological Challenges*, ESRC National Centre for Research Methods. Available at: http://eprints. ncrm.ac.uk/491/1/MethodsReviewPaperNCRM-012.pdf

ONS (Office for National Statistics) (2018) *Family Resources Survey 2016/17*, 1–12. Available at: https://assets.publishing.service.gov.uk/ government/uploads/system/uploads/attachment_data/file/692771/ family-resources-survey-2016-17.pdf

Pepper, P. (2018) 'I rely on plastic straws and baby wipes. I'm disabled – I have no choice', *The Guardian*, 9 July. Available at: www.theguardian. com/commentisfree/2018/jul/09/disabled-person-plastic-straws-baby-wipes

Polit, D.F. and Beck, C.T. (2010) 'Generalization in quantitative and qualitative research: Myths and strategies', *International Journal of Nursing Studies*, 47(11), 1451–8. Available at: https://doi. org/10.1016/j.ijnurstu.2010.06.004

Quinlan, K.J., Bowleg, L. and Ritz, S.F. (2014) 'Virtually invisible women: Women with disabilities in mainstream psychological theory and research', *Review of Disability Studies: An International Journal*, 4(3).

Rothman, K.J., Gallacher, J.E.J. and Hatch, E.E. (2013) 'Why representativeness should be avoided', *International Journal of Epidemiology*, 42(4), 1012–14. Available at: https://doi.org/10.1093/ ije/dys223

Sharman, J. (2019) 'Woman dies after being impaled by metal straw', *Independent*, 9 July. Available at: www.independent.co.uk/news/ uk/home-news/woman-dies-metal-straw-elena-struthers-gardner-inquest-coroner-a8996431.html

Stone, S.D. (2005) 'Reactions to invisible disability: The experiences of young women survivors of hemorrhagic stroke', *Disability and Rehabilitation*, 27(6), 293–304.

UN (United Nations) (2006) *United Nations Convention on the Rights of Persons with Disabilities*. Available at: www.un.org/development/desa/ disabilities/convention-on-the-rights-of-persons-with-disabilities. html

Vallely, E. (no date) 'Grasping at straws: The ableism of the straw ban', Center for Disability Rights. Available at: http://cdrnys.org/blog/ disability-dialogue/grasping-at-straws-the-ableism-of-the-straw-ban/

WHO (World Health Organization) and The World Bank (2011) *World Report on Disability*. Available at: http://documents1.worldbank.org/ curated/en/665131468331271288/pdf/627830WP0World00PUBL IC00BOX361491B0.pdf

Wilton, R. (2006) 'Disability disclosure in the workplace', *Just Labour*, 8(Spring), 24–39. Available at: www.justlabour.yorku.ca/volume8/ pdfs/02 Wilton.pdf

2

Research that includes disabled people

In this chapter we give a brief background to some of the key research models and methods in the field of disability studies, which has generated much of the conceptual work that informs the ideas presented in this book. The chapter includes:

- Definitions of disability, and how these relate to models of disability.
- The importance of using inclusive language and terminology, exemplified by the debate between the use of 'disabled people' vs 'people with disabilities'.
- An explanation of the distinction between research *on* disabled people and research *with* disabled people, and the wider implications of this distinction.
- The perception that disabled people are vulnerable, and the implications this has for research ethics.
- An overview of the research methodologies developed specifically for disadvantaged groups.
- An introduction to Universal Design (UD).

This book is focused on research with the general population. We argue that, as most samples will include a proportion of disabled people, research needs to be conducted in a way that enables them to take part. One of the assumptions we make is that readers will be looking for ways to make it easier for disabled people to take part in their research, but that their research topic does not relate to disability, and does not take a disability studies approach. It is assumed that people researching specifically with disabled participants will seek out focused training resources and guidance in the use of appropriate research methods, and will have or develop an in-depth understanding of the needs of their group of participants. This book is intended for researchers who are not working specifically with disabled participants, and so the description of research methods is presented at an introductory level, with links to original sources that readers can explore further if they wish.

19

Definition of disability

As discussed in Chapter 1, disability has been defined in various ways. Laws and the guidance that accompany them give a definition of disability that is used as a basis for deciding, for example, whether a workplace needs to make arrangements to accommodate a disabled employee, or whether a person is entitled to benefits.

Both the ADA (US) and Equality Act (UK) refer to a list of conditions that are defined as disabilities (ODI UK, 2010). While many people still think of the definition of a disability as a visible condition that mainly causes mobility impairment (Dixon et al, 2018), the types of conditions covered by the definition include chronic and genetic conditions, mental health conditions, cancer, HIV infection and multiple sclerosis, as well as acquired and congenital conditions. Some legal definitions go further than this by defining disability purely in terms of barriers rather than impairments: 'Disability is the process which happens when one group of people create barriers by designing a world only for their way of living, taking no account of the impairments other people have' (ODI NZ, 2016, p 12).

The friends and family of a disabled person may also be protected by law where they are treated unfairly due to their relationship with a disabled person,[1] which in the literature is referred to as 'courtesy stigma' (Goffman, 1963, p 30). Laws also protect against less favourable treatment, or harassment, based on the perception that someone is disabled when they are not.

Disability is a very diverse characteristic, and people can be affected in many different ways. The way in which someone is affected, and the degree to which they are affected, can vary depending on the individual and their specific life circumstances as well as on the condition itself (Oliver, 1990). It is also important to bear in mind that some health conditions have an impact on daily life but are not diagnosed as disabilities, since the definition of what constitutes a disability (as a protected characteristic) is a legal one and does not necessarily relate to a person's ability to function. Certain conditions are under-diagnosed, especially in disadvantaged groups (Kelly et al, 2019). Others, such as myalgic encephalomyelitis, took some time to be accepted as a disability by the medical profession. There may be people among our participants who do not define as disabled because they don't have a diagnosis, but who may still have access needs and would benefit from accommodations in the way we conduct our research. Finally, some people who have acquired disabilities don't consider themselves disabled – older people are especially likely to take this approach. If we are collecting demographic data that include disability, we may find that there is a gap between the proportion of disabled people we might expect to meet in a particular population and what people have disclosed or told us in advance.

Models of disability

As discussed in Chapter 1, a distinction is usually made between impairment and disability. The UK's Equality Act 2010 clarifies this distinction in the following way:

- Impairment can be defined as the effects a person experiences which arise from an injury, illness or genetic condition, and which affect their ability to fully function.
- Disability can be defined as the effect an impairment has on a person's ability to carry out daily activities.

Disability studies scholars and activists have critiqued the representation of an impairment as purely a condition of the body or mind, defined in contrast to the 'normally' functioning body of a non-disabled person, arguing that this framing is inherently stigmatising and reflects a bias towards one particular model of disability, the medical model. The medical model defines disability as a quality or feature of a disabled person, and views non-disability as normal and disability as impaired function or lack of function that needs to be remediated through medical or surgical intervention (Barnes, 2012). The focus is on the functioning of the individual person rather than seeing disability in a broader social context. In this model, the impairment is the same thing as the disability – both are remediated through treatment – and the intended outcome is normalisation with the non-disabled population.

Alternative models of disability have been developed that challenge the medical model (Goodley, 2016, Chapter 1). Three influential approaches are the social model, the relational model and the human rights model:

- *Social model:* first devised by Oliver (1983), and conceived as an evolving process of describing and understanding disability (Oliver, 1996; Bailey, 2004), this model locates disability in society's failure to acknowledge human diversity by organising and designing only for non-disabled people. Where the medical model tends to see disability as a problem for the individual to address, in the social model, impairment and disability are separated: disability has been created through society's lack of consideration for the needs of the whole population, which includes disabled people, and consequently it is society's responsibility to stop creating barriers so that disabled people can participate.

- *Relational model:* this model sees disability as both culturally constructed and as describing a reduced function (Reindal, 2008), with individual and social outcomes that reflect the diverse lived experience of disabled people. Using this model, an impairment is a physical or mental phenomenon rather than solely socially constructed, and cannot be separated from a person's embodied experience of it; 'impairment effects' are felt in the interaction with the social world, such as social stigma, and in physical effects, such as pain and exhaustion, as well as in the implications of physical and digital lack of access (Thomas, 1999). 'Disabled' describes 'a particular form of unequal social relationship which manifests itself through exclusionary and oppressive practices – disablism' (Thomas, 1999, p 40).
- *Human rights model:* this is based on human rights principles of dignity and equality enshrined in the UN CRPD (UN, 2006), stating that disability is a natural feature of human diversity – 'disabled people are people' – and that disability must not be used as a reason to deny or limit disabled people's rights.

Political action to promote the use of the social model has had a great influence over the way society approaches disability. For example, it has resulted in the introduction of legislation and best practice guidance that requires public services and businesses to proactively make adjustments to accommodate the needs of disabled people. But the considerable influence of the medical model can be seen in the fact that, in both the US and UK, the legal definition of disability takes the medical approach. The social model also has its weaknesses, one of them being that disproportionate attention is paid to particular types of disability (Goodley, 2016). Another is that it overlooks the diversity of disabled people, not just in terms of the condition they might have but also in all their other qualities. People may be disadvantaged for more than one reason, and an individual's approach to their disability, as well as the way it intersects with their sex, gender, class, poverty and other factors, may influence their experience. An awareness of the impact of intersectional discrimination (Crenshaw, 1989) is therefore important when considering participants' diverse life experiences.

Use of respectful language

The language used to describe disabled people remains contested: old-fashioned, stigmatising terms such as 'wheelchair-bound', 'handicapped' or 'retarded' are falling out of favour, but there is an ongoing debate around the use of terms, with different groups varying in their preferences for language usage. At the time of writing (2021), a major point of difference is around the use of people-first language (PFL) versus identity-first language (IFL). People-first language is a form of words that describes the disability as a feature of the person, for example a 'person with Down's syndrome'.[2] Identity-first language refers to the disability first, for example an 'autistic person' rather than a 'person with autism'.

The people-first language approach focuses on the person and not the disability, arguing that disabled people are often reduced to their disability while their humanity is overlooked, so it is dehumanising to refer to the disability first, as if it is more important than the person who has it. The identity-first approach comes from the perspective that the disadvantages experienced by disabled people are an outcome of society's exclusion of disabled people; in other words, it applies the social model of disability, seeing the person and the condition as integrated rather than separate, as may be implied by people-first language.

While in the UK 'disabled people' is the most commonly used general term, this is not the same in all English-speaking countries (see, for example, ACE Disability Network, 2020). Some communities have strong preferences for a particular approach. For example, Down's Syndrome Scotland (2017) prefers people-first language for people with Down's syndrome because the dehumanising terms 'Down's sufferer' or even 'Mongol' are still regularly used. In contrast, the autistic communities, as exemplified by Identity-First Autistic,[3] tend to prefer identity-first language, using the neurodiversity paradigm to describe autism as part of the normal range of human neurodiversity (Singer, 1999) rather than routinely pathologised as a disability (Bottema-Beutel et al, 2020).

Hearing loss is another example where approaches differ within a group of people affected by related conditions (BDA, 2015). As a generalisation, people who are born Deaf (capital D) or lose their hearing before they begin to speak, whose first language is sign language and who are part of the Deaf community, may see being Deaf as part of their identity and Deafness as a unique culture. If they largely socialise with other Deaf people or are activists, they may consider themselves part of a subculture of people who define themselves as 'culturally Deaf'. People whose hearing loss is acquired, whose first language is spoken rather than signed, and who lip-read rather than use sign language, may call themselves deaf (lower-case d) but may not consider deafness part of their identity. It's important for researchers to be aware of this distinction because of its impact on the way people prefer to socialise and communicate. It's also important to be aware that there are many different distinct sign languages that are a community's first language, and they are no more interchangeable than spoken languages (Padden, 2011) – British Sign Language (BSL), American Sign Language (ASL) and Australian Sign Language (AUSLAN) are just three examples.

For respectful communication we therefore need to be sensitive to the use of expressions that are inherently negative, presenting disabled people as abnormal, such as assuming disabled people are 'suffering' or 'afflicted', or using 'able-bodied' people as a contrast to 'disabled' or even 'non-able-bodied' people. Additionally, there are terms that are best avoided because they are 'insider' terms that are acceptable within the disabled community but are not acceptable when used outside it. For example, 'crip' in some settings is acceptable (when used as 'crip theory', it is a term that relates to a particular strand of critical disability studies) but it is inappropriate for researchers to use this term unless they belong to the community. Others such as 'gimp', 'mad' and 'mad studies' are insider terms that should also be avoided by outsiders (Lipson and Rogers, 2000).

VIGNETTE

Sam was born Deaf, and both their parents have also been Deaf from birth. Sam's parents have always been very active within the Deaf community, and Sam grew up with a big circle of Deaf friends and acquaintances. Their first language is British Sign Language. Their doctor recommended a cochlear implant that Sam has refused because they feel comfortable with how they are. Although Sam does use some assistive devices, they do not consider themselves disabled and, if asked on a survey, they will not indicate that they have a disability.

CHECKLIST 3: LANGUAGE TO REFER TO DISABILITY

☐ Not everyone sees their disability as part of their identity, and some people are relaxed about language usage as long as it is courteous. If you are unsure, consider asking individuals directly, and be guided by their own preference, behaviour and word choices, even if it differs from what disability-led organisations advise.

☐ If you are referring to a specific community of people, be guided by disabled people and related disability-led charities to establish preferences for communication and terminology.

☐ Avoid referring to someone by their disability alone, as this reduces the whole person to a single characteristic. Do not use, for example, 'an anorexic', 'an autist', 'a dyslexic'.

☐ Language use and terminology preferences change over time. When you are writing content that makes references to disability, check the current general guidance for your field offered by disability-led organisations.

A thoughtful discussion of the language used around disability, with useful reading suggestions, is available on the Down to the Struts podcast (2020).

Having discussed the use of language, we now move on to the related issue of whether researchers conduct research 'with' or 'on' participants.

Research 'with' or 'on' disabled people

What does it mean to conduct research 'with' participants? Disability activists have questioned the location of the participant within the research, and their relationship to the researcher, pointing out that the power dynamic between the two has often been exploitative (Humphrey, 2000). The term 'research on' disabled people describes the traditional research relationship: it presents disabled people as powerless research subjects who are simply sources of data. The consequence of this is that research evidence has been collected from disabled people according to agendas set by healthcare practitioners, researchers or research funders rather than disabled people themselves.

The findings are then used to make decisions that have not fully taken into account the varied, lived experience of disability, yet are used in ways that have a significant impact on disabled people's lives (Oliver, 2002). This history informs some disabled people's attitudes to research, meaning that they may, understandably, be wary of a researcher's motives.

This has changed over time, and this change in approach is similar to that developed in feminist research methods by researchers such as Finch (1984) and Oakley (1981). The explicit intention of feminist research is to empower women, and an important way of achieving that is to change the power balance of the research relationship, acknowledging that women are the experts in their own lives. There are various different ways to achieve this that have been adopted both in research with other marginalised groups and in mainstream research practices. For example, traditional research referred to 'research subjects' while feminist researchers adopted the term 'participants'. Feminist researchers stressed the importance of the quality of the research relationship and that research should work to co-produce knowledge in partnership with participants. It encouraged mutual disclosure as a way to equalise the researcher and participant: where both are sharing personal information, the aim is to create and maintain mutual trust and rapport. Finally, the feminist approach also stresses the importance of reflexivity, to ensure researchers are conscious of and give full consideration to their impact on the research process.

In this context, the campaigning slogan 'Nothing about us without us' (Charlton, 2000) challenges the disempowerment of disabled people within traditional research, and highlights the expectation that researchers should facilitate a much more equal research relationship with disabled participants. In the context of research, the underlying principle is that research that is conducted with disabled people should focus on topics that are important for them rather than important for the researchers; disabled people should have a significant involvement in research projects whose findings are used to make policy and practice decisions that affect the way they are treated.

Vulnerability, power and privilege

Certain groups of research participants are considered 'vulnerable' as a matter of course. People may be vulnerable because of intrinsic factors, such as mental ill health, or extrinsic factors relating to their social circumstances (Smith, 2008). In the context of ethics in research, vulnerability is closely linked to the capacity to consent, as it refers to people who are seen as being particularly susceptible to coercion or undue influence, who may not understand what is meant by informed consent, or who may not understand the implications of taking part in a research project (Liamputtong, 2007).

While capacity to consent or to understand the implications of research participation may be seen as more relevant to people with intellectual disabilities, it can also apply to other groups; for example, it may be difficult for participants to understand consent forms and information written in English if English is their second language. There is the potential for coercion in research settings where a third party mediates between the researcher and participants. For example, in researching employment in a workplace, if HR or line managers are the gatekeepers, they may put pressure on staff to take part and staff may not feel able to refuse a request from their line manager. Service users may feel they have to agree to research when asked by their healthcare worker or service provider. Group interviews where participants are a family or a social group already known to one another also have the potential to be coercive, or to put participants in the position where they only give responses that they know will be socially acceptable to the group. In a setting like this, it is particularly important to be careful about confidentiality – it may cause problems if an employee has disclosed a disability or other 'socially sensitive' information (Sieber and Stanley, 1988) in a research setting that they have not disclosed at work, and their employer finds out.

Other types of inequality might affect people's ability to consent. If the research topic is sensitive, concerns about vulnerability potentially apply to all participants and, where possible, support options should be made available. Participants who are in chronic pain may be willing to participate when their health is good but not when it is poor, so consent may fluctuate depending on circumstances. Some marginalised people may feel there is no benefit to them from taking part and that it will not change the circumstances that have led to their marginalisation, so they may not agree to participate.

Institutional ethics committees have also sometimes taken a conservative view as to who is capable of taking part in research, assuming that disabled people are vulnerable by default (Iacono, 2006). This perception is sometimes given as a reason for excluding disabled people from research on general topics (Feldman et al, 2013; Trevisan and Reilly, 2014).

VIGNETTE

Layla has end-stage amyotrophic lateral sclerosis (ALS) and requires a high level of medical care and attention. Because of the ALS she is no longer able to practise her job as a primary school teacher. She uses assistive devices to communicate, both with people online and face-to-face. The local council wants to evaluate the quality of the care service that is being delivered and has contacted Layla for participation. Layla would very much like to give feedback to the council, as she is unhappy with the care that she receives through her care team. She worries, however, that any such feedback will get back to her carers, as there are only a handful of cases of ALS in the entire region, and any details she might give of her experiences are likely to be identifiable.

Are disabled people vulnerable? Some may be, but not necessarily because they are disabled. Vulnerability is not only about capacity to consent but also about power disparities. In qualitative research in particular, it is commonly understood that, in the research relationship, researchers usually hold more power than participants (Creswell et al, 2007). Therefore, as researchers, we need to consider the participant's circumstances, and reflect on the ways in which they may be vulnerable in the context of the research relationship. Here we have to consider issues related to disability (whether or not they have told us about it), but also include other factors. Protection from harm is intrinsic to research ethics and the perceived risks of participation have to be weighed against the benefits by the researcher and participants; crucially, however, the participants should be part of this discussion rather than having a decision made without them. (There is a further discussion of reflexivity in Chapter 3.)

Questions of both vulnerability and power imbalance could be addressed, at least partially, by involving participants more actively in the research process. The next section looks at research approaches specifically designed to improve inclusion.

Research approaches designed to include disabled people

In this section we look at research approaches that have been designed for researching with disabled people; they are also used with other marginalised groups where there is a large power imbalance between researchers and participants.

The field of disability studies is 'an academic discipline that approaches disability from an interdisciplinary perspective and uses multiple theories to define disability and understand the disability experience' (DO-IT, 2019). The intention behind the development of these research approaches was not only to make the research process more open but also to acknowledge that disabled people have insider knowledge about their own situation, needs and lives, and this makes an essential contribution to research where disability is part of the research question. The emphasis is on increasing participants' autonomy and gaining a better understanding of their lived experience, particularly in sensitive subjects; the research findings can then be used to make relevant changes (Liamputtong, 2007). In this way, the *outcome* of co-produced research is better quality research findings, but the *goal* of research conducted using these approaches is to effect social change (Green and Thorogood, 2018).

Participatory and emancipatory approaches were developed to address ethical problems and power imbalances in traditional research and to empower disadvantaged groups. In traditional research, the research is entirely researcher-led, answering research questions devised by the researcher. Usually, the research findings are disseminated in academic publications with a restricted readership and access, and are not presented in a format that enables lay people to make use of them. 'Research subjects' are not involved in the design of the research, and are seen purely as sources of data.

Participatory research is designed to engage vulnerable or marginalised groups. The research is co-designed and co-conducted in collaboration with the research participants, where the intended outcome is to make positive changes to an existing process or setting. The presentation of research findings is also co-designed. In this way, the research topic is relevant to the participants' needs, addresses the issues that they think are important, is conducted in a way that is inclusive, and is disseminated in ways that don't require specialist or academic knowledge (Nind and Vinha, 2013).

Participatory research has the following benefits (IDS, 2020). It:

- acknowledges that disabled people have insider knowledge about their own situation, needs and lives, and their informed contribution is an essential way to produce relevant findings;
- gives opportunities for the less powerful to have their say;
- enables people to have a say in research that affects them;
- encourages the powerful stakeholders in the research project to allow others to participate equally;
- encourages researchers to let go of their preconceptions and be genuinely open to what participants have to say.

Over time, some aspects of participatory research have become mainstream in social research. For example, researchers are expected to involve the public in the research project at an early stage, and to plan for knowledge exchange with relevant lay organisations such as patient groups, local pressure groups, related charities, and so on.

The **emancipatory research** approach came out of disability activism and has the explicit intention of campaigning for greater equality for disabled people, creating social change and facilitating personal change for everyone taking part (Oliver, 2002). Researchers put their skills at the disposal of the community and become participants. All participants are co-researchers and research is co-produced. Participants define the research questions and have a say in how the research is conducted and communicated. The intention is to produce knowledge that benefits disabled people.

According to Barnes (2002), the core features are:

- Accountability: the project should be led by disabled people and accountable to disabled people, for example by involving organisations run by disabled people.
- Using the social model of disability: a focus on the social conditions that create disability.
- Addressing the problem of objectivity: acknowledges that experiences vary and data can be interpreted in more than one way. Stresses the importance of reflexivity in the research process, of clearly stating the epistemological and ontological position of the researcher, and being transparent about the research methods that have been used.
- Choice of methods: uses a range of appropriate research strategies.
- Role of experience: sheds light on the experience of disabled people as they navigate an ableist society.
- Practical outcomes: a meaningful outcome that benefits disabled people.

This section has briefly summarised research approaches that are designed to enable disabled people (and other disadvantaged groups) to have more control over research projects that explore, and subsequently affect, their lives. We now move on to a discussion of a widely used approach to accessibility and how it can be applied in practice.

Universal Design

Universal Design (UD) is not a research approach but a set of guiding principles that can be applied to increase access and potentially make a product, service or building more inclusive. The term was originally coined by Ronald Mace, a disabled architect who was involved for many years in initiatives to improve the accessibility of buildings (Britannica, 2020). A number of researchers have suggested using UD as a pragmatic way to make research practice more inclusive of disabled people (Williams and Moore, 2011; Rios et al, 2016; Ouellette, 2019). This book uses UD as a basis for presenting suggestions on how to include disabled people in research.

UD underpins much of the thinking around the accessibility of buildings. Originally expressed as a set of principles that applied in architectural design, it was an attempt to make sure that architects designed buildings to be as easy to use as possible by the widest range of different people. These general principles have been taken up and applied much more widely, for example, in the development of guidelines for Universal Design for Learning (UDL) (Rose et al, 2006; Mertens, 2014, pp 389–401) and in the World Wide Web Consortium's (W3C) Web Content Accessibility Guidelines (WCAG) (Caldwell et al, 2008).

There are seven guiding principles of UD (Story et al, 1998), and they have been adapted here to apply to research:

1. Equitable use, meaning the same method could be used by people with diverse abilities.
2. Flexibility in use, meaning the method accommodates a wide range of preferences and is adapted to the participant's preferred pace.
3. Simple and intuitive use, meaning the method should be easy to understand, requires no prior knowledge, and minimises complexity.
4. Perceptible information, meaning the method and research communication is available to participants regardless of their sensory abilities.
5. Tolerance for error, meaning that the method minimises hazards and the adverse consequences of accidental or unintended actions.
6. Low physical effort, interpreted as a method that accommodates different attention spans and timing requirements, accommodates breaks, minimises distractions and avoids causing any additional discomfort or fatigue.

7. Size and space for approach and use, meaning that the method is accessible regardless of the user's body size, posture or mobility.

UD is not linked with a particular research approach, but it aligns well with the social model of disability as it presents an inaccessible environment as the major barrier to better participation in society. The intention was to promote the 'design of products and environments to be usable to the greatest extent possible by people of all ages and abilities' and for this to be implemented in a way which 'respects human diversity and promotes inclusion of all people in all activities of life' (Story et al, 1998, p 2).

Although the aim was to create a more inclusive environment, UD has also been used in ways that are depersonalising. For example, because it is not explicit about preferred techniques, it is subject to varied interpretations. Its very openness lends itself to being operationalised to create guidelines that may be based on a restricted understanding of disabled people's needs (for example, by defining specific dimensions for wheelchair access and designing around those measures rather than thinking about how wheelchair users move around – an approach called anthropometrics). This has sometimes been privileged over experiential knowledge. Furthermore, the needs of some groups of disabled people conflict with those of others; while it may be more difficult to resolve this when designing a building, a flexible approach to research makes it possible to accommodate different people's needs.

UD has been critiqued because it does not explicitly consider factors such as socioeconomic status and the way this may limit access to technology – the so-called 'digital divide' (Abascal et al, 2016). As many disabled people are paid less than average, face considerable barriers to gaining employment, or are unable to work, research that considers access issues also needs to consider income, literacy level and social isolation (Warschauer and Newhart, 2016). UD, with its pragmatic focus on making adjustments to research design and data collection, may not be enough to meet the needs of all groups of disabled people, for example those with fluctuating conditions or intellectual disabilities (Berghs et al, 2016). Another weakness is that it does not address ways of countering ableist attitudes in the research team; it is important to address physical and communication barriers, but creating a welcoming and safe space is not only about easy access to toilets and good signage (Hofmann et al, 2020). (See Chapter 3 for a longer commentary on this issue.)

Last, disability is enormously varied, and often hidden. Stigmatised people are less likely to be open about their stigmatised features; people do not always disclose, so it is easy to assume they are not there. Disabled people can experience 'access fatigue' (Konrad, 2018), which describes the impact of the emotional labour involved in having to constantly ask for and then check that adjustments are in place; people may not want to do this in a setting that (to them) is non-essential. Potential participants may screen themselves out of research if it does not look as if they can participate. Some aspects of the way that research is conducted can present barriers to disabled participants: the principle of **active accessibility** is that, by examining the way we are conducting research, we can ensure that we proactively identify and then remove barriers, and respond positively when participants tell us their access requirements.

In this book we present checklists and guidance based largely on the principles of UD and tempered by reference to the social model of disability. The aim is to better understand the implications of our research approach and the ways that can potentially present barriers to participation; by identifying barriers, it should be possible to identify actions we can take to address them, so we can practise active accessibility.

Summary

In this chapter we have looked at how disability is defined, and at the implications of different models of disability. We have looked briefly at debates around the use of language and explained why terminology preferences can vary. We have discussed the perception that disabled people are vulnerable by default and implications this has for research practice. Finally, we have presented an overview of research methodologies developed specifically for disabled people, and given an introduction to Universal Design (UD), the principles that guide the advice given in this book. Chapter 3 will look at accessibility and research design.

Notes

[1] See, for example, ADA (Americans With Disabilities Act) (1990) Pub L 101-336, 26 July, 104 Stat 328; Equality Act 2010, available at: www.legislation.gov.uk/ukpga/2010/15/contents

[2] In the UK, 'Down's syndrome' is used more frequently; elsewhere, for example in the US, the preferred terminology is 'Down syndrome'.

[3] See www.identityfirstautistic.org

Further reading

NIHR (National Institute for Health Research)/INVOLVE (2012) *Strategies for Diversity and Inclusion in Public Involvement: Supplement to the Briefing Notes for Researchers*, May. Available at: www.invo.org.uk/wp-content/uploads/2012/06/INVOLVEInclusionSupplement1.pdf
A guide to strategies you can use to increase the diversity of the people involved in your research project, including advice about accessibility.

Story, M.F., Mueller, J.L. and Mace, R.L. (1998) *The Universal Design File: Designing for People of All Ages and Abilities*, Washington, DC: National Institute on Disability and Rehabilitation Research. Available at: http://files.eric.ed.gov/fulltext/ED460554.pdf
A well-written and clear explanation of the principles of Universal Design, with guidance on how it is applied in practice.

References

Abascal, J., Barbosa, S.D., Nicolle, C. and Zaphiris, P. (2016) 'Rethinking universal accessibility: A broader approach considering the digital gap', *Universal Access in the Information Society*, 15, 179–82.

ACE Disability Network (2020) 'The Language of Disability.' Available at: www.acedisability.org.au/information-for-providers/language-disability.php

Bailey, K. (2004) 'Learning More from the Social Model: Linking Experience, Participation and Knowledge Production', in C. Barnes and G. Mercer (eds) *Implementing the Social Model of Disability: Theory and Research*, Leeds: The Disability Press, pp 138–56.

Barnes, C. (2002) '"Emancipatory disability research": Project or process?', *Journal of Research in Special Educational Needs*, 2(1).

Barnes, C. (2012) 'Understanding the Social Model of Disability: Past, Present and Future', in N. Watson and S. Vehmas (eds) *Routledge Handbook of Disability Studies*, London: Routledge, pp 12–29.

BDA (British Deaf Association) (2015) 'What is Deaf culture?', 7 September. Available at: https://bda.org.uk/what-is-deaf-culture

Berghs, M.J., Atkin, K.M., Graham, H.M., Hatton, C. and Thomas, C. (2016) *Implications for Public Health Research of Models and Theories of Disability: A Scoping Study and Evidence Synthesis*, National Institute for Health Research. Available at: https://eprints.whiterose.ac.uk/103434/1/FullReport_phr04080.pdf

Bottema-Beutel, K., Kapp, S.K., Lester, J.N., Sasson, N.J. and Hand, B.N. (2020) 'Avoiding ableist language: Suggestions for autism researchers', *Autism in Adulthood*, 20 September.

Britannica (2020) 'Ronald L. Mace, American architect.' Available at: www.britannica.com/biography/Ronald-L-Mace

Caldwell, B., Cooper, M., Reid, L.G. and Vanderheiden, G. (2008) *Web Content Accessibility Guidelines (WCAG) 2.0*. World Wide Web Consortium (W3C).

Charlton, J.I. (2000) *Nothing About Us Without Us: Disability Oppression and Empowerment*, Berkeley, CA: University of California Press.

Crenshaw, K. (1989) 'Demarginalizing the intersection of race and sex: A black feminist critique of antidiscrimination doctrine, feminist theory and antiracist politics', *The University of Chicago Legal Forum*, 1989(1), 139. Available at: https://chicagounbound.uchicago.edu/uclf/vol1989/iss1/8

Creswell, J.W., Hanson, W.E., Clark Plano, V.L. and Morales, A. (2007) 'Qualitative research designs: Selection and implementation', *The Counseling Psychologist*, 35(2), 236–64.

Dixon, S., Smith, C. and Touchet, A.M. (2018) *The Disability Perception Gap*, Policy report, London: Scope. Available at: www.scope.org.uk/campaigns/disability-perception-gap

DO-IT (Disabilities, Opportunities, Internetworking, and Technology) (2019) 'What is Disability Studies?', 30 April. Available at: www.washington.edu/doit/what-disability-studies

Down's Syndrome Scotland (2017) '"People First" Language', March. Available at: www.dsscotland.org.uk/wordpress/wp-content/uploads/2017/03/People-first-language-guide.pdf

Down to the Struts (2020) 'Episode 2: The Language of Disability with Dr Sara Acevedo', 27 October [Podcast]. Available at www.downtothestruts.com/episodes/season-1-episode-2-sara-acevedo

Feldman, M.A., Battin, S.M., Shaw, O.A. and Luckasson, R. (2013) 'Inclusion of children with disabilities in mainstream child development research', *Disability & Society*, 28(7), 997–1011.

Finch, J. (1984) '"It's Great to Have Someone to Talk to": The Ethics and Politics of Interviewing Women', in C. Bell and H. Roberts (eds) *Social Researching: Politics, Problems, Practice*, London: Routledge & Kegan and Paul, pp 70–87.

Goffman, E. (1963) *Stigma: Notes on the Management of Spoiled Identity*, New York: Touchstone.

Goodley, D. (2016) *Disability Studies: An Interdisciplinary Introduction* (2nd edn), London: SAGE Publications Ltd.

Green, J. and Thorogood, N. (2018) *Qualitative Methods for Health Research*, London: SAGE Publications Ltd.

Hofmann, M., Kasnitz, D., Mankoff, J. and Bennett, C.L. (2020) 'Living Disability Theory: Reflections on Access, Research, and Design', in the 22nd International ACM SIGACCESS Conference on Computers and Accessibility, October, pp 1–13.

Humphrey, J.C. (2000) 'Researching disability politics, or, some problems with the social model in practice', *Disability & Society*, 15(1), 63–86.

Iacono, T. (2006) 'Ethical challenges and complexities of including people with intellectual disability as participants in research', *Journal of Intellectual and Developmental Disability*, 31(3), 173–9.

IDS (Institute of Development Studies) (2020) 'Participatory Methods.' Available at: www.participatorymethods.org/

Kelly, B., Williams, S., Collins, S., Mushtaq, F., et al (2019) 'The association between socioeconomic status and autism diagnosis in the United Kingdom for children aged 5–8 years of age: Findings from the Born in Bradford cohort', *Autism*, 23(1), 131–40.

Konrad, A. (2018) 'Reimagining work: Normative commonplaces and their effects on accessibility in workplaces', *Business and Professional Communication Quarterly*, 81(1), 123–41.

Liamputtong, P. (2007) *Researching the Vulnerable: A Guide to Sensitive Research Methods*, London: SAGE Publications Ltd.

Lipson, J.G. and Rogers, J.G. (2000) 'Cultural aspects of disability', *Journal of Transcultural Nursing*, 11(3), 212–19.

Mertens, D. (2014) *Research Methods in Education and Psychology: Integrating Diversity with Quantitative and Qualitative Approaches*, London: SAGE Publications Ltd.

Nind, M. and Vinha, H. (2013) *Practical Considerations in Doing Research Inclusively and Doing It Well: Lessons for Inclusive Researchers*, National Centre for Research Methods. Available at: http://eprints.ncrm.ac.uk/3187/1/Nind_practical_considerations_in_doing_research_inclusively.pdf

Oakley, A. (1981) 'Interviewing Women: A Contradiction in Terms', in H. Roberts (ed) *Doing Feminist Research*, London: Routledge & Kegan and Paul, pp 7–22.

ODI (Office for Disability Issues) UK (2010) *Equality Act 2010: Guidance*. Available at: https://assets.publishing.service.gov.uk/government/uploads/system/uploads/attachment_data/file/570382/Equality_Act_2010-disability_definition.pdf

ODI (Office for Disability Issues) NZ (New Zealand) (2016) *New Zealand Disability Strategy 2016–2026*. Available at: www.odi.govt.nz/nz-disability-strategy/about-the-strategy/new-zealand-disability-strategy-2016-2026/read-the-new-disability-strategy

Oliver, M. (1983) *Social Work with Disabled People*, London: Routledge.

Oliver, M. (1990) 'The individual and social models of disability: People with established locomotor disabilities in hospitals', *Joint Workshop of the Living Options Group and the Royal College of Physicians*, 23(7).

Oliver, M. (1996) 'Defining Impairment and Disability: Issues at Stake', in C. Barnes and G. Mercer (eds) *Exploring the Divide*, Leeds: The Disability Press, pp 29–54.

Oliver, M. (2002) 'Emancipatory Research: A Vehicle for Social Transformation or Policy Development', in Conference Proceedings: Using Emancipatory Methodologies in Disability Research, Inaugural NDA Disability Research Conference, Dublin, 3 December, pp 15–23.

Ouellette, A.R. (2019) *People with Disabilities in Human Subjects Research: A History of Exploitation, a Problem of Exclusion*, Albany Law School Research Paper. Available at: https://papers.ssrn.com/sol3/papers.cfm?abstract_id=3492078

Padden, C. (2011) 'Sign Language Geography', in G. Mathur and D.J. Napoli (eds) *Deaf around the World: The Impact of Language*, New York: Oxford University Press, pp 19–37.

Reindal, S.M. (2008) 'A social relational model of disability: A theoretical framework for special needs education?', *European Journal of Special Needs Education*, 23(2), 135–46.

Rios, D., Magasi, S., Novak, C. and Harniss, M. (2016) 'Conducting accessible research: Including people with disabilities in public health, epidemiological, and outcomes studies', *American Journal of Public Health*, 106(12), 2137–44.

Rose, D.H., Harbour, W.S., Johnston, C.S., Daley, S.G. and Abarbanell, L. (2006) 'Universal design for learning in postsecondary education: Reflections on principles and their application', *Journal of Postsecondary Education and Disability*, 19(2), 135–51.

Sieber, J.E. and Stanley, B. (1988) 'Ethical and professional dimensions of socially sensitive research', *American Psychologist*, 43(1), 49.

Singer, J. (1999) 'Why Can't You Be Normal for Once in Your Life? From a Problem with No Name to the Emergence of a New Category of Difference', in M. Corker and S. French (eds) *Disability Discourse*, Buckingham: Open University Press, pp 59–70.

Smith, L.J. (2008) 'How ethical is ethical research? Recruiting marginalized, vulnerable groups into health services research', *Journal of Advanced Nursing*, 62(2), 248–57.

Story, M.F., Mueller, J.L. and Mace, R.L. (1998) *The Universal Design File: Designing for People of All Ages and Abilities*, Washington, DC: National Institute on Disability and Rehabilitation Research. Available at: http://files.eric.ed.gov/fulltext/ED460554.pdf

Thomas, C. (1999) *Female Forms: Experiencing and Understanding Disability*, Buckingham: Open University Press.

Trevisan, F. and Reilly, P. (2014) 'Ethical dilemmas in researching sensitive issues online: Lessons from the study of British disability dissent networks', *Information, Communication & Society*, 17(9), 1131–46.

UN (United Nations) (2006) *Convention on the Rights of Persons with Disabilities: Articles*. Available at: www.un.org/development/desa/disabilities/convention-on-the-rights-of-persons-with-disabilities/convention-on-the-rights-of-persons-with-disabilities-2.html

Warschauer, M. and Newhart, V.A. (2016) 'Broadening our concepts of universal access', *Universal Access in the Information Society*, 15(2), 183–8.

Williams, A.S. and Moore, S.M. (2011) 'Universal design of research: Inclusion of persons with disabilities in mainstream biomedical studies', *Science Translational Medicine*, 3(82).

3

Research questions and research design

This chapter discusses accessibility as an overall consideration in research design. We start by examining how a research question might touch on questions of accessibility, and how accessibility can be built into the research design through suitable choices of methodology; we do this while acknowledging the limitations in scope and feasibility, particularly for student research projects. We outline which factors may affect participation generally, as well as in specific forms of research, such as case studies and longitudinal research. We talk about sources of support and advice at this stage and in this context we also cover the use of reference groups. We discuss the use of secondary data and its implications, and look at how accessibility issues might be approached in the context of applying for ethics approval.

In the social sciences we should make sure that the findings and any policy decisions based on them are applicable and useful to as many from the underlying population as possible. This translates into the requirement for a sample that is both sufficiently large and sufficiently representative of the corresponding population. That said, it has different implications for qualitative and quantitative research that we will make it explicit in subsequent chapters (in Chapter 4 we discuss recruiting strategies for both approaches).

The extent to which findings from a study's sample can be applied to the population as a whole is referred to as **representativeness** in quantitative research, and it is threatened when participation is biased through the absence of some groups or over-representation of others. It is a matter of sample composition, and, as such, it is independent from sample size and participation rate. Arfken and Balon (2011, p 325), for example, note that 'the [United States] census has a high participation using a mixed mode of data collection (postal survey followed by in person interviews) but systematically misses disadvantaged people. In contrast, the ongoing telephone-administered US Behavioral Risk Factor Survey has a participation rate below 60% but no evidence of bias.'

In our case, we want to address possible bias caused by the exclusion of disadvantaged groups by making research more accessible rather than boosting participation numbers in general. That said, it is entirely possible that, by designing accessible research, participation rates may increase across the board (see also the discussion of intersectionality in Chapter 1).

In this context, what we mean by accessible research design is one that is intentionally designed to remove barriers of access to disabled people so that they can participate, and where consideration is given to the accessibility of communication at all stages of the research process, from the conception of the research question up to and including research dissemination.

The choice of methodology and method for our research is normally led by the research question. This will guide us in identifying the most appropriate approach to find an answer. As we decide on this, consideration needs to be given to accessibility at the very beginning of the project so that it is planned in ahead, and any potential issues are anticipated and addressed as far as possible.

When might a research question touch on accessibility?

Very broadly speaking, the answer is: whenever the research methodology requires interaction with human participants, be it face-to-face or remotely. This holds true even if the research question does not explicitly relate to disability in any shape, form or fashion. We may assume that the very nature of the research question means that no disabled participants might possibly be included – and we have seen market research companies remark that because they were surveying working adults, they would not have to worry about accessibility! – but this assumption is simply incorrect.

Of course, there are disabled people who are successful chief executive officers (CEOs),[1] actors,[2] politicians[3] and world-class athletes.[4] It's easy to see how this can lead to the perception that no accommodations at all are necessary – clearly these CEOs, actors, politicians and athletes get by just fine, don't they? But, as researchers, we are asking our participants for a favour. We don't want them to just 'get by'; we want to make participation as easy and unproblematic as possible. To put it another way, if you were a shopkeeper and the door to your shop is old, warped and difficult to open, customers who really want to buy from you might be willing to push hard enough to come in. Others might just decide it's not worth the hassle, and some may be unable to get in at all.

But research can touch on accessibility in more than one way, from the conception of the research question itself right up to the dissemination of the findings:

- Who is asking?
- What is the question?
- Who are we asking?
- How are the data collected?
- How is the research funded?
- How are we asking?
- How is the answer disseminated, and who benefits from it?

We will now discuss these questions in more detail.

Who is asking? Being in a position to propose, develop or attempt to answer a research question is in itself an expression of privilege as many marginalised groups are underrepresented in academia. Privilege can manifest itself as being non-disabled and therefore in a position of not having to engage with issues of accessibility when considering research questions.

What is the question? Although we explicitly talk about research that does not look at disability, impairment or accessibility, the focus and scope of the question determines to what extent accessibility is considered. For example, if we are planning to conduct a survey on the usage patterns of the local library, we may miss out on relevant information if we don't also ask who is *not* using the library because it can only be accessed via stairs and no ramp is available, fluorescent light affects people with sensory processing disorders, or because there are no books in accessible formats. This touches on questions of sampling and representativeness, which brings us to the next point.

Who are we asking? This links to questions of sampling and representativeness. Are the recruiting channels more accessible to some groups than for others? If we use professional networks, can lack of access mean that some people are less well connected than others? (In Chapter 4 we will discuss questions of accessibility and sampling in more detail; in Chapter 5 we will look at how to approach people to recruit for our sample.)

How are the data collected? The choice of data collection method is important because different accessibility issues are related to different methods, and each will have an impact on who can take part. (We describe this in Chapters 5, 6 and 7, and suggest ways this can be approached.)

How is the research funded? This question overlaps with the previous four questions. Some research is easier to get funding for than others; some researchers find it easier to get funding than others; access to and research on some groups is easier to find than others. Publicly funded research often has more stringent requirements regarding accessibility, but not necessarily so. Consistently accessible research may be more expensive and thus more difficult to fund.

How are we asking? Even if research question, sampling and recruiting successfully navigate questions of accessibility, this doesn't necessarily mean that participation itself is free of any barriers. Are the premises where the experiment takes place accessible? Is the online survey screen reader-friendly? Do the group moderators use language that can be well understood by neurodiverse participants? (In Chapter 6 we will look at ways in which we can make face-to-face research more accessible; Chapter 7 looks at remote research; and in Chapter 8 we will talk about the use of mixed methods and how to maintain accessibility throughout.)

How is the answer disseminated, and who benefits from it? Research doesn't end once the last interview has been coded or the last statistical analysis has been run. Making research findings accessible to the public and to other researchers is an integral part of the scientific process. Who can access those findings and who benefits from the answers to the questions is therefore also an aspect of making research accessible (discussed in more detail in Chapter 9).

In practice, not all of these aspects are under our control. Funding is often elusive, and research questions are sometimes determined by institutions or departments or organisational strategies, or depending on our role, they may be determined by our supervisor or manager. This doesn't mean we shouldn't be trying to raise these issues and answer those questions. Instead, we need to keep asking, and where we don't find satisfactory answers, the limitations arising from this need to be acknowledged.

One helpful approach is to look at accessibility in terms of the planning we can do in advance and the way we can respond to participants who approach us with specific requests (Rios et al, 2016).

This means that we could use Universal Design (UD) principles to create an accessible research design, planning in accessibility in advance, and then make accommodations in response to a specific participant's needs. Accommodations change some of the features about the way a task is completed where they do not affect the outcome of data collection. This means considering where we could be flexible, for example in ensuring that an online questionnaire can be completed with keyboard commands as well as with a mouse, providing a paper version instead, and removing any time restrictions on completing it, unless they are a vital part of the research.

Factors affecting participation

From the numerous ways in which accessibility relates to the process of conducting research, a fair number of factors potentially affecting research participation can be derived. There is also a growing body of research examining which barriers exclude marginalised groups from participating in research. We will give some pointers towards relevant research at the end of this chapter.

1. Recruiting channels are not diverse or broad enough

We already know that not all groups are recruited equally well through particular channels or mediums of communication. Market research and voting intention surveys, for example, yield different results when people are contacted through landlines or mobile phones (see, for example, Link et al, 2007). Similarly, using landlines during the day yields different results than using landlines during the evening (see, for example, Vicente, 2015), and responses can differ between paper and online versions of the same survey (see, for example, Shin et al, 2012), but not necessarily so (Cole et al, 2006). For some communities having a personal connection and being seen to reach out is essential (see, for example, Olkin, 2004, p 341, on reaching out to the d/Deaf community). But it can also make a difference which newspaper an ad is published in, on which website a banner is shown, or which networks or groups are being approached for recruitment. (More information on how to reach out through different channels is given in Chapter 5.)

VIGNETTE

Myeengun is a student researcher in a politics department, working on his final year project. His supervisor, Chunhua, has asked him to evaluate how useful the university's open day events are for potential applicants to the department by running focus groups; she wants to know whether they get all the relevant information, and whether the events manage to convey the departmental atmosphere and spirit. Initially, Myeengun is given no budget for the project. However, he successfully argues with his supervisor that the evaluation should also include funds for making the study itself accessible – the events have been running in their current form for many years now, and anecdotal evidence suggests they present a few issues to visually impaired visitors. But, in order to verify these issues, the study itself needs to be accessible.

2. Communication is not accessible

Offering only a limited number of communication channels may similarly pose a barrier to participation. If we can only be contacted by phone, participants who prefer to communicate by email may not be willing to get in touch with us. In many ways, communicating online can make communication easier, but it is not a guarantee – a badly designed web form, for example, can make communication less accessible than offering to get in touch by phone. (We provide more information on this in Chapter 5.)

VIGNETTE

After an accident three years ago, George has a hearing impairment. He is using a hearing aid but find its use uncomfortable. When at home, he prefers to turn up the volume of the TV and the computer speakers rather than using the hearing aid. Although he could potentially participate in a phone call or video conference call, he would much prefer to have the interview conducted by email.

3. Participation itself is too difficult or risky

A main potential barrier to participation can be the set-up of the study itself. This can range from inaccessible premises, to material being available only in one form, to the participation itself being physically demanding or time-consuming. Equally, rigid participation requirements or schedules can constitute a barrier for potential participants with chronic illnesses or people who have carers or assistants whose schedules also need to be considered. Since the COVID-19 pandemic in 2020, there has also been increasing awareness of the risks of transmitting diseases while not being affected oneself, a risk that is magnified for people who are immunocompromised or who are regularly in contact with immunocompromised individuals. (Chapter 6 gives advice on how to conduct face-to-face research in a safer way.)

4. Getting there is too difficult

Even if the study is accessible, if participants can't physically reach the premises without much effort or cost, this can make recruiting participants difficult. Public transport is sometimes patchy, and not often joined-up, so travel that would be short and convenient by car can easily turn into a longer, arduous journey, with waiting time involved. But, even if public transport options exist, this doesn't necessarily mean it is available to everyone: buses usually only have limited space for passengers using mobility aids, and, if the allocated space is taken, other mobility aid users may have to wait for the next or later buses for one that has space (Velho, 2019). Sometimes the drivers have not been trained in using ramps to aid wheelchair users into the bus (Evelly, 2018). All of this can add substantial unpredictability and delays to travel times.

> **VIGNETTE**
>
> Yindi is a single mother of two young children. She has poorly controlled epilepsy and is therefore not legally allowed to drive. Because she is taking care of her children, she works part-time and relies exclusively on public transport. However, public transport options aren't very joined-up in the area she lives in, and so any travel takes a lot of time out of her day.

5. The benefit of the study is not clear

In many instances, the costs for participants (for example, in terms of time, effort and money for travel) outweigh any immediate, tangible rewards they may gain from participation. Rewards can, of course, be intangible: a sense of having contributed to research; an opportunity to learn more about a topic you are genuinely interested in; helping out a researcher; a sense of feeling valued or appreciated. For people with a disability or impairment, the cost–benefit calculation can become more pronounced – is participation worth the potential effort, discomfort or pain?

6. Participants don't trust the researcher or the institution

This is a potential issue for participants from marginalised groups, but also for people with little or no previous experience of research and what it entails. The extent of this may vary between different groups and also between different types of research. It is, for example, well documented in the case of recruiting African Americans to medical research (see, for example, Corbie-Smith et al, 2002; Rajakumar et al, 2009; Agoritsas et al, 2011). Research evidence suggests that people from minority ethnic groups may be less likely to participate in research (Redwood and Gill, 2013). Reasons for this are discussed by, for example, Wendler et al (2006), Scharff et al (2010) and Brown et al (2014), who argue that inclusivity is affected by factors such as trust, recruitment methods and participants' access to researchers – trust that previous large-scale instances of unethical and harmful research, such as the Tuskegee Syphilis Study,[5] have violated. Other historical examples include experimental vaccine research on children from indigenous Canadian populations without their parents' consent (Lux, 1998), hepatitis research on children with intellectual disabilities (see, for example, Murphy, 2004, p 149) or the use of cell lines without the knowledge and consent of the original patient[6] (superbly summarised in Skloot, 2017). The effects of these and similar cases are still felt by the community (Scharff et al, 2010), and are also reflected today in some people's reluctance regarding a COVID-19 vaccine, reluctance that is particularly high in marginalised groups (Letzing, 2020).

For many disabled people, this is compounded by their experiences of poor treatment by academic institutions (see, for example, Waterfield et al, 2017) and by healthcare professionals, including, but not limited to, being ignored, spoken to in a condescending manner, overlooking the complaint they present with to focus on the disability instead so the complaint is not treated, and receiving substandard care (see, for example, Wen, 2014; Findlay, 2016; Read et al, 2018).

Ethical research has many facets, and one less obvious is the researcher's responsibility to only recruit as many participants as are needed. Due to the physical and emotional work involved in taking part, it could be considered unethical to recruit more participants than are really required, especially in sensitive research areas where participants are discussing upsetting or traumatic experiences. Therefore, issues of sample size need to be carefully considered and reviewed:

> The question of sample size is also important because the use of samples that are larger than needed is an ethical issue (because they waste research funds and participant time) and the use of samples that are smaller than needed is both an ethical and a scientific issue (because it may not be informative to use samples so small that results reflect idiosyncratic data and are thus not transferable, and may therefore be a waste of research funds and participant time). (Francis et al, 2010, p 1230)

Last, participation may require completion of a range of documents such as consent forms. Although this is designed to make sure that participants are comprehensively informed of their rights, it can have the counterintuitive effect of making them more wary of the institution and its research, as reported by Arfken and Balon (2011, p 326):

> At least one study we know had a longer consent process than the intervention being studied. Informed consent forms in cancer research studies routinely reach double-digit numbers of pages. One of us recently reviewed a protocol with an informed consent form that was 34 pages long. We have also personally heard potential participants say they do not trust consent sheets because, in the words of the people approached, they are written by lawyers to protect the university.

(Guidance on language use is available in Chapter 6, Checklist 21.)

7. Power imbalances may make it difficult for participants to advocate for themselves

This is closely related to the issue raised in points 3 and 6: will participants feel able to speak up when requesting accommodations? Do they trust the researcher or the institution to listen to their concerns and then act on them? The practice of reflexivity is part of the process of thinking through how the power balance in the research relationship may affect what participants are comfortable discussing, or whether they decide to be there at all. People, particularly those whose disability is invisible, often experience that their exhaustion and pain is interpreted as them 'being lazy' (Kattari et al, 2018) or 'being difficult' (Inckle, 2018), and that the nature of their condition is trivialised. At the same time, even when the condition is taken seriously, people can't always rely on others to proceed with the care and attention to detail required, something people with life-threatening allergies often encounter (see, for example, Kale, 2019). It is therefore understandable if some people have negative expectations or are wary of researchers, conscious that in a research setting their requests and needs may be dismissed (Kale, 2019).

8. The paperwork to participate in the study is too difficult or too complex

As mentioned previously in point 6, depending on the institution and the context in which the research takes place, participation may require completion of a range of documents, sometimes written in complex, formal language and spanning several pages. This may cause difficulties for participants with memory or executive function issues, reading difficulties, anxiety and so on, as well as participants with low literacy levels.[7, 8]

9. Participants aren't adequately compensated

While compensation can (and often does) take the form of more intangible 'perks' such as useful information, networking opportunities, the researcher's gratitude or the chance to win a prize in a draw, a more tangible form is financial compensation, either in the form of reimbursement for expenses or payment for the time. Where no or little compensation is offered, this could mean participants would incur a financial loss – which not everyone is able to take. This topic is further discussed in the section on payment later in this chapter.

CHECKLIST 4: RESEARCH DESIGN

☐ Consider the costs of possible accommodations and include them in funding applications.

☐ Flag up the need to offer accommodations to your supervisee(s), if you have any; flag up the need to offer accommodations to your supervisor(s), if you have them. Remind colleagues of the need to offer accommodations.

☐ Communicate possible accommodations clearly during *recruitment*. Lessening the burden of (potential) participants is key, and one way to do this is to remove the need to ask or check for accommodations, and with it, the need to disclose. Be specific about what is possible and what isn't, so that potential participants can make an informed decision.

☐ Carefully monitor your methodology during *data collection*. Look out for ways in which it could be improved in a future iteration and pay particular attention to participant feedback.

☐ Keep the limitations in mind when *writing up and documenting* your research. If some aspects of your research constituted barriers to participation, note and discuss in your report or paper what the implications are for the validity and representativeness of your results.

☐ When *publishing and disseminating* your research, think about whether your findings reach the people for whom they are important, and aim to acknowledge the work and effort of your participants.

The researcher

Ableist attitudes are widespread across society (Friedman and Owen, 2017), playing a significant role in creating barriers to easy and respectful social relationships (Friedman and Awsumb, 2019). **Aversive ableism** (Friedman, 2018) describes how people who would not verbalise ableist prejudice nevertheless may still hold uninformed or stereotyped attitudes about disability, or feel uncomfortable around disabled people, meaning that they treat disabled people differently. There are two implications of this that we would like to talk about here. The first is the impact of ableist attitudes on the way we communicate our research and work alongside disabled participants, and the second is how we gain an insight into and then address our own ableism.

In addition to the channels in which participants are approached, the way in which we communicate with participants can itself communicate our approach to disability and accessibility, and, with it, potential barriers to participation. The perception that they will experience stigmatising attitudes may deter disabled people from taking part (Bedini, 2000). This can be communicated through our choice of words, as well as the volunteering (or absence) of potential accommodations. Ableist attitudes stigmatise disability by treating it as a condition that is outside the norm (Branco et al, 2019). This can be expressed in the form of **microaggressions** – brief comments, behaviour and language that convey ignorance, and negative expectations of or negative views about disabled people (Olkin et al, 2019). Because these attitudes are commonplace and based on stereotypes of the way a disabled person is expected to look and behave, they may not be called into question. Microaggressions can be expressed by researchers as well as by people in the wider community (Hofmann et al, 2020).

Interactions between research staff and disabled participants may also be characterised by an absence of easy, spontaneous interactions that researchers may feel able to have with non-disabled participants. Referred to as the 'Dinner Table syndrome', this is an experience D/deaf or hearing-impaired people often report: where the flow of conversations relies on auditory cues for turn-taking, people who cannot perceive those cues are effectively shut out of the conversation (Withey, 2018; Meek, 2020). One of the consequences may be that researchers will be less at ease and, in turn, less able to put participants at ease through their interactions – something that could also be perceived as a microaggression.

The impact of constantly having to deal with negative attitudes is anger, embarrassment and frustration, and, ultimately, the person is likely to lose trust that organisations and their staff will treat people respectfully (Keller and Galgay, 2010, Chapter 11; Lett et al, 2020). Consequently, signalling that accommodating disability is viewed as a problem, or that the disabled person will have to repeatedly justify what they need, is likely to deter participants altogether.

On the other hand, the perception that the researcher is knowledgeable and respectful, or disabled themselves, may affect participants' willingness to participate or disclose their own disability. Note that inexperience itself is *not* the issue; what is needed is the willingness to learn, reflect (graciously) on mistakes, and do better the next time.

Tackling our own attitudes is a process, and, while targeted training and education help reduce stereotypes and prejudice, the effectiveness of interventions, such as unconscious bias training, is contested (see, for example, Atewologun et al, 2018; Noon, 2018). In their review of prejudice-reduction interventions, Paluck and Green (2009) identify extended contact, whether through activities such as teamwork or cooperative learning, as one of the few empirically validated types of interventions to reduce prejudice and to have an effect on behaviour.

In addition to structured training we recommend a continuous approach to improving awareness and familiarity with disability by, for example, building research partnerships with disabled-led organisations (see Appendices 1 and 2) and following disabled authors and writers on social media. Rather than suggesting individual accounts, we recommend using hashtags like the ones below to start following the conversation:

- #disability, #disabled
- #ChronicIllness
- #a11y (particularly Twitter)
- #CripTheVote
- #ActuallyAutistic
- #InvisibleIllness (particularly Instagram)
- #DeafTalent
- #DisabledArtist
- #WeShallNotBeRemoved

Above all, we need to respect and believe what disabled people tell us about their experiences, even and especially if these experiences don't match our own.

Limitations

In the previous section we presented the factors affecting participation individually. In practice, they are interlinked and connected. Inaccessible communication can communicate the researcher's inexperience or unwillingness; unpaid participation exacerbates barriers caused by the lack of available and accessible public transport; undue burdens to participate may further distrust in the institution. In turn, this means that it is rarely enough to 'fix' one individual aspect, but that a systemic, holistic approach is needed.

At the same time, we are well aware that trying to address these issues can feel overwhelming and sometimes impossible within existing institutional constraints. And these constraints will be more restricting for some than for others. Established researchers may be in a better position to ask for more funding, hire additional staff, pay for participation or approach research questions that get overlooked or neglected. Ideally, costs to improve or provide accessibility should be an integral part of any project funding, but sometimes the budget is determined by external factors and is outside our control.

Early career researchers, or people who work for a company or a charity, may not have a choice of research question, or may not be in a position to influence some or all aspects of the research methodology. Students working on a course project or a final year dissertation may have been given the research question with no recourse to substantially change the question or method. There may be limited funds and/or limited time. But there are sources of help available. We have included a list of sources for help in this chapter, and have collected links to relevant organisations and charities in Appendices 1 and 2.

CHECKLIST 5: RECRUITMENT

☐ Reflect on your position as a researcher and to what extent the research questions may exacerbate existing inequalities. Which groups are excluded from participation? Who benefits from your research?

☐ Think about how to reach out to participants. Are there any groups or communities that may not be reached through the usual recruiting channels?

☐ Compare the practicality and accessibility of the means of recruiting. Are they accessible to all? Is it easier or more difficult for some than for others?

☐ Reflect on your institution's relationship with the wider community. How might your change in approach to research affect this relationship?

☐ Carefully consider the effort entailed by participation. This includes effort from enquiring for more information to participating to accessing any subsequent results. How much physical effort is required? Is the burden of participation heavier for some than for others? How much flexibility can you show?

☐ Identify the tangible and intangible benefits for the participant. Will the results be made available to participants?

Use of secondary data

In the previous section we mentioned some of the limitations that might apply to our research and that affect our ability to make our research accessible. Some of these limitations also apply when we use secondary data, as participant recruitment and data collection are outside our control. It's often difficult to determine how accessible the primary study was, since accessibility is very rarely mentioned in the writing up of research (an issue we will discuss in more detail in Chapter 9). Consider, for example, the following questions:

- How were participants approached and informed?
- How did researchers communicate with potential participants?
- Was participation remunerated?
- How flexible was the scheduling? Were participants able to drop in and out?
- Where material was used, how accessible was it? Were different formats available?

These questions relate primarily to empirical research where human participants are involved, but secondary data can also involve archival data or behavioural traces such as shopping receipts, tracking of webpage visits, purchasing patterns, letters and so on. Consider carefully whether any of the activities or items involved are equally accessible to all, or whether any systematic barriers might exist.

Many of the questions raised above require that we critically look at our own work and our approach. Our own assumptions and, of course, our own choices have a direct bearing on our research. Reflexivity is therefore a critical part of research.

Reflexivity

Qualitative research approaches see research findings as co-constructed, meaning that although the researcher collects data from participants, they also have an important influence on the research outcomes. This can happen in several ways:

- Through the researcher's selection of the topic, and what is seen as an important research question.
- Through their decisions about how the topic is approached and how the sample is chosen.

- Through their interaction with participants, which may have an impact on what the participants choose to tell them.
- Through their analysis of the data, as they make choices about what should be included.

Reflexivity is the process of acknowledging and documenting the impact this influence may have had. It involves the consideration of how issues, such as sex, class, disability, ethnicity or age, may affect the research. One example is of the impact of the researcher's gender on what participants are comfortable to discuss with them (see, for example, Kane and Macaulay, 1993). Researchers need to thoughtfully explore how their personal qualities and life experience might have affected the research approach, sample selection, analysis and findings.

Gaining access to participants depends not only on the researcher's ability to access but also on the participants' willingness to come forward; opportunities to access can reflect attitude, understanding of the field, research experience and good relationships with gatekeepers and potential participants (Riese, 2018). Having existing knowledge of the field can also affect the research. Merriam et al's concept (2001) of 'insider' and 'outsider' knowledge shows how being (perceived to be) part of the field may influence both the researcher's expectations of what they might discover and participants' expectations about what the researcher knows. The perception that the researcher is an 'outsider' might, for example, mean participants have to explain themselves in more detail, whereas they may gloss over those descriptions when talking to someone they think shares their level of knowledge. They might also take longer to build trust with someone they perceive as an outsider.

In some research methodologies, a reflexive process is part of the method, and the data collection or analysis may be planned to enhance researcher reflections. For example, in constructivist grounded theory (Charmaz, 2014), the processes of constant comparison and memo writing are intended to help researchers become aware of their preconceptions and biases.

Researchers' unconscious bias may account for a particular approach to data analysis. For example, sometimes researchers attribute responses to or decisions about fertility to ethnicity, religion or culture when they are made by patients from a minority ethnic group, while similar decisions made by majority ethnic participants may be attributed to individual choice and agency (Chattoo, 2015). There can be a temptation to focus on data when they consist of an interview or visual data that are expressed in a compelling way, while overlooking data that are just as important to the research but are expressed in ways that are less emotionally affecting (Mauthner and Doucet, 2003). Reflexive practices are intended to uncover such biases.

In the context of disability, reflexivity means that researchers need to be aware of the diversity inherent within the population, as well as within their sample, and to consider what that means for their research. Interdisciplinarity is also a factor: disabled people are often multiply disadvantaged, particularly compared to researchers, who are often, by comparison, highly educated and often middle class (Holloway and Jefferson, 2000). Disability stigma and unconscious bias may affect the researcher's attitudes, and this may lead to exclusionary practices – for example, the assumption that if a person is employed they are not disabled and, because of this assumption, failing to plan or offer any accommodations, which may mean that some people cannot take part.

Payment

Paying expenses for research participants presents different issues from that of payment of incentives, although both are often provided during recruitment to research because they increase research participation. Incentives may have a value that is unrelated to the financial cost of participation, or may be given as a voucher rather than cash, while expenses cover the actual cost of taking part.

There are pragmatic reasons for offering to cover expenses for research participants. It shows respect that there may be a financial cost to participation, particularly if taking part means participants have to travel to the researcher, take time off work or pay for childcare. This could particularly affect disabled participants for the following reasons:

- Disabled people are more likely to be employed in low-paid, precarious or part-time jobs (Powell, 2020), meaning that expenses may be a proportionately higher portion of their income.
- The 'disability employment penalty' (Berthoud, 2009), a measure of the extent to which disabled people are less likely to have a job, means disabled people are more likely to be unemployed due to misperceptions about their capability or employability.
- It may cost disabled people more to take part in research than other participants, as they may need, for example, to use a wheelchair-accessible taxi rather than public transport.

Asking any participants to spend time taking part, and to pay for their own travel, can place a financial burden on them if they are in low-paid or precarious employment (regardless of whether or not they are disabled). Providing expenses is a way to mitigate this disadvantage and to ensure that people who want to participate can still do so.

The issue of expenses could also be considered an aspect of the power relationship between researcher and research participant, particularly since researchers are paid to conduct research, and participants are taking part voluntarily and are (usually) unpaid. Ethics guidelines from professional associations such as the British Psychological Society (BPS) or British Sociological Association (BSA) generally caution against the payment of incentives as it may encourage people to take part in research that might cause distress. However, the National Institute for Health Research (NIHR, 2018) has a schedule of recommended payments for research participants as a way to acknowledge the effort involved. Practices may differ depending on the field, but it is important to make clear to participants whether any expenses and/ or payment are involved, and to document how this might affect recruitment. Any payment also needs to be included in the research budget from the start, and should be included in any funding bid (Breckenridge et al, 2017). Finally, given that disabled participants are often on a low income and may find it difficult to wait for their expenses to be repaid, any payment needs to be delivered promptly. This may mean making arrangements with an institution's finance team well in advance of the research data collection. Prompt payment of expenses and incentives also benefits other participants on a low income – bearing in mind that people may not want to discuss their financial circumstances with a researcher.

Advisory or reference groups

An **advisory group** is a panel formed to give knowledgeable guidance and a degree of oversight to a research project, to ensure it remains on topic, and to give reflections and a steer on research issues as they arise. It is made up of people with relevant experience in the field who can give an informed view.

Where the focus of the project is related to disability or another equality-seeking group, an advisory group might be part of a wider participatory research approach that seeks to enable marginalised groups to set the research agenda. Often, they are used more broadly to ensure that researchers have access to a breadth of experience in the field. For example, an advisory group for a research project on HR in the construction industry might consist of employees, HR specialists, construction specialists and trade union reps. In health and education research, the use of advisory groups can be part of a process called patient and public involvement (PPI) (NIHR and INVOLVE, 2012), where members of the public actively get involved with research projects, feeding back their views to influence the way the project is planned and conducted and to ensure the researchers maintain focus on the implications for affected groups (Turk et al, 2017). The underlying principle is that research that has an impact on members of the public should be conducted 'with' or 'by' them rather than 'to', 'about' or 'for' them (NIHR, 2020).

VIGNETTE

Two years ago, the county's health service established an early intervention team to support young adults aged 14–17 who received their first diagnosis of depression. Tanisha's research group has been tasked with examining the young adults' experience with the intervention. Although Tanisha herself has a background in clinical psychology, she is well aware of the complexity and sensitivity of the research, and begins to assemble an advisory group including young people from local depression support groups and parents of young adults with depression.

There are advantages to setting up or having access to a reference group. Members can help to ensure that research questions are relevant to the topic and advise on recruitment, on the most appropriate ways to conduct research and what may be likely to work (or not work) for participants, and on the use of appropriate plain language for presenting research findings. However, similar considerations apply to members of advisory groups as to sampling – participation needs to be open to people at a time and at a level that suits them and works with their existing commitments (Pandey et al, 2015).

Help is available if we are looking for people to take part. Organisations such as Involve specialise in helping research projects find volunteers to take part in research projects, as co-researchers, advisory group members, for PPI, and as participants in the research itself.

Using an advisory group could be seen as a form of quality assurance similar to **respondent validation** (Bryman, 2012, p 391). This practice happens after the research has been completed, when the researcher provides participants with a summary of the research outcomes and asks for their views, to see whether and how far participants corroborate the research findings. (This was discussed further in Chapter 2.)

Accessibility and ethics approval

Although we think that accessibility (or the lack thereof) should play an integral role in applying for and receiving ethics approval for a study, the reality is that most institutions don't ask whether research that does not explicitly include disabled participants is accessible.

As part of our earlier research, we looked at how accessibility was addressed in publicly available higher education (HE) institutional ethics guidelines and ethical guidance provided by research funding bodies (Aidley and Fearon, 2020). We found that most guidance was vague about whether researchers needed to address this and what they needed to do. Where it mentioned disability at all, it did so in one of two contexts:

- A requirement that research should be conducted in a non-discriminatory way, but without giving guidance about what this meant in practice.
- A reference to disability only in the context of vulnerability (BSA, 2017, p 6) or in ways that appeared to conflate all cognitive impairments with intellectual disabilities, assuming that these participants would have issues with capacity to consent and vulnerability (ESRC, 2015, p 8).

The BSA and the Economic and Social Research Council (ESRC) are not alone in conflating disability and vulnerability. It's a view that's as pervasive as it is insidious in the way it perpetuates harmful stereotypes on disability: 'Wherever operative, the ableist conflation flattens communication about disability to communication about pain, suffering, hardship, disadvantage, morbidity, and mortality' (Reynolds, 2017, p 152), which is why people are calling for an end to its use (see, for example, Deane, 2020; Pring, 2020).

It seems, then, that there may be a tension between the need to document practices that make research more accessible and a lack of clarity about the way that might impact a research ethics application. We need to take advice about how this is addressed in our own institution to guide what we say about the accommodations that are being made; for example, how aware is our institution that dyslexia is not an intellectual impairment and does not carry the same issues of potential vulnerability and consent?

Part of the definition of ethical research is that it is high-quality research, with questions about sampling being a frequent reason why ethics committees request changes to ethics applications

(Bryman, 2012, Chapter 6). In some cases, receiving ethics approval requires an assessment of the extent to which research touches on issues of gender equality, or where protocols can be adjusted to provide equal access to research participation. Ideally, we would like to see a similar requirement added concerning accessibility. We are well aware, however, that in asking this we would be adding to the ever-increasing workload of researchers, particularly in academia. But, equally, the situation as it is now is unsatisfactory. Considering the ethics of inaccessible research is a first necessary, but not sufficient, step.

Approaches to applying for ethical approval

If we are in a position to give approval, bear accessibility in mind and consider ways in which we could use our power and privilege as a supervisor or ethics reviewer to ensure researchers consider research accessibility.

CHECKLIST 6: APPLYING FOR ETHICAL APPROVAL

☐ Design the research process so that opportunities for reflexivity are embedded into it at each stage.

☐ Take advice on how the research is conducted to identify potential areas where participants might need to be accommodated.

☐ In the ethics application, relate any anticipatory steps taken to demographics about the general population.

☐ Consider and document your decisions regarding incentives and expenses.

☐ Make the payment arrangements clear to participants and, if relevant, consider the potential implications of receiving vouchers and expenses for participants who claim benefits.

☐ In the research proposal, describe the data quality issues that you are addressing through measures such as accessible research practice.

☐ Be transparent about your role in the research and the way you, as an individual researcher, may influence it.

When applying for ethics approval, the ethics approval process can be used as a lever for accommodations we need to make, or the institution needs to be able to make, so we can conduct our research in an ethical manner. This means being mindful of the language we use in our ethics application because disability is so often conflated with vulnerability (see Chapter 2 for a longer discussion on this topic).

Sources of support and advice

Navigating these steps can be challenging and complex, but there are some potential sources of advice and guidance that may be available:

- Supervisor: students undertaking research have an academic supervisor who can advise on all aspects of the research process. They will also be able to signpost to further sources of advice if needed.
- Researcher training: your institution's researcher development team is likely to offer courses to research skills and may be able to advise on funding for courses outside the institution if training is not offered by them. The Graduate School or Doctoral College is the point of contact for student research training, and should be able to advise where specific types of help and training can be accessed.
- Check with national and regional organisations that provide researcher training as they often also offer sessions on accessibility.
- Disability support office: most universities have staff with this area of expertise. Although they are mainly focused on supporting students, members of staff may be able to allow time to give advice on research accessibility issues.
- Your own institution's online learning and web teams: again, these staff are mainly focused on supporting staff and students in online learning, but they also have a great deal of expertise in digital accessibility, and may be able to give guidance.
- Software providers: if we are using institutionally provided tools (such as Qualtrics), we should be able to get technical support and advice on accessibility for that tool or service.

Summary

In this chapter we looked at some of the ways in which a research question touches on questions of accessibility, from the development of the research question to who gets to ask it in the first place – and how the question gets answered. We then discussed a number of factors affecting participation, particularly for disabled participants, and how researchers might address these. We stressed the importance of reflexivity and clear communication throughout the entire research process, and acknowledged the limitations within institutional and organisational frameworks. We talked about accessibility in the context of ethics approval, and introduced further sources of support.

Notes

1   For example, Bram Cohen of BitTorrent (Asperger syndrome), David Neeleman of JetBlue (attention deficit hyperactivity disorder, ADHD) and Ralph Braun of BraunAbility (muscular dystrophy).

2   For example, Marlee Matlin (hearing impairment) and Lauren Potter (diagnosed with Down's syndrome).

3   For example, Lenín Moreno (president of Ecuador, 2017–to date; uses a wheelchair) and Kelly Vincent (sat in the Parliament of South Australia; has cerebral palsy).

4   For example, every single athlete participating in the Paralympics.

5   The Tuskegee syphilis study ran between 1932 and 1972, tracking the health and lives of several hundred Black men who were actively and maliciously deceived into thinking they had participated in a long-term study monitoring their health. In reality, they had been infected with syphilis so the researchers could observe the progression of the illness over time, and treatment was actively withheld. It is important to note that, while the Tuskegee study is one of the most well known instances of the abuse and deception of Black patients, it is by no means the only nor the most severe case, as is meticulously documented in Harriet A. Washington's (2006) *Medical Apartheid: The Dark History of Medical Experimentation on Black Americans from Colonial Times to the Present*, New York: Random House.

6   A cell line refers to the use of an initial cell sample in a growth medium to create a supply of identical cells for use in research.

7   This guide by the University of Pittsburgh gives a range of recommendations on how to inform and gain consent from participants who have low literacy. However, we should point out that the conflation of guidance for low literacy and disabled participants in one document is, in our view, misleading: www.hrpo.pitt.edu/guidance-forms/low-literacy-disabled-participants

8   We are aware, of course, that many institutions impose a similar, if not more complex, burden of documentation and approval onto the researcher, but here we are focused on the perception of people outside the system.

Further reading

Goodley, D. (2016) *Disability Studies: An Interdisciplinary Introduction*, London: SAGE Publications Ltd.
See Chapter 3 of Goodley's book for a longer discussion on the intersection between disability and other equality-seeking groups.

Landrine, H., Klonoff, E.A. and Brown-Collins, A. (1992) 'Cultural diversity and methodology in feminist psychology', *Psychology of Women Quarterly*, 16, 145–63.

Martin, D., Gholson, M. and Leonard, J. (2010) 'Mathematics as gatekeeper: Power and privilege in the production of knowledge', *Journal of Urban Mathematics Education*, 3(2), 12–24.

McCorkel, J.A. and Myers, K. (2003) 'What difference does difference make? Position and privilege in the field', *Qualitative Sociology*, 26(2), 199–231. Available at: https://doi.org/10.1023/A:1022967012774
On privilege and the power to ask questions.

Merriam, S.B., Johnson-Bailey, J., Lee, M.Y., Kee, Y., Ntseane, G. and Muhamad, M. (2001) 'Power and positionality: Negotiating insider/outsider status within and across cultures', *International Journal of Lifelong Education*, 20(5), 405–16.
A classic work reviewing the perception of the researcher's 'insider' or 'outsider' status and how it affects the research.

NIHR (National Institute of Health Research)/INVOLVE (2020) *Briefing Notes for Researchers*. Available at: www.invo.org.uk/resource-centre/resource-for-researchers
Ten briefing notes from NIHR on how to involve the public in every stage of research, including case studies from existing projects.

Olkin, R. (2004) 'Making research accessible to participants with disabilities', *Journal of Multicultural Counseling and Development*, 32, 332–43.
A good overview on accessibility in research.

Patrick, J.H., Pruchno, R.A. and Rose, M.S. (1998) 'Recruiting research participants: A comparison of the costs and effectiveness of five recruitment strategies', *Gerontologist*, 38(3), 295–302. Available at: https://doi.org/10.1093/geront/38.3.295
A comparison of different recruitment strategies in their effectiveness to recruit a more racially diverse sample.

Reid, P.T. (1993) 'Poor women in psychological research: Shut up and shut out', *Psychology of Women Quarterly*, 17(2), 133–50. Available at: https://doi.org/10.1111/j.1471-6402.1993.tb00440.x
How psychological research excludes poor women.

Rios, D., Magasi, S., Novak, C. and Harniss, M. (2016) 'Conducting accessible research: Including people with disabilities in public health, epidemiological, and outcomes studies', *American Journal of Public Health*, 106(12), 2137–44.

A discussion of how to approach accessible research design in the context of health research.

Scharff, D.P., Mathews, K.J., Jackson, P., Hoffsuemmer, J., Martin, E. and Edwards, D. (2010) 'More than Tuskegee: Understanding mistrust about research participation', *Journal of Health Care for the Poor and Underserved*, 21(3), 879–97.
A qualitative study exploring some of the reasons African Americans in particular are reluctant to participate in research.

References

Agoritsas, T., Deom, M. and Perneger, T.V. (2011) 'Study design attributes influenced patients' willingness to participate in clinical research: A randomized vignette-based study', *Journal of Clinical Epidemiology*, 64(1), 107–15.

Aidley, D. and Fearon, K. (2020) 'Does Empirical Research on Work and Employment Consider the Needs of Disabled Participants? An Empirical Investigation', in S.N. Just, A. Risberg and F. Villesèche (eds) *Routledge Companion to Organizational Diversity Research Methods*, London: Routledge, pp 75–90.

Arfken, C.L. and Balon, R. (2011) 'Declining participation in research studies', *Psychotherapy and Psychosomatics*, 80(6), 325–8. Available at: https://doi.org/10.1159/000324795

Atewologun, D., Cornish, T. and Tresh, F. (2018) *Unconscious Bias Training: An Assessment of the Evidence for Effectiveness*, Research Report, Equality and Human Rights Commission.

Bedini, L.A. (2000) '"Just sit down so we can talk": Perceived stigma and community recreation pursuits of people with disabilities', *Therapeutic Recreation Journal*, 34(1), 55–68.

Berthoud, R. (2009) *Measuring the Impact of Disability Benefits: A Feasibility Study*, No 2009-06, ISER Working Paper Series, Colchester: ISER, University of Essex.

Branco, C., Ramos, M.R. and Hewstone, M. (2019) 'The association of group-based discrimination with health and wellbeing: A comparison of ableism with other "isms"', *Journal of Social Issues*, 75(3), 814–46.

Breckenridge, J.P., Devaney, J., Duncan, F., Kroll, T., et al (2017) 'Conducting Sensitive Research with Disabled Women Who Experience Domestic Abuse During Pregnancy: Lessons from a Qualitative Study', in *SAGE Research Methods Cases Part 2*, London: SAGE Publications Ltd.

Brown, G., Marshall, M., Bower, P., Woodham, A. and Waheed, W. (2014) 'Barriers to recruiting ethnic minorities to mental health research: A systematic review', *International Journal of Methods in Psychiatric Research*, 23(1), 36–48.

Bryman, A. (2012) *Social Research Methods*, Oxford: Oxford University Press.

BSA (British Sociological Association) (2017) *Statement of Ethical Practice*. Available at: www.britsoc.co.uk/media/24310/bsa_statement_of_ethical_practice.pdf

Charmaz, K. (2014). *Constructing Grounded Theory*, London: SAGE Publications Ltd.

Chattoo, S. (2015) 'Mapping race: Critical approaches to health disparities research', *Ethnic and Racial Studies*, 38(13), 2417–19.

Cole, M.S., Bedeian, A.G. and Feild, H.S. (2006) 'The measurement equivalence of web-based and paper-and-pencil measures of transformational leadership: A multinational test', *Organizational Research Methods*, 9(3), 339–68.

Corbie-Smith, G., Thomas, S.B. and St George, D.M.M. (2002) 'Distrust, race, and research', *Archives of Internal Medicine*, 161(21), 2458–63. Available at: https://doi.org/10.1001/archinte.162.21.2458

Deane, K. (2020) 'Don't call me vulnerable', SRHE (The Society for Research into Higher Education), 3 August. Available at: https://srheblog.com/2020/08/03/dont-call-me-vulnerable

ESRC (Economic and Social Research Council) (2015) *Framework for Research Ethics*. Available at: https://esrc.ukri.org/files/funding/guidance-for-applicants/esrc-framework-for-research-ethics-2015

Evelly, J. (2018) 'City buses are wheelchair-accessible, but disabled riders still face obstacles', City Limits, 2 July. Available at: https://citylimits.org/2018/07/02/city-buses-are-wheelchair-accessible-but-disabled-riders-still-face-obstacles

Findlay, C. (2016) 'Getting it right: What people with disabilities want from their health care', ABC Health & Wellbeing, 19 December. Available at: www.abc.net.au/news/health/2016-12-20/what-people-with-disabilities-want-from-their-health-care/8127416

Francis, J.J., Johnston, M., Robertson, C., Glidewell, L., et al (2010) 'What is an adequate sample size? Operationalising data saturation for theory-based interview studies', *Psychology & Health*, 25(10), 1229–45. Available at: https://doi.org/10.1080/08870440903194015

Friedman, C. (2018) 'Aversive ableism: Modern prejudice towards disabled people', *Review of Disability Studies: An International Journal*, 14(4).

Friedman, C. and Awsumb, J.M. (2019) 'The symbolic ableism scale', *Review of Disability Studies: An International Journal*, 15(1).

Friedman, C. and Owen, A.L. (2017) 'Defining disability: Understandings of and attitudes towards ableism and disability', *Disability Studies Quarterly*, 37(1).

Hofmann, M., Kasnitz, D., Mankoff, J. and Bennett, C.L. (2020) 'Living Disability Theory: Reflections on Access, Research, and Design', in the 22nd International ACM SIGACCESS Conference on Computers and Accessibility, October, pp 1–13.

Holloway, W. and Jefferson, T. (2000) 'Researching the Fear of Crime', in W. Holloway and T. Jefferson (eds) *Doing Qualitative Research Differently: Free Association, Narrative and the Interview Method*, London: SAGE Publications Ltd, pp 7–24.

Inckle, K. (2018) 'Unreasonable adjustments: The additional unpaid labour of academics with disabilities', *Disability & Society*, 33(8), 1372–6.

Kale, S. (2019) '"Eating that meal could kill you": When cooks don't take food allergies seriously', *The Guardian*, 11 September. Available at: www.theguardian.com/society/2019/sep/11/take-food-allergies-seriously-people-can-die

Kane, E.W. and Macaulay, L.J. (1993) 'Interviewer gender and gender attitudes', *Public Opinion Quarterly*, 57(1), 1–28.

Kattari, S.K., Olzman, M. and Hanna, M.D. (2018) '"You look fine!" Ableist experiences by people with invisible disabilities', *Affilia*, 33(4), 477–92.

Keller, R.M. and Galgay, C.E. (2010) 'Microaggressive Experiences of People with Disabilities', in D.W. Sue (ed) *Microaggressions and Marginality: Manifestation, Dynamics, and Impact*, Hoboken, NJ: John Wiley & Sons Inc, pp 241–68.

Lett, K., Tamaian, A. and Klest, B. (2020) 'Impact of ableist microaggressions on university students with self-identified disabilities', *Disability & Society*, 35(9), 1441–56.

Letzing, J. (2020) 'How a history of "medical racism" may fuel mistrust in COVID-19 vaccines', World Economic Forum, 9 December. Available at: www.weforum.org/agenda/2020/12/how-a-history-of-medical-racism-may-fuel-mistrust-in-covid-19-vaccines

Link, M.W., Battaglia, M.P., Frankel, M.R., Osborn, L. and Mokdad, A.H. (2007) 'Reaching the US cell phone generation: Comparison of cell phone survey results with an ongoing landline telephone survey', *Public Opinion Quarterly*, 71(5), 814–39. Available at: https://doi.org/10.1093/poq/nfm051

Lux, M. (1998) 'Perfect subjects: Race, tuberculosis, and the Qu'Appelle BCG vaccine trial', *Canadian Bulletin of Medical History*, 15(2), 277–95.

Mauthner, N.S. and Doucet, A. (2003) 'Reflexive accounts and accounts of reflexivity in qualitative data analysis', *Sociology*, 37(3), 413–31.

Meek, D.R. (2020) 'Dinner Table syndrome: A phenomenological study of deaf individuals' experiences with inaccessible communication', *The Qualitative Report*, 25(6), 1676A–94.

Merriam, S.B., Johnson-Bailey, J., Lee, M.Y., Kee, Y., Ntseane, G. and Muhamad, M. (2001) 'Power and positionality: Negotiating insider/outsider status within and across cultures', *International Journal of Lifelong Education*, 20(5), 405–16.

Murphy, T.F. (2004) *Case Studies in Biomedical Research Ethics*, Cambridge, MA: MIT Press.

NIHR (National Institute for Health Research) and INVOLVE (2012) *Diversity and Inclusion. What's it about and why is it important for public involvement in research?* Available at: www.invo.org.uk/wp-content/uploads/2012/10/INVOLVEDiversityandInclusionOct2012.pdf

NIHR (National Institute of Health Research) (2018) *Reward and Recognition for Public Contributors: A Guide to the Payment of Fees and Expenses*, April. Available at: www.nihr.ac.uk/documents/reward-and-recognition-for-public-contributors-a-guide-to-the-payment-of-fees-and-expenses/12248

NIHR (National Institute for Health Research) (2020) 'How we involve patients, carers and the public in health research.' Available at: www.nihr.ac.uk/about-us/our-contribution-to-research/how-we-involve-patients-carers-and-the-public.htm

Noon, M. (2018) 'Pointless diversity training: Unconscious bias, new racism and agency', *Work, Employment & Society*, 32(1), 198–209.

Olkin, R. (2004) 'Making research accessible to participants with disabilities', *Journal of Multicultural Counseling and Development*, 32, 332–43.

Olkin, R., Hayward, H.S., Abbene, M.S. and VanHeel, G. (2019) 'The experiences of microaggressions against women with visible and invisible disabilities', *Journal of Social Issues*, 75(3), 757–85.

Paluck, E.L. and Green, D.P. (2009) 'Prejudice reduction: What works? A review and assessment of research and practice', *Annual Review of Psychology*, 60, 339–67.

Pandey, S., Porter, M. and Bhattacharya, S. (2015) 'What women want from women's reproductive health research: A qualitative study', *Health Expectations*, 18(6), 2606–15.

Powell, A. (2020) 'People with disabilities in employment', Research Briefing, No 7540, House of Commons Library, London: The Stationery Office. Available at: https://commonslibrary.parliament. uk/research-briefings/cbp-7540

Pring, J. (2020) 'Coronavirus: Peer calls for an end to use of "vulnerable" to describe disabled people', Disability News Service, 25 June. Available at: www.disabilitynewsservice.com/coronavirus-peer-calls-for-an-end-to-use-of-vulnerable-to-describe-disabled-people

Rajakumar, K., Thomas, S.B., Musa, D., Almario, D. and Garza, M.A. (2009) 'Racial differences in parents' distrust of medicine and research', *Archives of Paediatrics and Adolescent Medicine*, 163(2), 108–14. Available at: https://doi.org/10.1001/archpediatrics.2008.521

Read, S., Heslop, P., Turner, S., Mason-Angelow, V., et al (2018) 'Disabled people's experiences of accessing reasonable adjustments in hospitals: A qualitative study', *BMC Health Services Research*, 18(1), 1–10.

Redwood, S. and Gill, P.S. (2013) 'Under-representation of minority ethnic groups in research – Call for action', *British Journal of General Practice*, 63(612), 342–3.

Reynolds, J.M. (2017) '"I'd rather be dead than disabled" – The ableist conflation and the meanings of disability', *Review of Communication*, 17(3), 149–63. doi:10.1080/15358593.2017.1331255.

Riese, J. (2018) 'What is "access" in the context of qualitative research?', *Qualitative Research*, 19(6), 669–84. doi:10.1177/1468794118787713.

Rios, D., Magasi, S., Novak, C. and Harniss, M. (2016) 'Conducting accessible research: Including people with disabilities in public health, epidemiological, and outcomes studies', *American Journal of Public Health*, 106(12), 2137–44.

Scharff, D.P., Mathews, K.J., Jackson, P., Hofsuemmer, J., Martin, E. and Edwards, D. (2010) 'More than Tuskegee: Understanding mistrust about research participation', *Journal of Health Care for the Poor and Underserved*, 21(3), 879–97. Available at: https://doi.org/10.1353/hpu.0.0323

Shin, E., Johnson, T.P. and Rao, K. (2012) 'Survey mode effects on data quality: Comparison of web and mail modes in a US national panel survey', *Social Science Computer Review*, 30(2). Available at: https://doi.org/10.1177/0894439311404508

Skloot, R. (2017) *The Immortal Life of Henrietta Lacks*, New York: Broadway Paperbacks.

Turk, A., Boylan, A. and Locock, L. (2017) *A Researcher's Guide to Patient and Public Involvement*, Oxford: Oxford NIHR Biomedical Research Centre, University of Oxford.

Velho, R. (2019) 'Transport accessibility for wheelchair users: A qualitative analysis of inclusion and health', *International Journal of Transportation Science and Technology*, 8(2), 103–15.

Vicente, P. (2015) 'The best times to call in a mobile phone survey', *International Journal of Market Research*, 57(4). Available at: https://doi.org/10.2501/IJMR-2015-047

Waterfield, B., Beagan, B.B. and Weinberg, M. (2017) 'Disabled academics: A case study in Canadian universities', *Disability & Society*, 33(3), 327–48. doi:10.1080/09687599.2017.1411251

Wen, L. (2014) 'Doctor's ignorance stands in the way of care for the disabled', NPR, 17 May. Available at: www.npr.org/sections/health-shots/2014/05/17/313015089/doctors-ignorance-stands-in-the-way-of-care-for-the-disabled?t=1608378597251

Wendler, D., Kington, R., Madans, J., Van Wye, G., et al (2006) 'Are racial and ethnic minorities less willing to participate in health research?', *PLoS Medicine*. Available at: https://doi.org/10.1371/journal.pmed.0030019

Withey, R.-A. (2018) 'Dinner Table syndrome is for life, not just for Christmas', The Limping Chicken, 19 December. Available at: https://limpingchicken.com/2018/12/19/rebecca-anne-withey-dinner-table-syndrome-is-for-life-not-just-for-christmas

4

Sampling

Disabled people have frequently been excluded from research through an inflexible approach to sampling (Rios et al, 2016). This is the case even when, by making adaptations to the way the research is conducted, many disabled people could have taken part. Researchers argue that the reasons for exclusion relate to 'overestimation of vulnerability, underestimation of ability, lack of experience and discomfort with disability, devaluing and disrespecting attitudes, research requiring sample homogeneity, and lack of foresight and accommodation' (Feldman et al, 2013, p 1000). Some of these issues could be remedied by taking disability and accessibility into account when devising the sample. In this chapter we look at both qualitative and quantitative approaches to sampling, discussing each in turn.

Sampling and qualitative methods

In social science research, the aim is to discover, describe and theorise about what is happening in the field. When a researcher chooses a research sample, they seek to identify the group of people whose experience and views will produce answers to the research question, and, consequently, research findings that are authentic.

Sampling is approached very differently in qualitative and quantitative research, which reflects their different definitions of what constitutes knowledge. In qualitative research, the epistemological approach to knowledge is relativist (Braun and Clarke, 2013). This is the idea that, rather than being solely objective, knowledge is created and interpreted within a social and cultural context. So, while empirical research may still be based on observation and data, researchers using a relativist approach anticipate that participants will offer diverse perspectives that reflect their varying interpretations and understandings of the world.

Qualitative research explores and analyses subjective experiences, either through observation or by interacting with participants. It offers a 'thick description' of social phenomena (Geertz, 1973), a fuller description and interpretation of behaviour, feelings and interpretations. Rather than providing objective facts, the intention is to capture a complete range of different views and experiences that people might have and, in doing so, provide an in-depth understanding of the topic. This is the reason that the breadth of the sample is important: inaccessible research means that disabled people are prevented from taking part. Their experiences may be different from those of other participants, and, if they cannot participate, this additional richness will be missing from the research findings.

A qualitative methodology requires a research method that is suitable to collect qualitative data (see Chapter 2); qualitative sampling aims to choose participants with a wide variety of views and understanding of the research topic. These are some of the most common sampling strategies:

- Purposive/purposeful: recruits participants who can provide an informed response to the research question.
- Convenience: recruits participants who are easy for the researchers to access; a weakness is that participants may not reflect a breadth of experience.
- Snowball: recruits participants from the researcher's network of contacts and the wider social networks of existing participants by asking existing participants to refer others they know who might be willing to take part.
- Stratified: reflects the diversity of the researched group in order to reflect the diversity of experience. For example, a project may need to recruit people of a range of ages, so may aim to recruit a fixed number of participants from different age bands rather than accepting all potential participants.
- Theoretical: this usually relates to grounded theory, where sampling is iterative and may change as the research progresses and the researcher comes to understand more about the research topic. Data analysis begins as soon as data are collected, allowing the researcher to modify the sample to follow up promising lines of enquiry, or to stop recruiting in areas that turn out to be unproductive.

Purposive sampling usually guides the inclusion criteria for the project, as it is led by the need to access participants who know about or who have experienced the topic that is being researched. **Inclusion criteria** describe features that the participants must have, such as age, parenthood status or experience of working in a particular field. **Exclusion criteria** describe features that are excluded – for example, a study of fatherhood may exclude people who have not been fathers.

The factor that links the development of sampling frames in these approaches is that they are generally decided on by the researcher and, in epistemological terms, they all take the view that social phenomena exist independently of researchers' descriptions of them. By contrast, if using an emancipatory or participatory approach to research, the sample is discussed and agreed on – or decided by – the co-producers of the research and not the researcher alone; the group decides who would be the best source of data. As the co-producers of the research usually have insider knowledge of the field, this approach may produce a very effective sampling and recruitment strategy.

Issues with sampling

Sampling can be prone to bias; this is one of the reasons that researchers need to be reflexive about sampling as well as other aspects of their research. For example, most qualitative and, in fact, most quantitative samples are self-selected: participants choose whether or not to take part, and this in itself has an effect on the breadth of data that can be collected.

Snowball sampling and convenience sampling both rely on the subject matter of the research being a topic around which people can network. This may apply well to some topics but not to others. The digital or physical locations where people meet may not be accessible, and consequently, if disabled people cannot become part of the social network where research participation opportunities are shared, they will be excluded. Snowballing relies on existing participants' decisions as to who to talk to about the research, and they may discount the disabled people in their network (Browne, 2005).Alternatively, given that social media works on the principle of homophily,[1] and that many people feel awkward around disabled people and sometimes avoid them (Pring, 2015), social sharing may not be an effective way to reach a balanced sample. Despite the potential for snowball sampling to produce a narrow sample, it can also leverage existing trusted relationships between participants and their contacts, potentially giving access to participants who might not otherwise have decided to take part.

If we are looking for a sample that is a sub-set of the general population, the sample frame may not explicitly include or exclude disability if we are researching another topic. However, if we do not make it clear that disabilities will be accommodated, disabled people may assume they will not be able to take part. Active accessibility requires proactive and explicit communication.

VIGNETTE

Keiko is a 24-year-old student who is about to graduate and embark on her first full-time job. A few weeks back she participated in a study on graduates' experience of transitioning from university to work. About six months ago, Keiko had an accident that led to a speech impediment she is still quite self-conscious about. Because of this, she had asked to conduct the interview by email rather than in person, and, for a couple of weeks, had exchanged emails with Sean, the researcher, responding to follow-up questions, providing clarifications, elaborating on some answers, and so on. She receives an email from Sean today. He gives her an update on the progress of the study and summarises his findings from the interview, asking Keiko whether she feels fairly and adequately represented by Sean's work.

From this description of potential issues of sampling, it becomes clear that the way the research is presented in communication with potential participants (Becker et al, 2004) is an important factor in successfully recruiting a broad sample. This means that the way we recruit participants has an impact on reaching the right sample group for our research. (Chapter 5 goes on to look at ways to make sure our recruitment is targeting a broad group of potential participants.)

CHECKLIST 7: QUALITATIVE SAMPLING

☐ Ensure accessibility is built into the data collection process, for example by making your recruitment advertising and participant information accessible (see Chapters 5 and 6).

☐ Ensure that clear guidance on accessibility is included in the recruitment material.

☐ Do not include disability in the exclusion criteria unless there are sound, justifiable and evidenced reasons for it.

☐ Collect self-reported demographic data (with permission) to keep track of the number of disabled participants in your sample (bearing in mind the factors that affect the accuracy of self-reported disability status).

Research quality in qualitative studies

Measures of research quality differ between qualitative and quantitative research. Reliability, generalisability and validity, which are realist measures that are used in statistical research, are less easy to apply to qualitative studies because, in a relativist approach, it is expected that research will elicit more than one account of social reality. Research findings may vary depending on participants, setting and researcher, and have limited generalisability because of this. In this section we look at how accessible research can enhance some of these quality criteria for qualitative research.

Research quality is such an important topic that, by convention, every publication that reports research will include a discussion of the way in which it meets research quality criteria. The rigour of the study, as evidenced by the way it meets research quality criteria, also determines how useful the study may be to other researchers (Bryman, 2016, Chapter 17). When documenting research quality, it is important to consider both the strengths and the weaknesses of the study: the study limitations also help to contextualise the quality of the research by describing and analysing the reasons for its weaknesses.

Some quality criteria require evidence that the research has been conducted to high standards, which requires ongoing attention to specific ways of documenting research practice. In health research, for example, the quality of qualitative studies may be systematically evaluated to see whether it provides evidence of a high enough standard to influence practice (Rendle et al, 2019), and it is worth looking at the criteria that evaluators use if this is our field. So, it is important to plan in advance the kinds of activities and actions we will take, in the same way as we are expected to plan for impact in advance (as far as is feasible). Before we discuss what we might do, we begin by describing two commonly used qualitative approaches to research quality: Guba and Lincoln's (1994) two criteria of trustworthiness and authenticity, and Charmaz's (2014) four criteria for constructivist grounded theory studies.

Trustworthiness is made up of four criteria: credibility, transferability, dependability and confirmability:

- **Credibility** describes how well the research reflects participants' experiences. Credible research is demonstrably carried out according to best practice (established by descriptions of how it follows good research practice). In addition, credibility can be established through other steps such respondent validation, peer debriefing or triangulation, which act as ways to validate the findings.

- **Transferability** is the extent to which the research findings or the analytic concepts developed within the research can be applied to other research contexts. It is similar to generalisability in quantitative research. Transferability can be hard to achieve, as qualitative research tends to use small sample sizes for interview studies or case studies. Providing a 'thick description' (Geertz, 1973) is one way for researchers to assess whether research findings can apply to other settings.
- **Dependability** is assessed through methodological and theoretical transparency (Anney, 2014), meaning researchers need to keep complete records of the research process and (if possible) conduct a peer auditing processes that would establish how well the research findings related to the data.
- **Confirmability** refers to the researcher having recognised and (where possible) limited the extent to which their own personal views and life experience have affected the way that the research has been conducted and ultimately the findings that are presented.

Authenticity is also defined via a set of criteria: **fairness, ontological authenticity, educative authenticity, catalytic authenticity** and **tactical authenticity**. These criteria were proposed as a way to balance the trustworthiness criteria, which are focused mainly on methodological rigour, with criteria that reflect ethical issues such as the power relationship between researcher and participants, whether the range of values expressed by participants is reflected in the findings, and accountability.

For example, in Shields and Synnot's (2016) research on the barriers disabled children experienced when participating in physical activities, the children who took part were asked if they agreed with the researcher's interpretation of the focus group data. The data were also analysed by a team of researchers, a strategy to increase confirmability. Thomas et al (2019) describe how the transferability of their study on the social impact of visible disabilities might be limited due to the homogeneity of the sample, and how that may restrict the generalisability of the concepts they developed, while credibility was supported by a detailed description of the way the research was conducted.

Constructivist grounded theory (Charmaz, 2014, pp 336–8) proposes the criteria of credibility, originality, resonance and usefulness.

- **Credibility** relates to the quality of the research practice and whether the analysis follows on logically from a description of the findings.

- **Originality** refers to the requirement for the research to provide new insights about existing knowledge, or to extend the boundaries of academic knowledge in the field.
- **Resonance** refers to the extent to which the research question and research findings make sense to participants or others in their circumstances.
- **Usefulness** relates to research impact, both in academic terms of expanding existing knowledge, and for participants in terms of increasing understanding of their situation and improving practice.

These criteria combine a focus on evidencing high standards of methodological rigour with an acknowledgement of the social setting in which the research is conducted, and the impact this might have had on both the research and on the participants.

Researchers do not use all of these criteria in one study (Morse, 2015) and, in addition, some criteria relate well to specific research approaches (Amin et al, 2020). However, it is useful to consider each individual criterion and to decide which ones are useful for our study and which ones are less relevant or perhaps cannot be achieved.

So, how can accessible research practice potentially enhance the work we do towards creating high-quality research? These are some ways in which it could be included, both for methodological criteria and for authenticity and relevance.

Methodological criteria

For methodological criteria this might mean:

- **Thick description:** the experience of disabled people can differ from that of non-disabled people. Consequently, including disabled people in research could potentially improve the richness of the account by eliciting views and experiences that might not otherwise have been available.
- **Triangulation:** this could be evidenced by the use of different methods, different data sources or by using different members of the research team to collect and analyse the data (Braun and Clarke, 2013). The use of different methods can potentially enable participation from people who might find one method inaccessible but are able to use another.
- **Reflexivity:** this can be evidenced through strategies such as acknowledging the existence of ableism in the academy and its impact on, for example, perceptions of the trustworthiness of

disabled participants when relating their own experiences (Bogart and Dunn, 2019), journaling our own reflections on the process of planning and conducting accessible research, documenting what we have done to address the power relationship between researcher and participant, and considering the impact that may have had on the research relationship. For example, conducting research in an accessible way, and being flexible about participation, can build participants' trust in the researcher (Kidney and McDonald, 2014)

- **An audit trail:** the steps taken to make research accessible should be documented at every point where it is relevant. This could be contextualised by a discussion of the demographic data and feedback from participants, if this has been collected.
- **Peer debriefing:** this could involve a discussion with an experienced researcher who is not involved in the project, or with someone who is familiar with accessible research practice, looking at the data collection and analytic development to help uncover biases and assumptions.
- **Auditing:** where researchers who have not been involved in the project look at the data collected and check whether the findings and analysis are reasonable and fair. It is a huge amount of work, and may not be feasible for small projects.

Authenticity and relevance

For authenticity and relevance, accessibility could enhance the following:

- **Fairness:** research should be fair to participants, meaning that it should not exploit them and should accurately represent the full range of experiences and views in the findings and analysis. This includes ensuring that people who want to participate aren't excluded.
- **Participant validation:** asking participants to comment on the findings. Researchers have identified a number of problems with presenting a full analysis of the data in academic language to lay participants (discussed further in Bryman, 2016; Braun and Clarke, 2013). Not least of these is that participants may not be aware of the diversity of views expressed by others. However, presenting key research findings to participants in a format and language they can easily understand may elicit some useful feedback.
- If **research advisers** are employed who are part of the group we are researching with, they may be able to comment on any misunderstandings or lack of clarity within the findings and analysis.
- An **advisory group**, set up to give informed feedback, can provide commentary on the research findings.

As Braun and Clarke (2013, p 285) point out, 'quality criteria are not theoretically "neutral." They are also underpinned by assumptions about the goals of research.' For example, a research project that uses a methodology that stresses the co-production of knowledge will have more involvement from participants during the planning, data analysis and write-up phases, while one that is researcher-led may only involve participants in data collection. It is important to use quality measures that reflect the type of project we are doing.

In this context, research dissemination could be considered an expression of **accountability**: an ethical approach to conducting research that takes into account both its impact on the participants and their access to the research findings (Shakespeare, 2002; Barnes, 2009). (Chapter 9 discusses how to disseminate and present research findings in an accessible way.)

CHECKLIST 8: QUALITATIVE RESEARCH QUALITY

☐ Choose and justify the quality criteria that you are going to apply to your research.

☐ When writing up the research, compare the characteristics of the actual research sample with those of the planned sampling frame, and describe how and why they are different.

☐ Document the limitations of the sample frame (both potential and observed).

☐ Plan and schedule the activities related to achieving quality criteria. For example, if you are using member checking, check with participants whether this is feasible for them and they are willing to do this, when they will be needed, and whether they are available.

☐ When writing up or publishing research, include disability as a demographic characteristic of the study sample in the methodology section, and say how you approached this.

☐ Describe the action you have taken towards ensuring accountability, both to participants and to the research community.

Having looked at sampling from a qualitative perspective, we now turn to the quantitative approach.

Sampling and quantitative methods

Sampling is a key aspect of our research as the composition of our sample directly influences the quality of our findings. In quantitative methods, adjacent terms that spring to mind are **validity** and **reliability**. Of the two, validity is the one relating most to sampling and its implications. As a short introduction, let's think about using a measuring tape to measure someone's height. Reliability means that – assuming the person doesn't actually change their height – a measuring tape will give us the same result on repeat measurements; a tape measure is a fairly reliable instrument. But high reliability is not everything: using the tape measure to measure intelligence would still give us excellent reliability – but no validity at all.

When we talk about sampling, we are concerned with validity: to what extent do the results we find reflect the true facts? For example, if two-thirds of our sample reject tuition fees, does this mean we can reasonably expect to find widespread rejection of tuition fees in the relevant population? We also refer to this as **representativeness**: to what extent does the sample represent the population we are ultimately interested in? If our sample consists exclusively or primarily of students or their parents, our answers will probably differ from answers given by a sample primarily consisting of pensioners or people from very affluent backgrounds. The range and diversity of answers will differ again if we take a sample that appropriately represents the population – some supporting tuition fees, some vehemently opposing them, some feeling quite indifferent. The composition of the sample matters, and so, systematically excluding some groups of people, for example through inaccessible methods, puts the representativeness of the research and thus its validity at risk.

VIGNETTE

Lawrence is an autistic single father in his thirties. He keeps informed of new studies, reports and articles on autism because he likes to gain a broader understanding. In his research he comes across a study that describes the experiences of autistic people in a way that jars with his own experiences, because it presents participants as hoping to prevent or eliminate autism and hoping for a 'cure'. He finds that this study was funded by Autism Speaks, an organisation that has been criticised by autistic people as following a negative and unrepresentative approach towards autism that does not represent the views of most autistic people.

In the tuition fee example earlier, we have referred to a sample representing the **population**, which is an ambiguous term since it can refer both to a country's citizens but also the group of people for whom we are trying to answer a question. These groups can overlap but don't always, and the degree to which they do may also reflect our assumptions and biases. For example, one might argue that when talking about tuition fees, we should primarily be concerned with past and present students, and therefore less with the opinion of those who left school without gaining the necessary qualifications for university attendance, or those who chose vocational training. Not only would this be a problematic, classist view; it also risks perpetuating a bias in who attends university and who doesn't by not eliciting the opinions of those who might be put off by the existing requirements and limitations – therefore not collecting information about precisely those barriers we are trying to lower. Defining the scope of representativeness is therefore not a trivial task, and some argue that it can be to the detriment of a study's overall validity to focus too much on representativeness (see, for example, Rothman et al, 2013).

Neither is checking whether our sample is, in fact, representative. We can only check that which we are aware of, and so checking representativeness is easier for clear quantifiable criteria such as age, income or occupation, and there is a limited number of criteria for which a sample can be representative of the underlying population within the available limits of time, effort and space. In addition, some criteria of representativeness are used more frequently than others – and, just as inclusion and accessibility are often neglected, so is disability as a representativeness criterion. At the same time, some criteria are much more difficult to ascertain than others, and disability is one of them. We might want to check, for example, whether our sample is representative of the general population in terms of disability and impairments, but, as already mentioned in Chapter 1, not everyone who would be classified as disabled under the relevant legal definitions self-identifies as disabled and vice versa. Asking 'Are you disabled?' is therefore not enough if we want to compare sample statistics with population statistics. Instead, it might be necessary to ask whether individual criteria are met, or whether the participant presents with one of a long list of conditions that are covered under the term.

For quantitative research, we generally distinguish between probability sampling and non-probability sampling. With **probability sampling**, the method of sampling is chosen in a way that every item – or, here, participant – has the same chance of being included in the sample. Probability sampling methods also have in common that the chance of every participant to be included in the sample can, at least theoretically, be calculated. The randomness of selection minimises the possibility of any systematic bias, particularly compared to non-probability sampling, although it does not fully eliminate it. Its success hinges on the assumption that everyone has the same chance of being included, and we have shown in previous chapters that there are systematic factors excluding disabled people from participation in a range of activities and experiences. Without active accessibility, probability sampling is likely to result in samples skewed towards non-disabled participants.

Non-probability sampling, in contrast, does not use reliably random selection methods and does not allow for the calculation of an item's (here, participant's) probability of inclusion in the sample. However, there can be good reasons to use non-probability sampling, depending on the scope of the question and the resources of the researcher.

Each method comes with its own advantages and disadvantages, and as with many aspects of research and methodologies, the sampling approach might be influenced by factors outside our control. In the next section, we will discuss the most frequently used sampling methods and the barriers they might pose, as well as possible ways to mitigate those barriers.

Probability sampling

With **simple random sampling**, participants are randomly chosen for inclusion, for example by using random number generators to select participants from a numbered list, such as, for example, a list of employees, an electoral register, a visitors' log and so on. Whether the resulting sample is (relatively) representative depends on both the research question and the individual's chance to make it onto the list in the first place. If there are systematic biases at work that prevent some groups more than others from being on that list, their voices will remain underrepresented. As an example, consider the low percentage of minority ethnic academic staff in the UK HE system. A study sampling randomly from members of the UK HE system would likely lead to lead to a statistically (relatively) representative sample but it would say little about systematic barriers and disadvantages for minority ethnic staff, and thus contribute little to lowering those barriers.

Systematic sampling combines the element of random selection with a systematic application. Simple examples would be: repeatedly using a dice to choose one participant from a group of six; picking every 10th entry in a list of names such as the electoral register; asking every fifth visitor of a museum for feedback, and so on. While this is likely to produce a fairly random sample, it does not fully exclude the possibility of bias. In an example from Harris and Jarvis (2014), a systematic sampling method using house numbers could potentially introduce a bias. If, for example, the house number 5 is picked as a starting point, and every 10th number thereafter, we would end up only with residents from houses with odd house numbers. In an area where odd and even house numbers are on opposite sides of the road, there is a chance (small, but non-zero) that there is a difference in affluence or social status between the two sides of the road.

CHECKLIST 9: QUANTITATIVE SAMPLING AND RESEARCH QUALITY

☐ Think about whether your research question allows you to identify potential barriers to participation.

☐ Check whether it includes any assumptions about observable behaviour being a reflection of a free choice rather than a consequence of other, limiting factors – in other words, are participants not interested in a particular activity, or are they unable to participate?

☐ Consider whether your data collection can be expanded to include data that allow checking for potential bias, such as demographic data.

☐ Consider the source of any data on which you might rely for sampling; ideally, identify who created the list or compilation.

☐ Try to understand the process by which the list was created, maintained and distributed.

☐ Try to understand the process by which individual items or people were included on or excluded from the list. Could any parts of the process systematically exclude certain groups of people?

☐ If you suspect systematic bias, aim to (in order of preference) eliminate, mitigate, reduce or quantify the bias by using appropriate statistical analyses.

☐ Aim to validate the composition of the sample against other, known parameters such as demographic data of the underlying population, if available.

Although random sampling can prevent some bias creeping into the sample, the nature of randomness can also mean that particular subgroups are over- or underrepresented. For example, a random selection of employees in an organisation may result in the sample by pure chance comprising only managers, or only women, or only employees aged 48 and above. One way to address this would be to use **stratified sampling**, where the resulting sample contains a number of 'strata', that is, specified subgroups. In the previous example, we could define strata as, for example, the different hierarchy levels, or age groups, or departments. We would then have to decide whether we wanted each stratum to be equally represented, that is, having a similar proportion of managers, team leaders, team members and so on, or whether we wanted the strata proportions to mirror their proportions in the population they are drawn from. Stratified sampling can thus be used to ensure all known groups are represented in the sample and all their voices heard – the emphasis being on 'can ... be used' and 'known'. Its success greatly depends on the way in which strata are identified by, known to, or salient to the researcher. A stratified sample that mirrors the strata proportions of the population may perpetuate biases that created the strata in the first place; an equal-sized stratified sample will boost some voices and dampen others.

There is one more potential disadvantage of random sampling that we haven't mentioned so far, and that is the potential wide dispersion of participants in terms of location. Consider a scenario where we are using random sampling to recruit 300 participants for a study within an organisation with 10,000+ employees across 150 locations. Although unlikely, it is nevertheless statistically possible that by sheer luck of the draw we recruit participants from each of the 150 locations. This is feasible if all we need to do is post a questionnaire, but requires far too much effort and resources if we want to meet each participant in person. Here, we could employ **cluster sampling**, where we use repeated rounds of random sampling on subsequent levels of entities or items. In this example, we could use random sampling to first select a number of locations (for example, 20), and then random sampling again to select 15 participants each from all 20 locations. Alternatively, if the 150 locations were further split into five regions with 30 locations each, we could also first randomly select regions, then locations, and then participants. In that way, cluster sampling strikes a compromise between the benefits of random sampling and the real-life restrictions on resources.

Non-probability sampling

Whenever participants are recruited through a process that doesn't give everyone – from the relevant population, that is – the same probability to be included, or where that probability cannot be calculated, even hypothetically, we speak of non-probability sampling. Sometimes this means that the resulting sample is of inferior quality because it is potentially less representative of the population, and more biased. But it can also provide a means of sampling where probability sampling would not be possible or feasible because we simply don't have full access to the relevant population to then draw a random sample from it.

This is often the case for populations that are very narrowly defined and therefore quite small, but also for populations the members of which are not easily identifiable or known – for example, bilingual twins with synaesthesia; experts in early 18th-century Parisian fashion; all teenagers aged 15–17 with an interest in model trains; female CEOs from a working-class background, and so on. Having identified and approached at least one member of the target population, we could employ the method of **snowball sampling**, which means asking each contacted and/or recruited participant to provide one or more further contacts of people fitting the same criteria, thereby increasing the sample much as a snowball quickly gathers in size when rolling downhill. The strength of this method lies in the way in which it allows recruiting from otherwise less accessible populations, essentially using the similarity between participants and their contacts as a means of recruitment. However, this also carries the risk of excluding individuals who are not part of the existing participants' network of contacts. If there is any systematic bias in how this network is formed and maintained – in addition to the criteria that define the population – the resulting sample may also be biased.

VIGNETTE

Natalya is an extremely competent tax accountant. She runs her own business and has managed to grow quite a large clientele. Despite her success, however, she is known only to a very few colleagues in the profession – because she has difficulties reading body language, she finds personal interactions stressful and tends to avoid large gatherings. This means she tends not to attend professional conferences or networking events. There is a prestigious association of successful women accountants, but, in order to join, candidates need to be recommended by at least three existing members and, thus far, Natalya's networking has been unsuccessful.

Most sampling methods described so far are based on carefully planned and executed procedures to maximise the quality of the sample, and with it, the quality (or rather, validity) of its conclusion. Other sampling methods, however, may be used in contexts that prioritise speed, sample size or use of resources over representativeness or validity. **Convenience sampling**, **haphazard sampling**, **opportunity sampling** and **accidental sampling** all refer to the same method of selecting those who are easily available through proximity in time and space, be it by virtue of, for example, being acquaintances of the researcher, respondents to an online questionnaire, or pedestrians who happen to be passing a researcher with a clipboard – the examples all being methods quite commonly used in, for example, student projects. At the same time, it's easy to see how the resulting samples can be substantially and systematically biased, for example by demographic similarity to the researcher, by access to the specific media through which the study is conducted, or by their opportunity to be at a particular place at a particular point in time. Last, convenience sampling of this and similar types may be influenced by the researcher's potential unease about interacting with disabled people (see, for example, Lenney and Sercombe, 2002; Sasson et al, 2017), and subsequent reluctance to approach disabled people for participation.

VIGNETTE

Pablo has cerebral palsy and struggles with balance issues. He sometimes uses a wheelchair but also walks quite often. However, both on foot and by wheelchair he tries to avoid the busy high street in the city centre. Although it is centrally located and home to some really interesting shops, the pedestrian zone is cobbled throughout to fit the medieval town architecture. When walking, the cobblestones make it difficult for him to keep his balance, and navigating the wheelchair takes much more effort, carrying a high risk both of injury and of damaging the wheelchair. The city occasionally conducts surveys on how to make the high street more attractive to visitors, but these surveys are usually done by people with clipboards walking along the high street – and, because it is so inaccessible, Pablo rarely gets the chance to participate.

In the discussions so far, we have conflated non-probability sampling with non-representative sampling. In **quota sampling** we see an odd mixture of a non-probability sampling method creating something that can look very much like the result of probability sampling. Quota sampling means recruiting participants such that a specific number of participants fulfilling certain criteria is met, for example 51 per cent women, 15 per cent of participants in the 10–15 age bracket, and so on. With detailed enough quotas, such a sample may even look like a representative portion of the population. But quota sampling does not specify how the participants are recruited, and thus they may still be drawn, for example, from limited or biased recruitment channels. It also means that criteria for which quotas are not defined may be entirely ignored – and thus be vastly under- or overrepresented.

CHECKLIST 10: PROBABILITY AND NON-PROBABILITY SAMPLING

☐ When using cluster sampling:
  ○ Make sure that individual clusters are similar enough that the selection of specific clusters doesn't introduce too much of a bias.
  ○ Consider the way in which clusters are formed. Are some clusters different from others in a way that would influence your conclusions?
☐ Can you push for more refined stratification to improve inclusion of minority groups?
☐ Think about the ways in which members of the relevant population gain entry to that particular population. Are there potential members of that population who are less likely to be well connected and suggested as potential participants? If this is the case, try to specifically reach out to those individuals, or encourage them to get in touch.
☐ Consider whether potential similarity between participants is an intended outcome or a potential source of unwanted bias.
☐ When using quota sampling:
  ○ Make sure you know who defines the quotas, why, and through which process. Try to identify any underlying assumptions.
  ○ Examine the quotas against criteria relevant to your research. Can the quotas be amended to ensure (more) representativeness?
  ○ Consider whether the quotas are purely in service of the underlying research question or whether they are likely to be influenced by (potentially faulty) assumptions.
☐ Where feasible, look beyond snowball and convenience sampling for participants to broaden out the range of experiences and perspectives that you hear about.

Last, **panel sampling** initially relies on a (usually random) selection of participants, and then draws from the same panel of participants several times over a longer period of time, thus enabling researchers to track changes and developments over time. In addition to potential bias arising through the selection of participants, further bias may arise through the way in which the panel operates. Some groups of participants may find it easier than others to repeatedly make time for participation, such as, for example, by having a job that allows them to take time off, stable enough circumstances that mean they are willing and able to participate over a longer period of time, or a lack of underlying health issues that may make continuous participation more likely.

Mitigation strategies

Having had a look at the most commonly used sampling methods, we are now going to look at some of the strategies we can pursue to lower barriers to participation and thus increase the chance that all voices are heard. We acknowledge that researchers may not always have the opportunity to ask for or implement these changes, particularly where constraints exist in forms of funding, modes of cooperation, organisational hierarchies or availability of resources. Where funding is limited and tightly controlled, including additional questions on a market research survey may not be possible, or there may not be any scope to change a given research question. But asking might be the start to a productive conversation.

- *Identify the complete relevant population:* if the relevant population is an organisation such as a company, acquiring a full list of its members may be relatively straightforward (assuming, of course, the organisation's records are complete and up to date). If the relevant population is all women aged between 29 and 39 undergoing fertility treatment, getting a full list will be impossible, and different sources may have different biases. Drawing from a patient list of private fertility clinics (notwithstanding any issues of patient confidentiality) will likely bias the sample towards more affluent women; drawing from participants in online forums might bias towards a certain age range. For most sampling methods, but particularly for probability sampling, their success is based on the completeness of the population from which the sample is drawn. Any existing bias will be perpetuated. The closer we are to a comprehensive data basis, the higher our chances of developing a good sample.

- *Validate and iterate:* depending on the scope of the study and the resources available, it might be feasible to use existing data (for example, from a census) to check to what extent the sample mirrors a known (sub)population and then adjust sampling procedures accordingly. Again, this is easier to do for smaller populations: it is easier to check the age composition of a sample drawn from a particular company than to check whether the distribution of handedness is representative of the handedness of the population at large. But it may give some indication. If an online questionnaire resulted in 90 per cent of the participants being 30 years old or younger, it is fair to say that the topic of the questionnaire, the way in which it was distributed or the way in which the questions were asked did not appeal equally to all age groups. A possible approach can also mean proceeding in different stages with different approaches, for example using surveys or focus groups first to establish potential sampling issues that can then be addressed in the next stage.

Summary

In this chapter we looked at qualitative and quantitative sampling, and the varying definitions of research quality according to the type of research we are doing. We discussed the importance of choosing quality measures and collecting evidence for them throughout the study, and the way a broad sample can contribute to good quality research. We introduced different sampling methods and their individual drawbacks and how they might be mitigated.

In Chapter 5, we move on to look at participant recruitment, advertising and communication.

Note
1   Homophily describes the tendency for people to associate with a social group which resembles them, which might be colloquially described as a 'bubble' or expressed in the saying 'birds of a feather flock together'.

Further reading
Ezzati, T.M., Hoffman, K., Judkins, D.R., Massey, J.T. and Moore, T.F. (1995) 'A dual frame design for sampling elderly minorities and persons with disabilities', *Statistics in Medicine*, 14(5–7), 571–83.
Discussing the implications, in terms of practicalities but also statistical implications, of using a dual-frame design.

Morse, J.M. (2015) 'Critical analysis of strategies for determining rigor in qualitative inquiry', *Qualitative Health Research*, 25(9), 1212–22.
While this does not mention accessibility, it is a useful and clear description of quality criteria and provides a summary of the strategies used to achieve academic rigour in research.

Olsen, R.B. and Orr, L.L. (2016) 'On the "where" of social experiments: Selecting more representative samples to inform policy', *New Directions for Evaluation*, 2016(152), 61–71.
Four recommendations to increase representativeness, particularly of impact evaluation studies.

Rad, M.S., Martingano, A.J. and Ginges, J. (2018) 'Toward a psychology of Homo sapiens: Making psychological science more representative of the human population', *Proceedings of the National Academy of Sciences*, 115(45), 11401–5.
Analysing to what extent papers still relied on WEIRD participants, and developing recommendations for authors, editors and reviewers. (WEIRD here refers to the observation that participants in studies tend to be predominantly White, Educated, from primarily Industrialised, Rich and Democratic countries.)

References

Amin, M.E.K., Nørgaard, L.S., Cavaco, A.M., Witry, M.J., et al (2020) 'Establishing trustworthiness and authenticity in qualitative pharmacy research', *Research in Social and Administrative Pharmacy*, 16(10), 1472–82.

Anney, V.N. (2014) 'Ensuring the quality of the findings of qualitative research: Looking at trustworthiness criteria', *Journal of Emerging Trends in Educational Research and Policy Studies*, 5(2), 272–81.

Barnes, C. (2009) 'An Ethical Agenda in Disability Research: Rhetoric or Reality?', in D.M. Mertens and P.E. Ginsberg (eds) (2009) *The Handbook of Social Research Ethics*, London: SAGE Publications Ltd, pp 458–73.

Becker, H., Roberts, G., Morrison, J. and Silver, J. (2004) 'Recruiting people with disabilities as research participants: Challenges and strategies to address them', *Mental Retardation*, 42(6), 471–5.

Bogart, K.R. and Dunn, D.S. (2019) 'Ableism special issue: Introduction', *Journal of Social Issues*, 75(3), 650–64.

Braun, V. and Clarke, V. (2013) *Successful Qualitative Research: A Practical Guide for Beginners*, London: SAGE Publications Ltd.

Browne, K. (2005) 'Snowball sampling: using social networks to research non-heterosexual women', *International Journal of Social Research Methodology*, 8(1), 47–60.

Bryman, A. (2016) *Social Research Methods* (5th edn), Oxford: Oxford University Press.

Charmaz, K. (2014) *Constructing Grounded Theory*, London: SAGE Publications Ltd.

Feldman, M.A., Battin, S.M., Shaw, O.A. and Luckasson, R. (2013) 'Inclusion of children with disabilities in mainstream child development research', *Disability & Society*, 28(7), 997–1011.

Geertz, C. (1973) 'Thick description: Toward an interpretive theory of culture', *Turning Points in Qualitative Research: Tying Knots in a Handkerchief*, 3, 143–68.

Guba, E.G. and Lincoln, Y.S. (1994) 'Competing Paradigms in Qualitative Research', in N.K. Denzin and Y.S. Lincoln (eds) *Handbook of Qualitative Research*, London: SAGE Publications Ltd, pp 105–17.

Harris, R. and Jarvis, C. (2014) *Statistics for Geography and Environmental Science*, London: Routledge.

Kidney, C.A. and McDonald, K.E. (2014) 'A toolkit for accessible and respectful engagement in research', *Disability & Society*, 29(7), 1013–30.

Lenney, M. and Sercombe, H. (2002) '"Did you see that guy in the wheelchair down the pub?" Interactions across difference in a public place', *Disability & Society*, 17(1), 5–18.

Morse, J.M. (2015) 'Critical analysis of strategies for determining rigor in qualitative inquiry', *Qualitative Health Research*, 25(9), 1212–22.

Pring, J. (2015) 'Backlash from activists over Scope's attempt to "end the awkward"', Disability News Service, 7 August. Available at: www.disabilitynewsservice.com/backlash-from-activists-over-scopes-attempt-to-end-the-awkward

Rendle, K.A., Abramson, C.M., Garrett, S.B., Halley, M.C. and Dohan, D. (2019) 'Beyond exploratory: A tailored framework for designing and assessing qualitative health research', *BMJ Open*, 9(8), e030123.

Rios, D., Magasi, S., Novak, C. and Harniss, M. (2016) 'Conducting accessible research: Including people with disabilities in public health, epidemiological, and outcomes studies', *American Journal of Public Health*, 106(12), 2137–44.

Rothman, K.J., Gallacher, J.E.J. and Hatch, E.E. (2013) 'Why representativeness should be avoided', *International Journal of Epidemiology*, 42(4t), 1012–14. Available at: https://doi.org/10.1093/ije/dys223

Sasson, N.J., Faso, D.J., Nugent, J., Lovell, S., Kennedy, D.P. and Grossman, R.B. (2017) 'Neurotypical peers are less willing to interact with those with autism based on thin slice judgments', *Scientific Reports*, 7(1), 1–10.

Shakespeare, T. (2002) 'Rules of engagement: Doing disability research', *Disability & Society*, 11(1), 115–21. Available at: https://doi.org/10.1080/09687599650023380

Shields, N. and Synnot, A. (2016) 'Perceived barriers and facilitators to participation in physical activity for children with disability: A qualitative study', *BMC Paediatrics*, 16(1), 9.

Thomas, E.V., Warren-Findlow, J., Webb, J.B., Quinlan, M.M., Laditka, S.B. and Reeve, C.L. (2019) '"It's very valuable to me that I appear capable": A qualitative study exploring relationships between body functionality and appearance among women with visible physical disabilities', *Body Image*, 30, 81–92.

5

Recruitment and the research setting

This chapter examines how the recruitment process and communication with (potential) participants can be made more accessible. We provide recommendations on how to reach out more actively to disabled participants, discuss advertising and recruiting strategies, and deal with the question of how to access a population with specific needs that does not define itself as 'disabled'. As part of the participant recruitment process we explore the issue of emotional labour provided by participants, and how this relates to issues of compensation for participation. Throughout the chapter we stress the researcher's responsibility to communicate the (un)availability of accommodations proactively.

Before we start, however, we need to point out that the research setting includes not only the participant but also the researcher, and in this context we want to acknowledge disabled researchers. They often face substantial barriers in their workplace as ableism in academia is still prevalent (see, for example, Brown and Leigh, 2018; Inckle, 2018; Lourens, 2020). At the same time, interactions with participants are influenced by the researcher's disability:

> Felicity [Boardman]'s identity as a disabled person operated differently depending on whether she was interviewing non-disabled or disabled people. At times a "disabled identity" appeared to signal shared experiences, the "right" to research, and take on board the concerns and issues of disabled populations, providing her with "insider status". (Brown and Boardman, 2011, p 25)

It is important to keep in mind that disabled researchers may also be dealing with barriers to access, and that we need listen to and believe them. Navigating multiple identities amid often disabling work and research environments is complex, challenging and highly individual – making it not just extremely difficult but also inappropriate for us to advise disabled researchers on how to manage their work and research environment. In the remaining chapters, we will therefore focus on considering, anticipating and meeting the needs of the disabled participant.

Recruiting and communicating with participants

We have previously argued (see, for example, Chapter 1) that it is necessary to improve access to research, not only for ethical but also methodological reasons. Successful research therefore relies on successful recruiting, which relies on successful advertising and reaching out to potential participants in an act of active accessibility. Before we begin, let us briefly summarise some of the reasons for non-participation previously discussed:

- Distrust in the institution and in procedures as protecting the institution rather than the participant.
- Scheduling that conflicts with work or the availability or expenses of participants' assistants or carers.
- Communication from researchers that reveals a lack of understanding or lack of accessibility.
- Failure to value research.
- Transportation issues.
- Health problems.
- Desire for privacy or confidentiality.

We have noted before the relative lack of research on barriers to participation for potential participations. As such, it is more than likely that this list is incomplete – but even the incomplete list is challenging. Some of these issues are easier to address than others. Conducting research in a central location with good connections to public transport can make it easier for some to participate, but reducing someone's distrust in an institution can be much more difficult and take more than a single researcher can provide. There is a further difference between the items on the list, in that some of them help convince potential candidates to participate, while others will likely make participation itself easier.

In other words, addressing the issues on the list is one thing; communicating that we are addressing them is another. Active accessibility requires both. It is the communication of our efforts that can help us improve our chances of recruiting a diverse sample. In this chapter we are particularly concerned with measures that make it easier to reach participants and subsequently positively influence their decision to participate in research.

For most potential participants, our recruiting message in the form of a flyer, social media post, email or video is the main source of information about our research. It is also the main source of information on how we (and, implicitly, our research) might handle issues of accessibility. A flyer that uses white font on a soft yellow background thus shows little awareness of the problems visually impaired users might face, as would a video with no subtitling, or a social media post with no alt text provided for the images contained therein. The language used might also convey a lack of awareness (see Chapter 6, Checklist 21). Equally, the lack of alternative communication channels offered is something that potential participants can and will pick up on. Our recruitment message thus communicates accessibility in more than one way. First, the accessibility of the message itself gives potential participants clues on how we might approach other aspects of research; and, second, any mention of possible accommodations will communicate our awareness and willingness to address potential issues (see, for example, Olkin, 2004).

Offering and communicating available accommodations also reduces the need for participants to actively reach out, and, by asking for available accommodations, to disclose personal information. Mingus (2017) uses the term 'forced intimacy' to describe 'the common, daily experience of disabled people being expected to share personal parts of ourselves to survive in an ableist world'. The term **ableist** (from able-ist, by analogy to sexist, racist and so on) is often used to refer to environments, attitudes or behaviours that favour or privilege non-disabled people over disabled people and contribute to the latter's exclusion or discrimination (see, for example, Kattari et al, 2018; Bitman and John, 2019). An ableist environment might also require additional effort from disabled people. For example, Mingus (2017) points out that merely asking for 'accessibility requirements' is not enough since the need for requirements very much depends on what accommodations are already in place:

> ... if you don't provide any accessibility information about your event, then I cannot assess what my access needs will be. *Am I supposed to list out every single access need I might ever possibly have, simply because of your ignorance?* (Mingus, 2017; original emphasis)

The way we communicate with our participants therefore provides cues as to what extent our research environment is ableist – and how much labour, physical or emotional, our participants are expected to expend on our behalf.

There are several things we can do to send the right message:

- Use diverse channels to reach out.
- Avoid microaggressions and reduce unconscious bias.

- Constructively deal with mistakes.
- Seek input from experts and incorporate it.
- Use several routes of communication.
- Make information available in accessible formats.
- Clearly communicate the purpose and benefit of the research for the public.
- Communicate accessibility or lack thereof.
- Consider immunocompromised participants.
- Pay for participants' time.
- Stress any measures taken to ensure confidentiality and anonymity.
- Monitor the process to avoid any 'leaky pipeline'.
- Use debriefing to improve the process.

We will now discuss each of these in turn.

Use diverse channels to reach out

When trying to recruit from particular communities through using their professional networks, consider to what extent people from within the community have access to these networks, or whether these networks are likely to perpetuate the exclusion of marginalised communities (see, for example, Gray et al, 2007; Greguletz et al, 2018). One way to minimise or avoid either potential exclusion or the general underrepresentation of disabled people from these types of network is to use networks formed specifically for and by people with disabilities. Thus, when trying to recruit, for example, teachers for a study, we might also specifically try to recruit teachers with a disability by approaching the Disabled Teachers' Network. (We have included a list of associations for disabled people based on profession or personal interest in Appendix 1.)

A note on charities: it is important to point out that not all charities are equally appropriate sources of information and support. Charities run *for* disabled people may have a substantially different perspective from charities run *with* disabled people, in some cases directly contradicting people's lived experiences. A case in point is the charity Autism Speaks, which presents autism as something that negatively affects families and people with autism, and for which a cure should be sought and developed – a view that is certainly not shared by many autistic people and their families (see Luterman, 2020). Where we have given links to charities or resources provided by them, this does not necessarily imply endorsement. While we are aware of the problematic views of, for example, Autism Speaks, we may not be aware of other problematic views held by other charities. We would therefore generally advise giving preference to charities run by and with disabled people.

Avoid microaggressions and reduce unconscious bias

For many people, disability still carries a stigma (see, for example, Green, 2007; Buljevac et al, 2012; Grue, 2016). The effects of this stigma are visible in many areas. In the context of healthcare provision, people with disabilities are sometimes presumed less competent by medical staff, or interactions are expected to be more time-consuming and exhausting (see, for example, Sabatello, 2019). But stigma can have far worse (Lusli et al, 2015) and potentially deadly consequences (Vigdor, 2019). It is equally important for researchers and people who interact with participants with visible or invisible disabilities to avoid so-called 'microaggressions' – 'brief and commonplace daily verbal, behavioural or environmental indignities, whether intentional or intentional' (Sue et al, 2007, p 273). Although originally coined in the context of the experience of racism, microaggressions are also experienced by disabled people, such as, for example, having to defend their use of disabled seats in public transport or the non-use of hearing aids; being told they don't try hard enough; or ableist language being used in their presence (Kattari et al, 2018; see also Chapter 2).

Constructively deal with mistakes

Learning new things is difficult, and mistakes are bound to happen. If we make a mistake – for example we used a turn of phrase we realised is offensive, we sent out inaccessible material, we misgendered a participant – we need to apologise and then correct our behaviour. This can require a delicate balance. Mingus (2019a) argues that apologising for mistakes is a necessary part of developing accountability, and that a thorough apology requires acknowledgement, a naming of the hurt or harm and a naming of the impact the behaviour had. It also requires taking responsibility and committing to not doing the harm again (Mingus, 2019b), for example, 'I am sorry for saying you don't look disabled; that was offensive and minimised your disability/implied you weren't telling the truth. I will not question your and other people's disabilities again.' Equally important, however, is to accept that an apology may not be accepted, and nor is it incumbent on the person receiving the apology to do so. DiAngelo (2015, 2018) uses the term 'white fragility' to describe, among other things, the observation that white people would often dominate discussions of racism with proclamations of guilt and shame. This usually meant that Black people were expected to provide comfort and absolve white people of their guilt, effectively centring white people's experiences and feelings. Although to our knowledge there has been no systematic theorising of the term 'ableist fragility', as a behaviour it is widely known within the community (see, for example, Simmons University Library, 2020), and could be considered an aspect of 'non-disabled privilege' (Wolbring, 2016) that requires similar active work to overcome: if we feel guilty or bad that our behaviour has caused harm to a participant, it is not the participant's responsibility to make us feel better.

Seek input from experts and incorporate it

If we want to make it easier for people to participate, or if we want to specifically reach out to participants with impairments and disabilities, we might also consider reaching out to any of a number of charities that may be able to further advise – but see the caveats mentioned earlier. (A list of such charities and organisations is included in Appendix 2.) Note that, while many of these organisations explicitly offer training, advice or consultation, it is generally our responsibility to educate ourselves, and not their responsibility to teach us. Again, this comes down to expecting other people to perform free labour on our behalf. It is not on those who are marginalised to educate those who are not. Therefore, where advice is not explicitly given in the context of a paid consultation, payment for time expended should nevertheless be offered.

CHECKLIST 11: INCLUDING EXPERT KNOWLEDGE

☐ Check the plans with your institution's disability specialists to ensure they are sound and to anticipate any potential difficulties or barriers, and/or employ a research adviser or a researcher with this specialism on the team.

☐ Include disabled people in the pilot and specifically request that all participants give feedback on the accessibility of the method and recruitment communication.

Use several routes of communication

This gives potential participants a choice of medium to communicate rather than relying on one single channel that may or may not suit their requirements. Asynchronous means of communication, such as an email or letter, allow the interested party to use whatever communication aids or adjustments may be required, and at their own pace. If this is not possible, and communication relies primarily or exclusively on phones, offering a Textphone[1] route can enable communication with d/Deaf participants (see, for example, Parsons et al, 2000). Appendix 4 provides a brief explanation as well as information on a range of text relay service providers.

CHECKLIST 12: SETTING UP RECRUITMENT CHANNELS

☐ Set a budget for making accommodations and include this as part of the funding bid, so if it is necessary, for example, to employ a signer, there is no barrier to making arrangements.

☐ Ensure that accommodations are mentioned in recruitment material and invite people to contact you if they need to check accessibility.

☐ Consider that some participants might need more time, and timetable some extended slots (Harris and Roberts, 2003).

☐ Include local disability organisations in your call for participants.

☐ Enable participants to contact the research team via telephone/ SMS as well as via email.

☐ Disabled people might not be able to access your call for participants if it is not presented in an accessible format. Offer mixed modes for information provision and, for example, for survey completion (see Chapter 8 for more on mixed methods). Include alternative methods of communication, such as video and audio as well as printed (see Chapter 7 for more about how to do this).

Make information available in accessible formats

The content of our recruiting material may show us talking about accessibility, but the form will show whether we are following through: our material, including the information about the research, any sign-up forms or websites, and, later, the material used in the research itself, all needs to be accessible.

Online material

If we provide our research information via a website and/or ask participants to sign up via a web form, we need to make sure they are accessible, in terms of colour scheme, structure and navigability by a screen reader. This requires the website to follow a set of requirements concerning structure and labelling as well as navigating within the website.[2] We can check whether our website meets those requirements on the Web Accessibility in Mind (WebAIM) website[3] (note that Chapter 6 provides more information on the accessibility of websites and online tools).

VIGNETTE

Sina is a young woman in her mid-twenties who just purchased her first property, a fixer-upper with charm and a lot of work still required. She has visual impairments and finds that website accessibility is generally still very poor. When surfing the internet, Sina comes across a banner ad from a study on homeowners' attitudes towards solar power and the installation of solar panels. This is a topic close to Sina's heart, and so she clicks on the ad, wanting to know more about the study. However, the website has been designed with the study's topic in mind, and so presents itself with grey text on a yellow background – and, to make matters worse, the website is poorly coded and the text cannot be read by a screen reader.

Print material

Printed documents need to be designed to suit a wide audience. Unlike electronic documents, research participants cannot change the font size or weight, layout, colour scheme or contrast of a printed document to suit their own preferences. 'Clear print' guidelines give suggestions aimed at making it easier for people to read and follow printed documents (Print Disability, 2011; Sensory Trust, 2020). A summary of the guidance is given in Checklist 13.

If we find we are trying to compromise between font size, line space and page limit, we might consider editing the text down so it fits the space available rather than making the document harder to read in order to cram the text into it.

The Royal National Institute of Blind People (RNIB, 2020) describes 'large print' documents as being displayed in no less than 16pt or 18pt in a sans-serif font. Bear in mind that the larger the font, the longer the document, and consequently the more effort it will take a participant to read through it. The document may need to be laid out differently as tables, images and text boxes will reflow. Do also bear in mind that, although some users may need to increase the font size to make a document accessible, others may require a decrease in font size.

The Dyslexie font is designed specifically to increase readability for dyslexic people, and many people report that it improves the legibility of the text for them. However, empirical studies have so far found mixed evidence of improvements.[4] While, generally, a clear sans-serif font such as Arial should also work effectively, we may still wish to explore this option if it is relevant to our participants.[5]

CHECKLIST 13: ACCESSIBLE PRINT MATERIALS

☐ Use a minimum font size of 12pt.

☐ Choose a sans-serif font such as Arial or Helvetica.

☐ Use a medium font weight rather than a light font weight, such as Calibri rather than Calibri Light, as text can 'disappear' into the page. Increase the weight of the font if the text is displayed as a light colour against a dark background, to maintain legibility.

☐ Ensure the document uses at least single line spacing, and, if you have enough space available on the page, increase the line spacing.

☐ Text should be left aligned rather than justified or right aligned. This gives an equal amount of space between every word, making it easier to read along the line of text.

☐ Turn off hyphenation to avoid participants having to read one word across two lines of text.

☐ Ensure that the text is legible against a background colour, watermark or tinted panel. Avoid using images under text, as this can make it harder to read the text.

☐ Aim for high contrast text against the background colour in general, but bear in mind that some people find this combination hard to read. If you can, offer versions printed on different coloured paper (for example, cream).

☐ Keep line lengths to about 50–65 characters. If you are using a landscape layout, running the text across the full width of the paper is likely to make it illegible; consider using columns or display boxes.

☐ If the text is presented in columns, use a maximum of 50 characters and allow enough space between the columns so that users can clearly distinguish between them.

☐ Matt paper is preferable to gloss: gloss paper reflects the light, making it harder to read. If documents are printed on both sides, ensure the paper is thick enough so that the ink does not show through it, as this also makes it hard to read.

☐ If documents need to be bound, use a binding that allows the pages to lie flat, such as spiral binding.

Electronic documents

Providing documents to participants in their original format, or in Portable Document Format (PDF), has a number of advantages. It keeps the original page layout intact, which can be important to clearly communicate the structure and content. The participant can also save the document to their computer hard drive so they can complete it in their own time and email it back.

It is easy to enlarge the page on screen, so participants can read it at a size that is comfortable for them. However, it also means that participants can see the document formatting.

PDF forms

A word-processed form that has been used to create a PDF file can be made into an interactive, fillable form by using the Form tools in Acrobat Pro. PDFs can be set up as forms that can be downloaded, completed and emailed back to the sender. Acrobat also has accessibility checkers that enable you to clearly label form fields, buttons and images. Digital signatures are available, which may be important for security or for verifying identity. It is possible to change the view (in either way) so that the text is legible without the rest of the page content reflowing (which may happen with online forms).

However, when typing text into a PDF form text input box, the text reflows, so the margins of text input boxes and the overall size of the printable page will remain the same. This is useful for forms that need to be printed, but it is a disadvantage if the participant needs to type in paragraphs of text: they may have more to type in than space will allow.

CHECKLIST 14: ACCESSIBLE ELECTRONIC DOCUMENTS

☐ Identify the main language of the document. This helps, for example, with spell checking, and ensures a screen reader will read the text in the correct language (see also Appendix 5 on how to assign languages to whole documents or sections of documents).

☐ Format text with styles. For example, use Heading 1 for the main document heading, and lower-level headings appropriately. This creates a clear document structure that helps people understand what is in the document and how sections of content relate to each other.

☐ Format lists with list styles and multi-level styles.

☐ Add alternate text to images.

☐ Format table headings with styles.

☐ Understand how to export from one format to another.

☐ If you are using Microsoft (MS) Word, it has a built-in accessibility checker that will flag up any of these issues that you need to address.

☐ Use clear, direct language in all the recruitment material, the consent form and participant information sheet, etc.

☐ Make consent forms available in advance so participants can read them before the session.

Clearly communicate the purpose and benefit of the research for the public

This is important for two reasons. One, it is part of the information that enables a participant to give informed consent for participation. But it is particularly necessary for reaching out to historically marginalised communities by providing transparency and building up trust in the researchers and in our institution or organisation (see, for example, Bhopal, 2010; Kingsley et al, 2010). It also makes it all the more important to be clear about the limitations of the study and not to exaggerate the benefits of our study in order to convince people to participate. Part of this transparency can be demonstrated by offering to make the findings of the study available to participants, if this is possible within the institutional and funding constraints. However, we must then make absolutely sure to follow up on such offers, otherwise the failure to meet our promise will only serve to further potential participants' distrust in research institutions and the researchers therein.

Communicate accessibility or lack thereof

There is, sadly, a plethora of reasons why some aspects of participation cannot be made accessible. Some premises are inaccessible because they are old, and building regulations prohibit the fitting of an elevator or stair lift; accommodations for different types of impairments may contradict each other; for example, bright lighting to help with visual impairment could make it more stressful for participants with sensory processing disorders; a student researcher may not be able to access funds to pay for a sign language interpreter and so on. Active accessibility also means that, where accommodations cannot be made, this is communicated clearly and well ahead of time. We are asking our participants to volunteer their time and effort for something that is of more benefit to us, at least in the short term – any benefit for the participants will arise at a later time, if at all. For that reason, we rely on our participants' goodwill. We want to avoid them either starting their participation only to realise that the questionnaire isn't screen reader-friendly, the focus group is too noisy to understand everyone, or there is no lift to the room in which the study takes place. Equally, we want to put the burden of reaching out on us, which is why we need to tell participants what's available so they don't have to ask and, in the process, disclose their disability.

In all of this, we need to take care that in explaining reasons for the lack of accommodations we do not cause further harm. A failure to budget for accommodations can be (rightfully) interpreted as not having considered accommodations important enough at the start of the study; talking about the added effort demonstrates that we are prioritising convenience over accessibility. Similarly, mentioning that, although the building is very pretty, it isn't accessible is dismissive and a harmful microaggression (see Chapter 3). For the same reason, expressions of pity or overly apologetic manners that would require the disabled person to expend emotional labour to console us need to be avoided at all costs.

Consider immunocompromised participants

We introduced the concept of invisible disabilities earlier in Chapter 1. One type of invisible disability is a compromised immune system, whether by congenital immunodeficiency or acquired later in life, by, for example, having lupus, becoming HIV positive, undergoing cancer treatment or having undergone transplant surgery. For immunocompromised participants, exposure to crowded spaces or close contact with other people can pose a serious risk to their health. If we want to reduce or remove barriers to participation, taking precautions to reduce the risk of spreading infections has to become another best practice for empirical research. Immunocompromised participants need to be able to assess whether the research setting is safe and whether necessary precautions are being taken to protect their and other people's health.

Like many other issues that regrettably only make it into mainstream societal awareness once non-disabled populations are affected, the issue of reducing risk of infection wherever people meet has only become widely discussed with the advent of COVID-19. What we used to think of as something primarily required by immunocompromised people suddenly became a consideration for many more people. Research organisations, professional (see, for example, Market Research Society, 2020) and academic (for example, BPS, 2020) alike, have issued guidance on how to minimise risk – guidance that was developed for COVID-19 but which is likely to remain useful beyond the pandemic.

At the same time, we need to remain aware of how increased hygiene measures might impede accessibility: greater distances between participants or the use of masks or visors might impede accessibility for people who are hearing-impaired, and wearing masks may make it more difficult for participants with anxiety issues, sensory processing issues or with respiratory illnesses, or for participants who rely on lip-reading to aid understanding (a possible solution for the latter are visors or face masks that are partially or entirely transparent).

CHECKLIST 15: WAYS TO REDUCE INFECTION RISK

☐ Reduce or avoid physical contact.

☐ Provide sanitiser or disinfectant.

☐ Consider providing personal protective equipment, such as single-use gloves and face masks.

☐ Make sure that the premises are clean, and that material changing hands can be cleaned after each use.

☐ Properly dispose of cleaning equipment.

☐ Communicate clearly to participants that they should postpone or cancel participation in a group setting if they are currently showing symptoms of transmittable diseases such as a cold or flu.

☐ Consider using research methods that do not involve face-to-face data collection or travel using public transport.

Pay for participants' time

Payment can serve several purposes: providing an additional incentive for participation, compensating participants for their time, or an acknowledgement or demonstration of gratefulness. Critical voices argue that offering payments may give the wrong incentives for participation, that people may participate even when not interested or not participate faithfully and with their best effort. We have outlined this discussion and the strong case for paying participants in Chapter 4. Having said that, there is some evidence that people may feel obliged to participate beyond what is healthy if they are paid (Turner and Beresford, 2005). It follows that payment needs to be made in advance and/or it needs to be made clear that withdrawal from participation is still possible and absolutely acceptable, at any point in time. The right compromise is described by Becker et al (2004, p 474): 'The amount of incentive was not enough to be coercive yet did serve the objective of providing some recognition and compensation for the participant's time.'

Stress any measures taken to ensure confidentiality and anonymity

Ensuring the confidentiality of participants' information is a vital aspect in research in general. It is all the more important if we are trying to recruit participants who, for the purpose of participating, need to disclose information to us that may put them at a disadvantage in their personal life, or their workplace (Pearson, 2003; Wilton, 2006). It doesn't matter whether that disclosure is made for reasons of asking for accommodations, or because we asked participants for the information in order to monitor recruiting. In the context of intersectionality this becomes even more important to the point of being, potentially, a matter of life and death, as transgender people, people from minority ethnic backgrounds, victims of domestic violence or people from particular religious groups are still at risk of physical and psychological abuse (Haller et al, 2020).[6] Ethical research therefore requires absolute confidentiality.

VIGNETTE

Sebastian runs a small construction business in rural England. He's a haemophiliac and received a contaminated blood product during a treatment he underwent in the early 1980s. As a result, he became infected with human immunodeficiency virus (HIV). His condition is stable and very well controlled with medication. Sebastian heard about a study recruiting small business owners and would like to participate, but he is very reluctant to disclose that he's immunocompromised as he worries about the stigma associated with HIV, and what would happen to his business if any of his customers in the small rural town learned of this.

CHECKLIST 16: CONFIDENTIAL DATA COLLECTION

- ❏ Encrypt your documents (see Appendix 6 for help).
- ❏ Try to use tools or apps that offer end-to-end encryption.[7]
- ❏ When sending emails to several participants, make sure to use a setting so that recipients can't see other recipients' emails, such as 'blind carbon copy' or BCC.
- ❏ Store participant IDs and identifying information separately.
- ❏ Collect monitoring information separately.
- ❏ Restrict access to documents, and document who has access to what.

Monitor the process to avoid any 'leaky pipeline'

Research is an iterative process. If we want to improve our recruiting and recruiting strategies, we need to find out where we are losing participants, in order to adjust and improve the process accordingly. The idea of the 'leaky pipeline' has long been used to describe the process by which the share of women in the STEM subjects (Science, Technology, Engineering, Mathematics) diminishes with every step along the way, from girls being interested in STEM subjects in school, to young women choosing STEM subjects in university, to entering the workplace and advancing in their careers (for an early discussion of this term, see, for example, Pell, 1996; Wickware, 1997). We are using this concept here in analogy to the gradual diminishing in representation, from the first contact with participants to the full completion of the study.

As briefly mentioned in Chapter 3, this could also be followed up by conducting substudies with some of the participants who drop out before the final step or who drop out in higher rates than other identifiable subgroups. The keyword here is 'identifiable subgroup': this relies, of course, on having already collected enough information, that is, demographic data, to identify any such groups. Without such information, however, we can still collect valuable information by identifying stages in the recruiting process where numbers are reduced perhaps disproportionately: do most of the (potential) participants withdraw after the initial contact, after they receive information, after the first meeting and so on?

Use debriefing to improve the process.

In a narrow definition of the term, **debriefing** refers to the researcher informing participants of any deception that was part of the study, outlining why the deception was necessary and what the true nature or research question of the study was. In a broader sense of the term, debriefing can also refer to the researcher checking in with participants about the way they experienced the study, in terms of method but also about organisation and administrative issues. In this way, the debriefing is part of the monitoring process – almost like an exit interview. We can ask participants how easy or difficult it was to find information, participate, raise questions or concerns with the researcher or their colleagues. The knowledge gained this way can inform future research.

CHECKLIST 17: REVIEWING YOUR RECRUITMENT PROCESS

☐ Make sure you have a comprehensive overview of the specific effort required for participation.

☐ Reflect on whether some of the methods constitute a barrier for potential participants, such as multiple sessions, long sessions, heavy reliance on particular material (audio, video, written, etc), group sessions, etc. If so, which of these barriers can be mitigated?

    ○ Can group sessions be broken up into smaller groups?

    ○ Can participants sit out one or more of the sessions?

    ○ Can material be provided in different forms?

    ○ Can sign language interpreters be hired?

    ○ How flexible are you in terms of locations or premises?

☐ Focus on means of communications that can reliably be offered, for example email, phone, letter, online video conferencing (such as Skype, Zoom, Discord, WebEx, AdobeConnect, etc), Messenger etc, and which complement each other, that is, some for written contact, some for spoken etc.

☐ Know which accommodations can be offered to participants, and, of those, which ones are consistently available and which ones can be offered on prior arrangement.

☐ Offer financial compensation. If this is not possible, find alternatives to convey genuine appreciation or recognition; consult with potential sources of support what may be appropriate.

☐ Clearly lay out the benefits of the research for the participants.

☐ Offer to make a summary of the results available to participants.

Summary

In this chapter we discussed accessibility issues related to recruiting participants, including why people may be reluctant to take part in research. We talked about how to communicate to participants that our research is accessible, and also the importance of being honest about where and how it may not be accessible. We described the particular importance of keeping participants' data confidential where it contains information that is stigmatising and may not have been shared with others. We offered ways to monitor when and (potentially) why people are dropping out of the recruitment process. We stressed the importance of using multiple methods of communication so that participants can choose the method and timing that works best for them.

In Chapter 6 we consider the practicalities of making face-to-face research more accessible.

Notes

1   A Textphone service allows d/Deaf participants to communicate with other phone or Textphone users by having sound translated to text and vice versa, via either software or a relay interpreter.

2   A good example of a website offering different accessibility options is www. disabilitynewsservice.com, which offers options to change contrast and font size, and using WebReader text-to-speech software to make written text accessible.

3   https://webaim.org

4   Kuster et al (2018) and Wery and Diliberto (2017) found no evidence of benefits of a special dyslexia font; Marinus et al (2016) found some benefit but concluded it was due to the spacing, not the shape of the letters.

5   This book uses a serif font. However, the publisher Policy Press participates in the RNIB Bookshare scheme and explicitly offers to make books available in accessible electronic formats.

6   See www.pfc.org.uk and www.hrc.org

7   End-to-end encryption (E2EE) means that only the sender and recipient can read the message – something that, for example, WhatsApp or Signal offer, but regular text messages don't. E2EE therefore offers a higher degree of data security. Be aware that for some tools or apps E2EE may be available but not switched on by default.

Further reading

Agarwal, P. (2020) *Sway: Unravelling Unconscious Bias*, London: Bloomsbury Publishing.
A comprehensive introduction to the causes and consequences of implicit bias.

Ellard-Gray, A., Jeffrey, N.K., Choubak, M. and Crann, S.E. (2015) 'Finding the hidden participant', *International Journal of Qualitative Methods*, 14(5), 160940691562142. Available at: https://doi. org/10.1177/1609406915621420
A literature review on ways to approach hard-to-reach populations.

Ibrahim, S. and Sidani, S. (2014) 'Strategies to recruit minority persons: A systematic review', *Journal of Immigrant and Minority Health*, 16(5), 882–8. Available at: https://doi.org/10.1007/s10903-013-9783-y
A systematic review of recruitment strategies.

Sabatello, M. (2019) 'Cultivating inclusivity in precision medicine research: Disability, diversity, and cultural competence', *Journal of Community Genetics*, 10(3), 363–73.
On unconscious bias and the need for disability culture competency in research.

Singer, E. and Bossarte, R.M. (2006) 'Incentives for survey participation. When are they "coercive"?', *American Journal of Preventive Medicine*, 31(5), 411–18. Available at: https://doi.org/10.1016/j.amepre.2006.07.013
A review of the ethical issues surrounding payment for participation.

References

Becker, H., Roberts, G., Morrison, J. and Silver, J. (2004) 'Recruiting people with disabilities as research participants: Challenges and strategies to address them', *Mental Retardation*, 42(6), 471–5.

Bhopal, K. (2010) 'Gender, identity and experience: Researching marginalised groups', *Women's Studies International Forum*, 33(3), 188–95.

Bitman, N. and John, N.A. (2019) 'Deaf and hard of hearing smartphone users: Intersectionality and the penetration of ableist communication norms', *Journal of Computer-Mediated Communication*, 24(2), 56–72.

BPS (British Psychological Society) (2020) 'Ethics best practice guidance on conducting research with human participants during Covid-19.' Available at: www.bps.org.uk/sites/www.bps.org.uk/files/Policy/Policy%20-%20Files/Conducting%20research%20with%20human%20participants%20during%20Covid-19.pdf

Brown, L. and Boardman, F.K. (2011) 'Accessing the field: Disability and the research process', *Social Science & Medicine*, 72(1), 23–30.

Brown, N. and Leigh, J. (2018) 'Ableism in academia: Where are the disabled and ill academics?', *Disability & Society*, 33(6), 985–9.

Buljevac, M., Majdak, M. and Leutar, Z. (2012) 'The stigma of disability: Croatian experiences', *Disability and Rehabilitation*, 34(9), 725–32.

DiAngelo, R. (2015) 'White fragility: Why it's so hard to talk to white people about racism', The Good Men Project, 9 April. Available at: https://goodmenproject.com/featured-content/white-fragility-why-its-so-hard-to-talk-to-white-people-about-racism-twlm

DiAngelo, R. (2018) *White Fragility: Why It's So Hard for White People to Talk about Racism*, Boston, MA: Beacon Press.

Gray, M., Kurihara, T., Hommen, L. and Feldman, J. (2007) 'Networks of exclusion: Job segmentation and social networks in the knowledge economy', *Equal Opportunities International*, 26(2), 144–61.

Green, S.E. (2007) 'Components of perceived stigma and perceptions of well-being among university students with and without disability experience', *Health Sociology Review*, 16(3–4), 328–40.

Greguletz, E., Diehl, M.R. and Kreutzer, K. (2018) 'Why women build less effective networks than men: The role of structural exclusion and personal hesitation', *Human Relations*, 72(7), 1234–61.

Grue, J. (2016) 'The social meaning of disability: A reflection on categorisation, stigma and identity', *Sociology of Health & Illness*, 38(6), 957–64.

Haller, M.B., Kolind, T., Hunt, G. and Sard, T.F. (2020) 'Experiencing police violence and insults: Narratives from ethnic minority men in Denmark', *Nordic Journal of Criminology*, 21(2), 1–16.

Harris, J. and Roberts, K. (2003) 'Challenging barriers to participation in qualitative research: Involving disabled refugees', *International Journal of Qualitative Methods*, 2(2), 14–22.

Inckle, K. (2018) 'Unreasonable adjustments: The additional unpaid labour of academics with disabilities', *Disability & Society*, 33(8), 1372–6.

Kattari, S.K., Olzman, M. and Hanna, M.D. (2018) '"You look fine!" Ableist experiences by people with invisible disabilities', *Affilia*, 33(4), 477–92.

Kingsley, J., Phillips, R., Townsend, M. and Henderson-Wilson, C. (2010) 'Using a qualitative approach to research to build trust between a non-Aboriginal researcher and Aboriginal participants (Australia)', *Qualitative Research Journal*, 10(1), 2–12.

Kuster, S.M., van Weerdenburg, M., Gompel, M. and Bosman, A.M. (2018) 'Dyslexie font does not benefit reading in children with or without dyslexia', *Annals of Dyslexia*, 68(1), 25–42.

Lourens, H. (2020) 'Supercripping the academy: The difference narrative of a disabled academic', *Disability & Society*, 1–16.

Lusli, M., Zweekhorst, M., Miranda-Galarza, B., Peters, R.M., et al (2015) 'Dealing with stigma: Experiences of persons affected by disabilities and leprosy', *BioMed Research International*.

Luterman, S. (2020) 'The biggest autism advocacy group is still failing too many autistic people', *The Washington Post*, 14 February. Available at: www.washingtonpost.com/outlook/2020/02/14/biggest-autism-advocacy-group-is-still-failing-too-many-autistic-people

Marinus, E., Mostard, M., Segers, E., Schubert, T.M., Madelaine, A. and Wheldall, K. (2016) 'A special font for people with dyslexia: Does it work and, if so, why?', *Dyslexia*, 22(3), 233–44.

Market Research Society (2020) 'MRS post-Covid-19 lockdown guidance: Undertaking safe face to face data collection.' Available at: www.mrs.org.uk/resources/covid-19-lockdown-restrictions-january-2021

Mingus, M. (2017) 'Forced intimacy: An ableist', Leaving Evidence, 6 August. Available at: https://leavingevidence.wordpress.com/2017/08/06/forced-intimacy-an-ableist-norm

Mingus, M. (2019a) 'The four parts of accountability: How to give a genuine apology part 1', Leaving Evidence, 18 December. Available at: https://leavingevidence.wordpress.com/2019/12/18/how-to-give-a-good-apology-part-1-the-four-parts-of-accountability

Mingus, M. (2019b) 'How to give a genuine apology part 2: The apology – The what and the how', Leaving Evidence, 18 December. Available at: https://leavingevidence.wordpress.com/2019/12/18/how-to-give-a-good-apology-part-2-the-apology-the-what-and-the-how

Olkin, R. (2004) 'Making research accessible to participants with disabilities', *Journal of Multicultural Counseling and Development*, 32, 332.

Parsons, J.A., Baum, S. and Johnson, T.P. (2000) *Inclusion of Disabled Populations in Social Surveys: Reviews and Recommendations*, Chicago, IL: Survey Research Laboratory, University of Illinois for the National Center for Health Statistics.

Pearson, S. (2003) 'Promoting sexual health services to young men: Findings from focus group discussions', *BMJ Sexual & Reproductive Health*, 29(4), 194–8.

Pell, A.N. (1996) 'Fixing the leaky pipeline: Women scientists in academia', *Journal of Animal Science*, 74(11), 2843–8.

Print Disability (2011) *Guidelines for Producing Clear Print*. Available at: http://printdisability.org/guidelines/guidelines-for-producing-clear-print-2011

RNIB (Royal National Institute for the Blind) (2020) 'Large and giant print.' Available at: www.rnib.org.uk/information-everyday-living-reading/large-and-giant-print

Sabatello, M. (2019) 'Cultivating inclusivity in precision medicine research: Disability, diversity, and cultural competence', *Journal of Community Genetics*, 10(3), 363–73.

Sensory Trust (2020) 'Designing with clear print and large print.' Available at: www.sensorytrust.org.uk/resources/connect/infosheet_clearlargeprint.pdf

Simmons University Library (2020) 'Anti-oppression: anti-ableism.' Available at: https://simmons.libguides.com/anti-oppression/anti-ableism

Sue, D.W., Capodilupo, C.M., Torino, G.C., Bucceri, J.M., et al (2007) 'Racial microaggressions in everyday life: Implications for clinical practice', *American Psychologist*. Available at: https://doi.org/10.1037/0003-066X.62.4.271

Turner, M. and Beresford, P. (2005) *User Controlled Research: Its Meanings and Potential. Final Report*, Eastleigh: INVOLVE.

Vigdor, J. (2019) 'Fatal accident with metal straw highlights a risk', *The New York Times*, 11 July. Available at: www.nytimes.com/2019/07/11/world/europe/metal-straws-death.html

Wery, J.J. and Diliberto, J.A. (2017) 'The effect of a specialized dyslexia font, OpenDyslexic, on reading rate and accuracy', *Annals of Dyslexia*, 67(2), 114–27.

Wickware, P. (1997) 'Along the leaky pipeline', *Nature*, 390(6656), 202–3.

Wilton, R.D. (2006) 'Disability disclosure in the workplace', *Just Labour*.

Wolbring, G. (2016) 'Ability Privilege: A Needed Addition to Privilege Studies', in P. Devlieger, B. Miranda-Galarza, S.E. Brown and M. Strickfaden (eds) *Rethinking Disability: World Perspectives in Culture and Society*, Antwerp, Belgium: Garant, p 463.

6

Face-to-face research

In this chapter we discuss accessibility in the context of face-to-face research with people. This focuses mainly, but not exclusively, on qualitative research data collection.

The advice in this chapter covers choosing a suitable location, ensuring participants can reach the venue, closing and follow-up for the session, and ways to address accessibility issues in individual and group interviews. The guidance is based on the principles of Universal Design (UD) (see Chapter 2) and focuses on offering ways to participate that are flexible and that accommodate varying access needs. The aim is to make it as easy as possible for people to take part.

The checklists in this chapter cover several eventualities, so some points won't apply to every situation and others may not be feasible at the research location.

There are three important points to bear in mind:

- This book gives generalised advice so plans can be made in advance. The most important thing is to check with and listen to participants, consider ways in which researchers can be flexible to their individual needs, and find solutions that work for both participants and researchers.
- Make a back-up plan. For example, if someone can't come to a face-to-face interview, they may be able to continue with a telephone or video interview.
- If there is no choice about the location or the facilities that are available, it's important to be realistic with participants about what we can and cannot do to facilitate access, given the constraints of the setting.

The guidance in this chapter is based on a combination of academic references, professional or patient group guidance for specific needs (see Appendix 2) and personal experience.

We begin by looking at some of the features to check for when selecting a research location.

Choosing a suitable location

Although modern buildings are now constructed to higher standards of access, some may not be accessible for everyone. As well as considering access for wheelchair users, other issues can affect access, such as the lighting, the level of background noise in open plan spaces, how easy it is to find the building and how easy it is to find the room once participants arrive. The availability of suitable public transport options (for example, that the venue is on a bus route with wheelchair spaces) is also a consideration.

Timing

Bear in mind that it may not be easy for people to take part in interviews during the working day. Some disabled people work; some may rely on carers (with limited working hours) to support them in getting ready to answer a video call or to leave the house. People with chronic illnesses that limit their energy may have times of the day when they have more energy and times when they need to avoid exertion (Harris and Roberts, 2003). Similarly, long sessions may be exhausting or impossible for some (Barrett and Kirk, 2000). It is important to be open to people telling us their needs, and to work around them so that they are able to participate.

Meeting point

Participants need to know where they are meeting us, so choose a location that is clearly signposted and easy to find (Kidney and McDonald, 2014). It can be very helpful to provide photos of the venue, so it is easier to recognise.

Some participants may prefer to suggest a convenient meeting point themselves, such as a bus stop or a taxi drop-off point. Once they have arrived at the meeting point, they will need a way to let us know they have arrived, and a comfortable place to wait. We might like to suggest places to wait if participants arrive very early (as they may do if they are reliant on public transport), such as the location of nearby cafes. Unless the route there is very clearly marked, they should not have to find their way to a specific room inside a building.

Facilities in the building

The venue for the research needs to be an accessible building; there must be step-free access and facilities such as disabled toilets near to the room where the research is taking place. Ideally the room(s) where the research is being conducted would be near to, and on the same level as, the reception area, to avoid people having to find their way to a room in a distant part of the building. The route to the room needs to be well lit and free from obstructions, with additional signage where necessary.

It is helpful to have a clearly marked out waiting area, with seating for all the participants who need it, so that nobody has to stand. If a participant needs to bring a support person or animal, the waiting area should be suitable for them to attend along with the participant, and to wait for them during the session; we need to consider that they will also have comfort needs.

Participants need to know the location of toilets; they should be clearly signposted and the route described to participants when they arrive. Inside the disabled toilet, there needs to be enough turning space for a wheelchair. This is difficult if, as sometimes happens, it is also being used for storage. Some disabled toilets are kept locked, and the participant will need a key to use them – this needs to be checked in advance.

Some participants may need to be escorted from the meeting point to the interview location. Visually impaired people may need information about the route, such as a verbal description indicating steps, turning direction, warning about obstructions, where the seating is when they get to the meeting room, and so on. They may wish to take our arm or elbow for guidance. If we're unsure what to do, we need to ask the participant directly what they would like (RNIB, 2014).

If participants need to use a lift, it needs to be accessible in terms of both the size and the way it is operated. There should be enough space for a wheelchair plus at least one other person.

Facilities in the session room

The room should be in a peaceful location where there is no background noise and space has been cleared for participants to enter and move around easily, with little chance of being accidentally interrupted (Kroll et al, 2007). The room temperature should be well controlled and adequate for the weather and climate. The seating, if needed, should be comfortable, particularly for longer sessions. Bear in mind that some people may find that sitting down causes discomfort or pain or may need seating that supports their back. A 'stretch break' can be very helpful for people with painful joints, to avoid sitting in one position for too long. The requirement to sit down may limit the time some participants can spend in the session, so consider whether we can be flexible about this. For example, offering to talk at a standing desk or to use a walking or 'go-along' interview (Parent, 2016; Kinney, 2018) might work better for some participants.

Wheelchair users should be able to move in and out of the room without obstruction, and to position themselves comfortably at a table if they need to. Participants need to be able to easily see, listen to, or otherwise access the researcher's welcome, session instructions and any audio or video stimulus material. If we are using a portable hearing loop, it should be suitable for the size of the room; the ones that are designed for meeting rooms may not amplify sound as effectively in a larger space. Ensure there are plenty of electrical sockets, as there may be an additional need for them (for example, for charging a motorised wheelchair or to power any assistive technology that we or the participants might use).

The room's lighting can also enhance comfort for participants: fluorescent lighting can trigger migraines or be overstimulating, and flickering lights can put participants with epilepsy at risk. Boards and screens are easier to read if they are non-reflective. Good lighting is important for people who need to lip-read and for people with a visual impairment to see the researcher.

Refreshments

Consider the participant's comfort and provide water, at a minimum, and also provide for the needs of their carer or companion and service animal. For longer sessions, and if we are providing food, we may have to cater to a range of participants' needs, such as religious or dietary requirements, specific cutlery, drinks without caffeine or food allergies. Participants may want to bring their own food, and in that case, access to a sink to wash their container, and a bin for food waste, needs to be provided.

CHECKLIST 18: CHOOSING A LOCATION

☐ Give participants a meeting point to aim for and, if there is more than one entrance to the building, make it clear which one they need to find. Alternatively, ask participants to suggest a meeting point that suits them.

☐ Ensure it is easy to find the meeting point once people have reached the building entrance, or it is clearly signposted.

☐ If there is an entry system, check it is easy to use and at a wheelchair-friendly height.

☐ Ideally the waiting area would be a reception area with seating and space for wheelchair users to wait, immediately inside the building, on the ground floor, with room for everyone who will be there to sit down if they need to.

☐ Consider the feasibility of meeting participants at the entrance to escort them, if the meeting room is hard to find within the building. Be prepared to offer help or guidance on the way to the room, bearing in mind that participants may not need or want it.

☐ Ensure that you have a key if key access is needed to the disabled toilet, and check on the day that the toilet itself is clear of obstructions.

☐ Ensure you know the location of alternative facilities, how to get there, and roughly how long it may take to get there and back.

☐ Check that essential facilities such as chair lifts and power doors are working.

☐ Check that there is enough room for a wheelchair inside the lift; if you know in advance that a wheelchair user is participating, check that the lift is suitable, as wheelchairs come in different widths and heights.

☐ Check that the controls are at a height that puts them within reach for wheelchair users, and that the buttons are tactile (that they can be read by Braille readers).

☐ Consider the comfort level of the seating that will be provided and let people know in advance what this is.

☐ Ensure that tables, if used, are at the right height for wheelchair users, or can be adjusted or removed.

☐ Plan for the implications of infection risk, take precautions to minimise the risk of infection (minimising use of shared utensils or items, using hand sanitiser, coughing or sneezing into your elbow, wearing a face covering) and share them with the participants.

☐ Choose a room with natural lighting, if possible.

☐ Ensure the room is well lit and it is easy to read from any screens or boards.

☐ The room should have a hearing loop installed; if not, bring a portable hearing loop and ensure that it is switched on and working during the session.

☐ Check for the participants' needs and preferences in advance of the session, such as building access or refreshments.

☐ Remember to offer a drink, and take it to participants if needed.

☐ If you are providing other refreshments, offer options besides tea and coffee.

☐ Provide cups with lids and straws.

☐ If providing food, ensure it is clearly labelled or that a catering team member can give guidance if anyone has questions.

☐ Familiarise yourself with the building evacuation procedures for disabled people so you can assist participants.

If the session runs over a half or full day, a quiet space should be made available to participants who may need a comfort break, away from being with other people (Rios et al, 2016). A space that is being used for group research and refreshments may give some participants sensory overload.

Travel to the venue – what participants need to know

Travelling to an unfamiliar venue for a research session can be stressful; the aim is to make the experience of taking part in the research as easy and welcoming as possible. Participants will also need to know in advance about how they can travel to the venue, who is meeting them, and where.

It is important that the venue is easy to reach, and easy to find once participants are at the right location. Especially if we are not covering participants' travel costs, it should be cheap and easy for them to reach us. Participants will need to know how to get to the venue easily from public transport, whether the public transport has access options (such as wheelchair spaces on the bus or a lift at the railway station), the closest parking options and information about disabled parking options. Participants may need to rely on help, such as a wheelchair space being free on the bus they catch, or assistance to get off the train at the railway station, and, if these are not available or late, their journey will be delayed.

If participants need to find a building on a campus or within an office complex, they will need to know how to get to the right building from drop-off points. It would be helpful for them to know how to tell they are in the right venue, who to look out for when they arrive, and what to do if they get lost. Providing photos of the venue makes it easier for people to identify that they are in the right location; they may also be able to spot in advance any access barriers that we are unaware of, so other arrangements can be made. Participants also need to know if the entrance requires a key card or code, and if there is an entry system. See the RNIB guide (2014) for more information about guiding someone with low vision or blindness.

It would be helpful to offer participants an urgent contact name and number so they can let us know if there are transport glitches or if they get lost. Ensure the building management team, security or cleaners are aware of the research in advance, so they do not remove any temporary signage.

CHECKLIST 19: TRAVEL TO THE VENUE

☐ Provide participants with a map along with descriptive directions and make it available in more than one format (print and digital).

☐ Include a photo of the building so people can recognise that they have arrived at the right place.

☐ Give the postcode so it is easy for participants to make their own way there using GPS and so they can check out the location in advance if they need to; if necessary, include notes about how accurate GPS directions are.

- ☐ Give participants the nearest bus stop, station or taxi drop-off point, and the average walking distance or time from there to the meeting point.

- ☐ Check whether there are disabled parking spaces near to the venue, and whether the car park entry system is accessible and working.

- ☐ Let participants know whether they will need a parking permit, how long it will be valid for, and how you will arrange for them to receive it.

- ☐ Choose a venue that is well signposted.

- ☐ Alternatively, provide very clear signage along routes from public transport and car parks on the days you will be conducting the research.

- ☐ Give participants the details for a named urgent contact on the day of the session.

- ☐ Ensure that someone is always available to answer the phone and respond to emails straight away.

- ☐ Nominate someone from the team who can be free to meet lost participants or sort out any last-minute issues such as parking problems.

- ☐ Ensure the person meeting the participant knows whether they need support, or asks.

- ☐ Include a photo of the researchers in the participant information, and tell them who will be meeting and greeting them when they arrive so they know who to look out for.

- ☐ If appropriate, show ID or a name badge; if you do this, let participants know they can look out for this, and that they can ask and check.

- ☐ Introduce yourself by name, so it is clear who you are.

- ☐ Check the participant's name so they can be sure they are in the right place and talking to the right person. This is especially important if the reception or waiting area is a public place.

- ☐ Avoid wearing heavy perfume or strong fragrances.

- ☐ If relevant, consider wearing a mask to protect immunocompromised participants or participants at risk; consider one that has a transparent inset so participants can still see your lips move, or alternatively use a visor.

Using the participant's choice of venue

We may be travelling to conduct a session with the participant at or near their home, where we are not going to have much control over the suitability of a venue as a research space. In those cases, consider the issues that might arise in that setting and plan ways to work around them.

If the participant has chosen the venue because it meets their specific access needs, and is a place they know and are comfortable, that will ensure the session gets off to a good start and they are likely to be more relaxed. However, they could have chosen it for convenience without considering what it might be like as a place to have a semi-formal conversation that is recorded. If the venue is a public space, and it's feasible, it is a good idea to check it out in advance to identify potential issues with privacy, background noise and interruptions.

Participants need to feel comfortable talking about potentially personal issues in the interview setting, and that we will be able to have a peaceful and uninterrupted conversation. In a location with a lot of background noise, there's a potential impact on the interviewee's ability to hear or to understand us. This can affect rapport if we have to keep repeating ourselves (see, for example, Kazmer and Xie, 2008). While not necessarily an accessibility issue, it can seriously affect some participants, while noise also can affect the quality of the recording, if we are making one.

Safety

For researcher safety reasons, interviews may be conducted in public places such as cafes rather than the participant's home, but sometimes the participant needs to be interviewed in their own home. There are risks to lone research (discussed, for example, in Breckenridge et al, 2017) and similar issues of noise and privacy can also arise in the participant's home. We need to ensure that we follow the safety guidance issued by our university or employer; researcher safety should be described in the ethics application form and, when visiting a participant's home, make appropriate contact arrangements with our supervisor or manager.

At the time of writing, COVID-19 is an issue that affects the safety of face-to-face research for both participants and researchers, and shifting to using technology instead is not always possible. Professional associations, including the Market Research Society (UK), Research Society (Australia) and Insights Association (US) have responded with guidance that explains how to conduct face-to-face research safely based on their government's guidance on safe working practices (see, for example, the excellent and thorough guidance offered by the Market Research Society, 2020). This enables research to continue – where appropriate – in ways that also fulfil our responsibility as researchers to behave ethically and with care for our participants. This advice could also be relevant to working with participants who are immunocompromised, for example by HIV or other health conditions or by chemotherapy or radiotherapy (see also Chapter 5).

Before starting the session

As we welcome participants to the session and give our standard introduction, we need to make sure we are facing the person and they can lip-read if they need to. It is also very helpful to reiterate the timetable for the session, including any planned breaks and that participants can request a comfort break, as well as going through the fire safety regulations, details about refreshments, describing the room layout and giving the location of the nearest toilets.

When planning the session, we have to check that we are aware of any timing limitations for the participant and confirm this with them as the session starts. This will enable us to plan the timing to prioritise questions about all the essential topics early on, a strategy that will also be useful for participants with fatigue.

It is also worth bearing in mind that not everybody will be able to sign a consent form, or is comfortable doing so, even if they are keen to participate. Other ways in which their consent can be recorded (for example, by audio recording that part of the interview) need to be considered (see also further guidance from the University of Pittsburgh, 2019). Some researchers have found it is more effective to discuss the consent form at the end of the interview once rapport has been established (Gysels et al, 2008).

Closing and follow-up

> ### VIGNETTE
>
> Sean is 25 and works in the engineering department of an automobile parts supplier. He has been blind from birth. At work he knows his way around the building and the equipment; in town, he relies on his knowledge of the environment and his guide dog, Tiberius. Sean has been playing the piano for almost 20 years, the last 10 of which he has been playing in a community orchestra. He has been recruited by a fellow orchestra member to participate in a study examining the link between the amount of musical practice and the ability to differentiate pitch. The study takes place in a university building. Sean contacts the research assistant to say that he would like to be picked up at the entrance to the university campus. He also requests that information material be made available to him in advance, or in Braille, and asks whether provisions can be made for Tiberius – will he be able to stay with him for the duration of the study?

Whether we are running a session with one person or with several, it is important to clearly communicate to participants, explicitly in words, that the session is coming to an end. This will give them the opportunity to make any further comments they would like to share, without being brought to an abrupt halt. It means participants have a clear understanding of what is going on and don't have to rely on what may appear to them to be vague words or body language (Nind, 2008).

Aim to finish sessions on time unless the participant has said they can stay for longer or can easily change their arrangements for getting home. Some participants may have booked transport home at a fixed time or have people waiting to collect them. Others may prefer to avoid travelling on their own after dark or on public transport.

The participant's financial situation should also be considered. Even if it is not our usual practice, if they request expenses to be paid at the session, or if we know they are on a low income, arrangements should be made to accommodate them without embarrassment. There may be very little flexibility in their budget to allow them to wait for repayment to happen at some future date.

It is usual to close a session by describing what will happen next with the data from the research and, if they are interested in finding out the outcome of the study, when that is likely to happen. Participants will need to be able to access this information when it is eventually sent out to them. They will need to find their way back to their transport and, if they need or request it, to receive assistance with getting to the nearest public transport pick-up point or arranging a taxi.

CHECKLIST 20: CLOSING AND FOLLOW-UP

☐ Keep track of the timing of the session and finish when you have promised the participants you will finish.

☐ After the main part of the interview has ended and you have covered the final or housekeeping issues, formally draw it to a close.

☐ Include the information you cover post-session in the participant information sheet, so participants have a written record to refer back to, as well as your contact details.

☐ Check if they have a preferred format in which they wish to receive this information and that there is a record of their preference. (See Checklist 13 in Chapter 5 for print and Checklist 24 in Chapter 27 for digital access.)

☐ Initiate the discussion about how expenses (and, if relevant, any fee) are paid, and when, as participants may not feel comfortable asking.

☐ Escort participants back to the meeting point.

☐ If they need or request it, offer assistance with getting to the nearest public transport pick-up point or arranging a taxi.

☐ Remember to thank people for their valuable contribution to your research.

In the following sections we look at potential access issues related to face-to-face data collection. There are extensive resources that give information about methodology and the uses and limitations of these methods; this section focuses solely on issues related to accessibility.

CHECKLIST 21: LANGUAGE WHEN COMMUNICATING WITH PARTICIPANTS

☐ Use explicit language and plain English where possible, and be prepared to answer clarifying questions.

☐ Try to verbalise the information you might otherwise communicate through body language alone, such as encouragement to speak further.

☐ Use prompts and follow-up questions to explore any points.

☐ Begin by using plain, literal language that is free of metaphors, irony, sarcasm and other common forms of speaking that, for example, autistic people may find confusing – follow the participant's lead.

Individual interviews

These are some general things to consider when planning a one-to-one interview. Although some points may already be familiar, it is important to consider these issues from an accessibility perspective to understand how they might affect a disabled participant.

Speak directly to participants, even if they are speaking through a carer or signer. Participants whose first language is sign language may prefer an interview that is conducted in sign language, and this will need to be video recorded (Anderson et al, 2018). The interviewer will need to be a fluent signer, or will need to use a professional signer, and the video recording will need to be translated into a text transcription (Harris and Roberts, 2003). One positive of this approach is that it can be empowering for the participants, and go some way towards changing the power balance of the research relationship in their favour (Evans, 2017).

The welcome and introductory section of the interview is important for starting to build rapport with the participant. Using humour is one way to do this, but bear in mind some people take language literally and may miss a joke or feel upset that they have not understood. Stick to using unambiguous language until sure this is not issue, and always be guided by what the participant appears to be comfortable with – or ask if it isn't clear (Breckenridge et al, 2017).

If someone asks for another person to be present, such as a carer or supporter, find out their role and the kind of services they provide to the participant to consider how this might affect the session (Gysels et al, 2008). A one-to-one interview is very different from a dyadic interview, and would need to be accounted for in the methodology if that approach is chosen. However, the main purpose of a supporter is to enable the participant to get to the venue, and perhaps to facilitate participation in other ways, rather than to take part themselves. Their role needs to be discussed with both the participant and the supporter so it is clear, for example, that, if the supporter responds on the participant's behalf, they are doing so with permission. One way to achieve this could be to incorporate the supporter's role in the consent form and in pre-interview discussions, so their role is clear from the outset.

Some people have executive function difficulties, which means they are likely to have problems with time management and keeping on topic in an interview. Participants could be sent an agenda, such as an abridged version of the interview questions, so they know the topics that need to be covered in the time given. In the session, the agenda can be used to structure the conversation and bring the participant's focus back to the questions that need to be asked.

If it is likely to be a long session, decide when in the agenda would make a good point to stop for a break, if one is needed. This avoids breaking rapport at a sensitive point in the conversation, then needing to re-establish it. However, if participants seem to be getting tired, offer them a break when they seem to need it. Some people get tired quickly, need a stretch break to avoid getting stiff or find it hard to concentrate for long periods; building in a break allows a convenient point to pause and let the participant relax and refocus.

The researcher should be at eye level (or close) with the participant. Being at eye level is an important way of demonstrating that we are on equal terms with the participant, which is also important for wheelchair users, who regularly speak to people who are standing over them. At the same time, we need to ensure that we are sitting in a position where the participant can easily see our mouth while we speak, if they need to; people who have a natural habit of covering their mouth with their hand when they speak need to be aware that this might make it harder for a participant to understand what they are saying. Bear in mind that some participants might feel very uncomfortable with eye contact, so follow their lead.

Reassure participants they don't have to discuss a subject if they are uncomfortable and suggest a non-confrontational form of words for them to use if this situation arises, such as 'I'd like to move on'.

Structured interviews

A structured interview consists of the researcher asking participants a fixed set of questions. These are often used to collect quantitative data, to focus on a restricted range of questions and answers, rather than allowing a wide-ranging response, and to minimise the influence of the interviewer on the participant's responses. The interviewer is not able to reinterpret the question if the participant is struggling to understand it.

As general advice, consider:

- Wording questions so they are unambiguous and do not use metaphors.
- Developing a standard set of hints or prompts that can be used consistently by interviewers if participants are struggling to answer a question.
- Piloting the interview questions to identify and address any issues around lack of clarity.

Because the issues related to structured interviews are very close to those raised by methods such as questionnaires, see also the fuller discussion in Chapter 7.

Semi-structured interviews

Semi-structured interviews are sometimes presented as a naturalistic conversation that covers a range of topics, but which can move in any direction that the participant feels is relevant. Participants are encouraged to give in-depth responses and the conversation proceeds at a pace they are comfortable with.

As well as planning the interview topic and questions, it is useful to ensure that prompts and follow-up questions have been added for each key topic area. Prompts are important because, if the participant is asked a question and they are not sure how to answer it, we may be able to move things forward by using a different form of words or a different perspective.

Some participants may not be able to infer our meaning from body language or indirect prompts, or understand irony. Vice versa, consider whether we need to capture non-verbal behaviour as part of the interview process, and whether this might be affected by disability. Of course, we need to take account of the fact that we may be unaware of a disability, if the participant has decided not to disclose.

CHECKLIST 22: FACE-TO-FACE INTERVIEWS

☐ Speak directly to the participant, even when a carer or interpreter is present.

☐ Ensure the role of a helper or carer is clear and that the participant is taking part as fully as they are able to.

☐ Use a signature guide so a participant with low vision can sign the consent form; or obtain consent verbally, and audio record the process so there is a record; or obtain consent retrospectively, at the end of the interview.

☐ Ensure that everyone is comfortable, that the participant can move their seat or position if they wish to, that they can see and hear you if they need to, and that there is little or no background noise.

☐ Discuss the agenda for the session and the timing of each section.

☐ Make sure this is available to participants so they can keep track of where they are in the session.

☐ Keep track of the time and aim to finish the session at the time you agreed.

☐ Structure the interview so it works around the agenda that you have already sent the participant.

☐ Offer participants a break at the time you have planned, or if it appears to you that they are flagging and would like to pause.

☐ Give participants the option to contact you with points they would like to add to the interview afterwards.

Group interviews

A group interview is an interview with several participants, which is moderated by the researcher or a facilitator. Because they can be run in a way that is flexible and open, they can be a good way to include people who may otherwise not feel able to take part in research (Kroll et al, 2007). A standard group interview can be quite wide-ranging, as it is allowed to develop in a direction that interests the participants. A focus group, however, usually centres round a single topic; participants may be selected because they have similar life experiences or a similar background. In both cases the moderator's behaviour can influence how easy or hard it is for each participant to join in.

It can be more challenging to moderate a group of people than a single participant. There are different approaches to practice on this topic (Liamputtong, 2011), but in general, in an academic research setting, the moderator is there to facilitate the group discussion and encourage participation from everyone, not to lead the session. The aim is to create a friendly, open atmosphere where participants feel confident to do most of the talking. The moderator needs to balance the amount of talk time each participant has, encouraging quieter participants to speak, while keeping the discussion on topic and discouraging participants from talking over each other.

The room set-up can support this. Participants who lip-read need a clear view of the other participants and the moderators, and any screens that they might need to look at during the session (Kidney and McDonald, 2014). Although focus groups are often organised to sit around a table, this can be restrictive for people who use sign language or others for whom seeing and understanding body language is important to help them follow the conversation (Balch and Mertens, 1999).

All participants need to understand the role of the moderator and to appreciate that they will step in from time to time to clarify points or move the discussion forward. Ground rules for participants should cover treating others with respect, taking it in turns to talk and not talking over anyone else. This doesn't mean saying 'there's a disabled person in the group' (and this would be unacceptable, as it breaches participant confidentiality) but talk about the rules of engagement and expectations of behaviour that apply to everyone in the session, including the moderators.

Participants need to know the outline agenda for the session and the timing, particularly of the breaks or end of the session.

Focus groups can be a challenge for people with a hearing impairment who rely either partly or entirely on lip-reading to understand what is being said; it may be more effective to provide a signer (Balch and Mertens, 1999). That said, people who lip-read may not use sign language, or may object to the use of a signer, as it is a visible signal of disability. People who lip-read need to be in a well-lit room with a clear view of the mouth of every speaker in the room. They can only watch one person at once, so it can be very difficult to follow a discussion when several people are speaking at once (see also the discussion of the 'Dinner Table syndrome' in Chapter 3). The need to concentrate on a group conversation can be demanding and some participants may tire easily or lose focus (Barrett and Kirk, 2000). Waiting until another participant has finished speaking so we don't talk over them is a courtesy, but also aids people with hearing impairments and people who find it hard to concentrate, so is a good reason why moderating this behaviour is important for increasing participation.

It is helpful for moderators to make it clear when they're speaking to an individual participant. A person with low vision, who may not be able to see well enough to pick up on cues shown through body language (such as the moderator looking at them expectantly), might not realise the moderator is talking to them and would like them to respond. As well as helping people follow the discussion and prompting them to talk when someone has drawn them in, it can also make transcription easier. That said, some people take longer than average to consider what they think and feel about a topic, particularly if they have communication difficulties (Trevisan, 2020), and as a result the discussion may have moved on by the time they are ready to speak. Thoughtful observations may be missed if quieter participants are not drawn into the discussion and given sufficient time to respond.

VIGNETTE

Bindi is a mum of three teenage children. She is in her mid-forties and neuro-diverse. One of the ways this manifests for her is that she tends to miss jokes or metaphors in other people's speech as she takes language very literally; for the same reason, she struggles with polite small talk as she prefers precise, meaningful interactions. She finds direct eye contact very uncomfortable. Bindi volunteered to participate in a study organised by the local university; the city council wants to collect feedback on childcare provision, and this is a topic Bindi feels passionate about and can speak from personal experience. The initial call for participation only mentioned that feedback was to be collected, but more detailed information has indicated that this is to be done in the form of a focus group. Bindi contacts the research team to tell them that she often struggles with non-literal speech and is worried whether she will be able to participate in the focus group. Maya, the lead researcher, thanks Bindi for telling her this. She decides not to use the ice-breaker exercise she initially planned and instead asks participants to prepare a brief, one-paragraph description of themselves she can collate and distribute in a booklet. She asks Bindi whether she'd be comfortable talking in front of a group, and reassures her that she would be happy to incorporate her feedback on the topic even if she was to find participation in the focus group was not feasible.

There are many other issues that could affect the quality of data generated by focus groups, and these have been covered extensively elsewhere. For example, it can be very dependent on group dynamics: people do not speak out about sensitive matters if they do not feel they can trust other members of the group; some people dominate the group, while others are more reticent. Conversely, some people feel safe to share in a focus group and would avoid the scrutiny of a one-to-one interview (Liamputtong, 2011, Chapter 5). The steps discussed earlier are focused on removing barriers to participation. Group interviews can also be conducted online, and, although the level of engagement may differ in online groups compared with face-to-face, the quality of data collected is generally comparable (Synnot et al, 2014). Asynchronous focus groups, conducted in a private discussion group with participants given a set period of time to respond, are one potential adaption that does not involve a video call (Ripat and Colatruglio, 2016).

CHECKLIST 23: GROUP INTERVIEWS

☐ Ensure that participants are in a circle and, where relevant, everyone can easily see and hear the other participants and the moderator.

☐ Make enough space for wheelchair users in the circle so that they are not left out of the discussion.

☐ Consider whether participants really need tables, as this may act as a barrier (some people do prefer to have one, so they should be available if needed).

☐ Set ground rules for the session and explain how moderation works.

☐ Remind the group not to interrupt or speak over each other; however, where doing this would interrupt the flow of discussion, repeat points back so that everyone can understand them.

☐ If there is a break, use this as an opportunity to follow up with participants any observations you have made about their comfort or freedom to participate.

☐ Discuss the agenda for the session and the timing of each section.

☐ Make sure this is available to participants (for example, as a notice on the wall or as an email) so they can keep track of where they are in the session.

☐ Make it clear when you're speaking to an individual. Provide name placards for all participants, ask participants to introduce themselves by name.

☐ Ensure that you draw people in if they are not participating, and go back to follow up any points that might not have been covered at a later point in the session.

☐ Give participants enough time to express their views.

☐ Ask participants to complete a feedback form asking if there is anything else they have to say.

☐ Offer the option of a debriefing conversation at some point after the session, and include these data in the analysis.

Stimulus materials

There are a number of accessibility issues to consider if we are planning to use vignettes or other in-session stimulus material as a discussion point. These include the language level, the time allowed, the format it is presented in and the design (Mertens, 2014). This means thinking about how the material is going to work for people of different abilities (Williams and Moore, 2011). (See Checklist 13 in Chapter 5 and Checklist 24 in Chapter 7 for information about how to make print or digital stimulus materials accessible.)

Written material that has to be read in a fixed time frame may be a barrier for people who take a long time to read, have a limited concentration span, can't easily read from a paper print-out or happen to have forgotten their reading glasses that day, so alternatives need to be offered (Johnson et al, 2005).

A potential solution is to provide stimulus materials a few days in advance and ask participants to read them beforehand. They could be provided alongside any other material that will be presented to them in the session, so participants can read them in their own time using their preferred assistive technology, if needed. This would also enable them to view the materials in their preferred format or colour scheme. However, there is no guarantee that participants will read anything in advance. For methodological reasons, there is sometimes a research requirement that participants do not see stimulus materials beforehand. In that case, plan options for providing them in accessible formats on the day, in a way that is easy and quick to take in (Kroll et al, 2007).

There are also potential issues with visual aids, such as using a printed outline of a human body to elicit the location of physical pain (Hendershot, 2004). While this may work well with participants who can see the image and use a pen, other solutions need to be found for those who cannot, which will facilitate them to contribute the same information.

To sum up, flexibility should be applied to our approach to providing stimulus material. This means presenting it in multiple formats so that participants have a choice of which one suits them best: if they cannot use one, then another option may work.

Including participant-produced content

We may wish to conduct sessions using elicitation activities such as relationship mapping or card sorting, or to include participant activities, such as drawing a mind map, or writing a list on a flipchart summarising a group discussion. Generating these data may require manual or visual abilities that the participant does not have or cannot achieve without support and may therefore require flexible adjustments or alternative approaches. (Chapter 7 includes a discussion of accessibility issues related to different interview formats and research methods and Chapter 8 discusses the use of arts-based approaches.)

Summary

In this chapter we covered the main issues to consider when choosing a location, guiding participants to it, and making them feel welcome. We looked at how to make it easier for people to participate in face-to-face research, and how to provide accessible stimulus material. We covered how to close a session and follow up with participants afterwards. Finally, we looked at some of the access issues that relate to face-to-face interviews and focus groups.

In Chapter 7, we move on to discussing research methods that don't involve face-to-face interaction between the researcher and participants.

Further reading

Access is Love, www.disabilityintersectionalitysummit.com/places-to-start

An introduction to accessibility giving a resource list of links on techniques and disability justice compiled by US disabled academics Sandy Ho, Mia Mingus and Alice Wong.

Liamputtong, P. (2007) *Researching the Vulnerable: A Guide to Sensitive Research Methods*, London: SAGE Publications Ltd.

A wide-ranging look at methods used to research with vulnerable and disadvantaged groups, not focusing specifically on disability but covering many useful related issues.

Rios, D., Magasi, S., Novak, C. and Harniss, M. (2016) 'Conducting accessible research: Including people with disabilities in public health, epidemiological, and outcomes studies', *American Journal of Public Health,* 106(12), 2137–44.

A journal article which includes a useful table that summarises strategies for increasing the accessibility of research sessions.

References

Anderson, M.L., Riker, T., Gagne, K., Hakulin, S., et al (2018) 'Deaf qualitative health research: Leveraging technology to conduct linguistically and sociopolitically appropriate methods of inquiry', *Qualitative Health Research*, 28(11), 1813–24.

Balch, G.I. and Mertens, D.M. (1999) 'Focus group design and group dynamics: Lessons from deaf and hard of hearing participants', *American Journal of Evaluation*, 20(2), 265–77.

Barrett, J. and Kirk, S. (2000) 'Running focus groups with elderly and disabled elderly participants', *Applied Ergonomics*, 31(6), 621–9.

Breckenridge, J.P., Devaney, J., Duncan, F., Kroll, T., et al (2017) *Conducting Sensitive Research with Disabled Women Who Experience Domestic Abuse During Pregnancy: Lessons from a Qualitative Study*, London: SAGE Publications Ltd.

Evans, M. (2017) 'Empowering people experiencing Usher syndrome as participants in research', *British Journal of Social Work*, 47(8), 2328–45.

Gysels, M., Shipman, C. and Higginson, I.J. (2008) 'Is the qualitative research interview an acceptable medium for research with palliative care patients and carers?', *BMC Medical Ethics*, 9(1), 1–6.

Harris, J. and Roberts, K. (2003) 'Challenging barriers to participation in qualitative research: Involving disabled refugees', *International Journal of Qualitative Methods*, 2(2), 14–22.

Hendershot, G.E. (2004) 'Innovative Approaches to Interviewing People with Disabilities', in Proceeding of Statistics Canada Symposium, Innovative Methods for Surveying Difficult-to Reach Populations.

Johnson, M., Newton, P., Jiwa, M. and Goyder, E. (2005) 'Meeting the educational needs of people at risk of diabetes-related amputation: A vignette study with patients and professionals', *Health Expectations*, 8(4), 324–33.

Kazmer, M.M. and Xie, B. (2008) 'Qualitative interviewing in internet studies: Playing with the media, playing with the method', *Information, Community and Society*, 11(2), 257–78.

Kidney, C.A. and McDonald, K.E. (2014) 'A toolkit for accessible and respectful engagement in research', *Disability & Society*, 29(7), 1013–30.

Kinney, P. (2018) 'Walking Interview Ethics', in R. Iphofen and M. Tolich (eds) *The SAGE Handbook of Qualitative Research Ethics*, pp 174–87.

Kroll, T., Barbour, R. and Harris, J. (2007) 'Using focus groups in disability research', *Qualitative Health Research*, 17(5), 690–8.

Liamputtong, P. (2011) *Focus Group Methodology: Principle and Practice*, London: SAGE Publications Ltd.

Market Research Society (2020) 'Post-Covid-19 lockdown guidance: Undertaking safe face to face data collection.' Available at: www. mrs.org.uk/standards/undertaking-safe-face-to-face-data-collection

Mertens, D.M. (2014) *Research and Evaluation in Education and Psychology: Integrating Diversity with Quantitative, Qualitative, and Mixed Methods*, London: SAGE Publications Ltd.

Nind, M. (2008) *Conducting Qualitative Research with People with Learning, Communication and Other Disabilities: Methodological Challenges*, Southampton: ESRC National Centre for Research Methods.

Parent, L. (2016) 'The wheeling interview: Mobile methods and disability', *Mobilities*, 11(4), 521–32.

Rios, D., Magasi, S., Novak, C. and Harniss, M. (2016) 'Conducting accessible research: Including people with disabilities in public health, epidemiological, and outcomes studies', *American Journal of Public Health*, 106(12), 2137–44.

Ripat, J. and Colatruglio, A. (2016) 'Exploring winter community participation among wheelchair users: An online focus group', *Occupational Therapy in Health Care*, 30(1), 95–106.

RNIB (2014) *How to Guide People with Sight Problems*, March. Available at: www.rnib.org.uk/sites/default/files/How-to-guide-sight-problems.pdf

Synnot, A., Hill, S., Summers, M. and Taylor, M. (2014) 'Comparing face-to-face and online qualitative research with people with multiple sclerosis', *Qualitative Health Research*, 24(3), 431–8.

Trevisan, F. (2020) 'Making focus groups accessible and inclusive for people with communication disabilities: A research note', *Qualitative Research*, 1468794120941846.

University of Pittsburgh (2019) 'Low-literacy and disabled participants.' Available at: www.hrpo.pitt.edu/guidance-forms/low-literacy-disabled-participants

Williams, A.S. and Moore, S.M. (2011) 'Universal design of research: Inclusion of persons with disabilities in mainstream biomedical studies', *Science Translational Medicine*, 3(82).

7

Online and remote research methods

Following the previous chapter's focus on face-to-face research methods, this chapter now focuses on research involving no direct face-to-face interaction with participants, such as methods conducted via email, the web, online video, phone or SMS. This chapter looks at some of the challenges and benefits of collecting data asynchronously or using technology that bridges the physical distance between the researcher and participant. It begins by giving general information about digital accessibility that is common across different forms of media, such as mobile devices and computers, and the remainder of the chapter looks at accessibility issues relating to specific types of data collection.

Note: technology changes rapidly, and rather than including specific techniques here, links to further information are given at the end of this chapter. This information is easy to find online or in the help and support pages for the relevant technology. At times, some of the information given here may seem quite technical and possibly overwhelming, but, for anyone working within an organisation, either IT support or disability services should be able to offer help with what is required. We also need to keep in mind that any technology used in our research will have to meet relevant legal requirements, such as data protection standards, and will be scrutinised by any ethics-approving body.

Why use online methods to collect research data?

There are many benefits to online data collection, ranging from the green benefits of much lower carbon emissions,[1] and less time needed overall of participants, to enabling participation from people in other locations and time zones. It means disabled people can take part when they might otherwise be isolated or not be able to participate (Tsatsou, 2020), and includes the opportunity for at-risk participants to participate in the safest form of social distancing. Participants whose energy levels vary greatly have more flexibility if they are able to respond to an email rather than to a phone call. It can make it easier to interview participants who otherwise may be reluctant to be interviewed and who may fear for their safety, for whatever reasons. Knowing that the interview can be stopped at any time simply by hanging up the phone or closing the computer may put some participants at ease.

That said, online research is not a panacea, and can also present barriers. For example, it can be more difficult for the researcher to pick up on cues that would normally help them assess a participant's state of mind, such as whether they are upset, bored or tired, or whether they have understood the consent process; it can make it more difficult to establish rapport. 'Online' does not equal 'accessible'. A well-designed online questionnaire can make participation possible for a lot of people, but a poorly designed online questionnaire might exclude more participants than a paper questionnaire.

Note that when we talk about accessible design, we refer to research designed with the principles of Universal Design (UD) in mind (see Chapter 2).

VIGNETTE

José is an artist working as a freelance illustrator. He had a kidney transplant a couple of years back, and is now in good health. However, he has to take immunosuppressants because of the transplant, and thus takes great care to minimise risks for infection, for example by avoiding public transport as much as possible. When contacted to participate in a study on precarious work in the arts sector, he agrees to participate only under the condition that he can do so remotely to minimise the risk to his health.

General guidance

Different types of digital media have some features in common: all digital media use a screen to display content, so issues such as the colour of text against the background, colour contrast, text size and so on are common issues that need to be considered, regardless of the type of content and the device used to access it. This section gives general information about digital accessibility, while the remainder of the chapter looks at accessibility issues relating to specific types of apps.

Digital content accessibility standards

As discussed in Chapter 1, many countries have laws to say that buildings and services, including services offered digitally, should be accessible, and some offer guidance as to what that means (DWP/ODI, 2018; ODEP, nd; ODI, 2011). The definition of what 'accessible' means in practice is described through guidelines, such as the Web Content Accessibility Guidelines (WCAG) developed by the international standards body for the web, the World Wide Web Consortium (W3C), and used in many countries. The guidelines go into detail about how access can be achieved with different sorts of media (see Appendix 3). Because various different sets of guidelines offer similar kinds of advice, we have included a summary of recommended best practice here. This can be explored (much) further by looking up some of the references in Appendix 3.

Semantic coding

An important first principle is to make a distinction between the meaning of a piece of content and the way it looks. Content needs to be formatted according to its meaning, so a paragraph, bulleted list or heading needs to be formatted as such; this is called **semantic coding**. If we want to change the visual appearance of the bulleted list or heading, we can do so, for example, using Cascading Style Sheets (CSS) for a web page or styles for Microsoft apps.

The reason this is so important is that assistive technology often re-presents content in a format that is easier for certain groups of people to use. This sometimes means overriding the visual appearance of the content, so it's presented in a way that works better for them; for example, if the page displays black text on a white background, a dyslexic participant can view this with a lower-contrast colour scheme. If our content is formatted according to its meaning, such as heading levels set with the correct hierarchy (Heading 1, Heading 2, Heading 3 and so on), the software can easily do this, and the structure of the content will still be clear. In addition, some assistive apps present alternative ways to view a document, such as showing a document map giving all the headings in a hierarchical order. This lets people quickly skip to the content they are interested in, but, even more importantly, it means they can quickly grasp how the content is structured and get a feel for how long it is and the information it contains. This makes it much easier to understand.

CHECKLIST 24: GENERAL DIGITAL ACCESSIBILITY CHECKS

☐ Choose a descriptive document name or title; when the page is bookmarked, the content is then obvious.

☐ Set the language for the page appropriately. If the page contains content in different languages, this is tagged within the page. (This means, for example, that screen readers will read the content out using the correct language.)

☐ Use a combination of colours with a strong contrast.

☐ Edit and spell-check the content.

☐ Avoid presenting flickering or flashing content.

☐ Use sans-serif fonts to maximise the legibility of text.

☐ Ensure that text can be enlarged according to the participant's preferences.

☐ Where the content uses hyperlinks (as in, for example, web pages or Word documents), make sure the link wording describes what the link points to, that is, it says 'Research Report March 2021' rather than 'click here' or the URL.

☐ Don't convey meaning by colour alone; use bold or italic to draw attention to content.

☐ Allow navigation by keyboard alone, for example tabbing through form fields, selecting checkboxes and Likert scale options in a standard way, and submitting a survey with the return key.

☐ Ensure the content works with touch screens.

☐ Ensure that the survey can be read and completed with assistive technology, that is, a screen reader.

☐ Avoid presenting content that is timed, or enable participants to easily extend the amount of time allowed according to their needs.

☐ Write alternative text for images that describe the content and meaning of the image. Avoid presenting tables as an image; this can be very hard to access.

☐ Ensure that audio and video content is captioned and audio described and a transcript is provided.

☐ Make sure that text can be easily read against the background, and, where possible, avoid superimposing text on an image.

Automated checkers

Automated checkers can help identify some potentially inaccessible features of documents. They can be built in to the software, like Word's Accessibility Checker, be available as add-ons to existing software, such as extensions in a web browser, or be web-based, such as WebAIM's Wave, which will check web page accessibility from a URL. However, there are limitations to automated testing, and some things can only be checked manually.

These are some features that automated testers are not able to check:

- Whether important information is provided using colour-coding. For example, if red text is used to flag text that participants must read, this may not be picked up by people with colour blindness or screen reader users unless is it also made obvious in other ways.
- Whether the heading levels are used correctly and consistently, and whether elements (such as lists) are formatted appropriately.
- Whether colour combinations in the page design provide enough contrast to be easy to read; however, there are checkers that will give this information.
- Whether controls for video or audio can be operated with the keyboard as well as with a mouse.
- Whether images are used to display text, meaning the text cannot be read by a screen reader and cannot be copied and pasted.
- Whether there is any content that flashes or blinks.
- Whether the user is in control of changes to the page content; for example, when filling in a form, the user should be able to choose to scroll or follow a link to the next question rather than being moved on automatically.

The following sections summarise key things that need to be checked for different formats.

Designing accessible surveys

One option to increase accessibility of surveys is to offer them in a choice of format, for example offer the same survey both in paper-based and digital form (something that is also discussed in Chapters 4 and 8; it is also important to consider any implications for our research sample). In both forms, the choice of font can improve (and, conversely, hinder) readability, and style and language are important. In most institutional contexts, the design of websites is outside our control. For cases where we do have control over the design, accessible design should follow the recommendations (see Appendix 3). It is also important that the questionnaire can be read out by text-to-speech software (Goegan et al, 2018) for people who need to hear rather than read information; this should pose no problem for text, but image, video and audio access issues need to be addressed.

Online surveys potentially offer more customisation, but not all customisation is beneficial. Some survey providers offer templates that they describe as accessible, although they do not always make it clear what they mean by this in practice (Gottliebson et al, 2010). In addition to the survey provider, the scale of the research project itself sometimes restricts which software we can (or have) to choose from. Is it a simple text or form field collection, or do we need complex underlying features such as integrated email, branching and randomisation? Does it need to process several hundred responses or several thousand? Depending on the research question, we may have to distribute our survey via a specific site's distribution channel, or we can share an URL to a tool fully developed by ourselves.

Last, the survey software that is available might also be influenced by budget and by institutional policies regarding the use of in-house and external software, what kind of tech support is available for either, and whether an external solution meets data protection standards. Simplicity and ease of use for the participant should be preferred over overly complex technical solutions; make sure that whatever is used is flexible enough to respond to the needs of different people who might want to change the display settings to suit their preferences, and also when they might want to complete it (Nikivincze and Ancis, 2018).

VIGNETTE

Calliope suffers from debilitating migraines that appear without warning and can last for hours. This is incredibly frustrating for her because it makes it difficult for her to plan her day – she doesn't always know when she's going to have the energy to work on things or whether she will have to rest and wait for the pain to abate. Sometimes she can go for days without a single migraine and sometimes she has several on one day. Calliope is actively involved in local politics and keen to respond to a recent online consultation the city's Chamber of Commerce has started regarding initiatives to support the environmental sustainability of small businesses. Halfway through her lengthy response she gets a bad migraine and has to stop; she closes the window in the hopes of being able to pick it up again later. However, on her return she discovers that the online form is now closed and does not allow changing or expanding previously entered information.

Both SurveyMonkey and Google Forms provide accessible features, and, at the time of writing, Qualtrics offers accessible style sheets and a 'Check survey accessibility' feature. Sometimes these settings can be overridden with our own settings and we then need to check that the survey design is still accessible. Other academic survey providers such as, for example, Prolific Academic, apply a time limit. Usually it's much longer than is actually needed, but it does have to be checked because time limitations are a substantial barrier to participation.

CHECKLIST 24A: ACCESSIBLE ONLINE SURVEYS AND QUESTIONNAIRES

Make sure to also consider Checklist 24 for general advice on digital accessibility.

☐ Include a progress bar ('page 2 of 4') to encourage people to work through the questionnaire because they can see how much work there is to go.

☐ Keep the length to the minimum you need; people's attention often starts to stray after about 10 minutes (Goegan et al, 2018).

☐ Unless a time limit is part of the experimental design, consider extending any time limits for completion or not limiting time at all.

☐ Similarly, unless it is absolutely necessary for the participant to answer all in one go, consider allowing a save feature or repeated log-in to enable people to part-complete the survey and pause if necessary.

☐ Consider using a 'funnelling' approach (Brace, 2018), presenting general questions on a topic first, and then more specific questions later on.

☐ Provide clarifying information about questions, for example by writing tooltip text.

☐ Offer contact details so participants can get help with completion problems.

☐ Forms should highlight the field the cursor is in at any given moment, making it easier for participants to keep their place.

☐ Unless the study is explicitly about memory span, the instrument should allow users to navigate forwards and backwards, and to be able to come back to complete it later, to enable users with memory or concentration issues to complete the questionnaire or survey.

Alongside all the advantages that internet surveys can offer, there are some disadvantages. For example, when participants are recruited by offering links that are not specific to the individual (that is, not personalised for them alone), it is hard to calculate the response rate as we don't know who received the link but didn't follow it. We have also alluded in previous chapters to the fact that, though the internet seems ubiquitous, access to a computer and an internet connection is by no means guaranteed, particularly in some marginalised communities.

Data collection via email

Email can be a useful way to collect survey data or to conduct an interview. It has many benefits. It is convenient for participants, who can respond in their own time and take time to consider their answers. It is private. Both of these features mean it can work for difficult topics where people want time to reflect and want a sense of control over what they say. It can also increase participation from people who are on the autism spectrum (Gillespie-Lynch et al, 2014) or who have communication disabilities, who may find it difficult to take part in a verbal interview (Ison, 2009).

Without face-to-face communication, it may be harder to assess whether the participant is tired or upset when the researcher has little or no non-verbal cues to flag this up. However, because data collection is asynchronous, participants can choose at which time they engage with the research (McCoyd and Kerson, 2006). Because emails are received through the recipient's email program and on their devices, chances are much higher that the content can be accessed and read.

CHECKLIST 24B: RESEARCH USING EMAIL

Make sure to also consider Checklist 24 for general advice on digital accessibility.

- ☐ Let participants choose when they reply.
- ☐ Keep the format of emails simple – avoid using many images, avoid using images as a background to text, check the colour contrast and minimise formatting.
- ☐ Make sure that any attachments are accessible.

> ☐ Protect participants' data by creating a password-protected folder in your email to store research data, or downloading them into a password-protected folder and then deleting the original email. We have provided some guidance to encrypting documents in Appendix 6.
> ☐ Some email services offer an accessibility checker, such as MS Outlook, which has a 'Check accessibility' tool.

Data collection via SMS or WhatsApp

Like emails and online forms, short message service (SMS) and apps like WhatsApp or Signal may work well for people with a hearing impairment. The use of the SMS and, more recently, WhatsApp, has been shown to be effective in a range of contexts, for example, in health interventions, as a way for researchers to send short reminders (see, for example, Tolonen et al, 2014), by conducting short surveys for market research (see, for example, Andrews et al, 2011), or, with training, for data collection by peer researchers (Cumming et al, 2014). SMS has been shown to be beneficial for reaching groups that researchers sometimes term 'hard-to-reach', meaning researchers find it difficult to find a way to contact them and to persuade them to take part, such as minority ethnic and deprived communities (see, for example, Icheku and Arowobusoye, 2015).

An example technique using SMS effectively is SMS-ES, Short Message System Experience Sampling, in which the participant is frequently contacted throughout the day to either record what they are doing at that particular time, or to briefly answer a few questions on their current activities (used, for example, by Andrews et al, 2011). This technique was adapted to WhatsApp in the form of a Mobile Instant Messaging Interview (MIMI), used, for example, by Kaufmann and Peil (2020) to collect information in small bursts at different times during the day. While researchers using SMS or WhatsApp have no control over when and where their message reaches people, the upside is that recipients can respond at their own convenience. With WhatsApp, the researcher can easily send and receive both visual and audio data, and — assuming the recipient has enabled these functions — can check when and whether data were received. A desktop version of WhatsApp means that the conversation does not necessarily have to be typed on the phone, although at the time of writing it cannot be used for video or audio calls. WhatsApp and Signal are also examples of services that use end-to-end encryption (E2EE), meaning that nobody else can read any messages you exchange. This makes them useful tools for collecting sensitive or personal data, and for participants who are particularly concerned with privacy and confidentiality.

CHECKLIST 24C: RESEARCH BY TEXT/MESSAGING SERVICE

Make sure to also consider Checklist 24 for general advice on digital accessibility.

☐ Because these communications are so short, it is especially important to be concise and clear.
☐ Keep in mind the lack of non-verbal cues, and avoid the use of sarcasm or irony.
☐ Give preference to end-to-end encrypted tools (E2EE).
☐ When sending voice messages, ensure these are recorded against a quiet background.

Video interviews

Video interviews, whether by Skype, Zoom, Discord, Google Meets or other tools, can address a variety of different access requirements that can make participation easier (or possible at all). In addition, the lack of need to travel and the reduced cost make video interviews an appealing option. However, the lack of non–verbal cues means it can be more difficult for the interviewer to pick up on participants being upset, tired or distracted, and may make it more difficult to establish rapport (see, for example, a review by Nović, 2020), although the evidence is not clear (Irvine et al, 2013).

Depending on the quality of the internet connection, video or sound quality may deteriorate and make it more difficult, particularly for hearing-impaired participants, who may find it harder to follow all the participants unless there is a signer on screen too (Nović, 2020). While tools such as Google Meets offer automated live captioning, the quality can be questionable, and to be sure of good quality subtitles or closed captions you need to employ a captioner. Further advice on enabling hearing-impaired people to participate in online video meetings is available through ConnectHear (2020). However, video meetings allow interviewing while maintaining social distancing, and thus don't put vulnerable people at risk, be it the researcher or the participant. It is important to consider potential accommodations, such as interviews that are conducted asynchronously, for example by email, as this allows participants to proceed at their own pace (Egan et al, 2006).

Phone interviews may communicate more information, but it is not certain that all nuances in tone will be caught. Even with videoconferencing the visual information can be incomplete, more so if the quality of the connection is poor. Some services (for example, Zoom) offer a closed caption or automatic subtitling service at an additional cost. Another option is to have a three-way interview including a sign language interpreter (see also Appendix 4 for more information on text relay), but this is not straightforward, given there is no widely used written form of sign language (SignWriting, 2020), and questions may not translate directly (Parsons et al, 2001). Nor are test batteries and measurement scales easily translatable[2] or validated in this form (Kroll, 2011).

CHECKLIST 24D: VIDEO INTERVIEWS

Make sure to also consider Checklist 24 for general advice on digital accessibility.

- ☐ Ensure you set up the interview in a well-lit place so, if relevant, it is easy for the participant to see you.
- ☐ Test the sound quality of your microphone before conducting a video interview.
- ☐ Check with the participant that the audio and video is working for them.
- ☐ If recording the interview, make sure the recording is stored in a password-protected folder.

PDF accessibility

PDF has become the quasi-standard for sending documents as it can ensure that a document can no longer be altered, and provides a printable format that is consistent with the original document. In terms of accessibility, PDF documents can mitigate some of the issues, but much depends on the quality of the original document. It is worth the effort as it makes a big difference to the accessibility of the content (Bigham et al, 2016).

In order to be accessible, a range of requirements needs to be met so that the document can be read properly by assistive devices and software. At the time of writing, PDF Acrobat IX Pro can be used to create documents that comply with WCAG (see also Appendix 3 for more information about web standards).

This accessibility functionality can be accessed by adding the accessibility button to the tool bar (About Adobe Plug-Ins, then Accessibility, and then Add Accessibility button to the toolbar). This then offers a range of options, such as auto-tagging documents, or checking them for accessibility issues.

A separate set of specifications has been summarised in the standard ISO14289-1:2014, also referred to as PDF/UA.[3] Drümmer and Chang (2014) provide a good overview and introduction on how to comply with this standard, and additional information can be found at Accessible PDF.[4]

CHECKLIST 24E: PDF QUESTIONNAIRES

Make sure to also consider Checklist 24 for general advice on digital accessibility.

☐ Before converting a document to PDF, make sure that the structure can easily be read. In Word, this means using formatting templates to mark headings, rather than simply formatting them as bold.

☐ Specify the language of the PDF; screen readers can then read out the content in the correct language.

☐ Use the accessibility plug-in to check for and fix potential issues.

Data security

Data security is routinely required in order to gain ethical approval for research to take place, and consequently we will not go into detail here about how this can be achieved. Web technology and social media can facilitate tracing or hacking (van Doorn, 2013), while social media can provide identifiable information to other people or other sites (Rooke, 2013). It can be surprisingly easy to infer someone's identity from a few seemingly non-identifying characteristics – which can also give information about their social circle (Kosinski et al, 2013). Bearing in mind that disability is a stigmatised condition, and that participants may not have discussed this with friends and family or with their employer, it is essential to put measures in place so that you can protect participants effectively (Markham, 2013).

Testing and piloting

Testing means checking that recruitment, communications, data collection and follow-up activities are accessible before they are used. Piloting, in this chapter, refers to a process of ensuring the method is well understood by the researchers and participants and is collecting the information needed. Note that this chapter discusses the testing of digital materials; see Chapter 5 for access issues related to printed materials.

These are the tasks that need to be considered in order to ensure that testing and piloting is built into the project plan.

CHECKLIST 24F: PLANNING A PILOT STUDY

Make sure to also consider Checklist 24 for general advice on digital accessibility.

☐ In the project plan, allow time to apply for ethical approval for the pilot stage and then to apply again for the main phase, even if there are no amendments to data collection.

☐ Build in time for testing and piloting.

☐ Test communications and research materials for accessibility before they are sent out to anyone, as this can help identify and resolve some potential barriers before they affect recruitment.

☐ Consider employing a research adviser to review the accessibility of the data collection materials, or ask appropriate members of your stakeholder group, research partner or advisory board, if you have one.

☐ Create a pilot recruitment strategy, set inclusion and exclusion criteria for the sample, and decide on a target response rate or number of responses before the pilot is complete.

☐ Use a subgroup of your sample for the pilot as this most closely reflects the group of people who will be taking part.

Testing: What needs to be checked?

- Recruitment material, in any format.
- The project website, and any audio or video material.
- Stimulus material such as interview schedules or vignettes, particularly where it is shared with participants.
- Project reports and other documents published by the team that share the research findings.

Web pages

There are a lot of free web accessibility checkers that will identify any issues in your page – the Web Accessibility Initiative keeps a list (see Appendix 3). We suggest you begin by looking at the WebAIM free tester: this company is well established and the tester is free, with straightforward explanations of any problem. There are plenty of other options, however; the important thing is that we do check.

CHECKLIST 24G: CHECKING WEB PAGE ACCESSIBILITY

Make sure to also consider Checklist 24 for general advice on digital accessibility.

☐ If style sheets are switched off, the page structure still makes sense.

☐ All interactive elements (forms, audio players) can be accessed with keystrokes.

☐ Participants can tab through the page in a logical order.

☐ All form inputs have labels that describe the form field.

☐ Forms use tooltips that give clarifying information about the question.

☐ Tables contain tabular information and are not used purely for displaying content.

☐ Row and column headings are formatted as such.

☐ Content displays on a mobile device (for example, the page width is not fixed so it is too wide to show on a mobile screen) and functions such as submit buttons work with a touch screen.

VIGNETTE

Rangar has dyslexia. After much trial and error, he has found a combination of font and line spacing that feels more comfortable and less exhausting than other formats. He's agreed to participate in a study on mobile phone use that requires him to install a tracking app on his phone. Because of the privacy and data protection implications, the participant information (including consent forms and participant briefing) is quite lengthy. This is provided as a PDF file, which doesn't allow Rangar to set it to the font and the spacing he needs to read the text comfortably. He asks to be given the text in a Word document so that he can apply the document settings that work best for him.

Word documents

Word has a built-in accessibility checker that can be accessed through the 'Check accessibility' feature. It produces a list of 'Recommended actions' that will alert us to the following kinds of issues.

CHECKLIST 24H: CHECKING WORD DOCUMENT ACCESSIBILITY

Make sure to also consider Checklist 24 for general advice on digital accessibility.

☐ Add a descriptive title to the document properties.
☐ Where audio and video content is presented, include a link to a transcript.
☐ Format tabular content as a table, rather than with tabs. Use easy-to-understand wording for the table heading text. Table header rows and columns need to be formatted.
☐ If a table is broken over more than one page, use the Table settings to ensure that the heading repeats automatically at the top of the page.
☐ Give sub-sections meaningful names so when people navigate using links to section headings, it is obvious where they are going.
☐ Format images as 'Inline with text'. This means that if the text is edited or moves, the image moves with it, always keeping it in the right context.
☐ Include a table of contents in longer documents, making it is easy for people to navigate straight to the content they are looking for.

PDF files

Ideally, a PDF file is created from an original document that has all the accessibility features enabled; this is simpler than adding features in the PDF version. It produces smaller files and the text can be selected and read out by a screen reader. It is possible to convert a scanned document into text, but the level of accuracy of the tool depends on the quality of the scan, and it can be time-consuming to create and check. There are a number of PDF creation apps available, but Adobe Acrobat has an accessibility checker that will identify, and enable us to amend, any issues that it identifies.

CHECKLIST 24I: CHECKING PDF DOCUMENT ACCESSIBILITY

Make sure to also consider Checklist 24 for general advice on digital accessibility.

☐ Create PDF files from documents in other formats, rather than from scans.

☐ Create links within the document to make navigation easier and quicker. For example, when a Word document is set up with an automated contents page, those links will also work when it is saved as a PDF file.

☐ If the document has security settings (for example, to prevent copying of text), ensure that they are set so assistive technology can still access the text.

☐ Make sure that the 'Reading order' tool gives options for correcting headings.

☐ The 'Table inspector' can mark table header rows and columns, if they are missing.

Excel spreadsheets

Excel has its own automated accessibility checker that will pick up on some issues and suggest what is needed to do to resolve them. When checking the document, look at the following:

CHECKLIST 24J: CHECKING EXCEL DOCUMENT ACCESSIBILITY

Make sure to also consider Checklist 24 for general advice on digital accessibility.

☐ All the images that present information (for example, charts and graphs) need to have alternate text that explains the salient points of the image.

☐ Cells are set to wrap text so all the text is displayed without having to manually change the size of the cells, or select the cell, to read it.

☐ Heading styles are used for headings within the spreadsheet and headings are worded descriptively (for example, 'Section 3: Research findings' rather than just 'Section 3'), so it is easy to understand the document structure.

☐ Ensure that heading rows and columns are marked.

☐ Set up tooltips that give more information about links if the cell that forms the link contains numbers rather than words.

☐ Name each worksheet tab in plain language so the contents are clear, and delete any blank worksheets.

☐ The Excel 'Accessibility Checker' identifies colour contrast issues.

Video and audio

Most (but not all) mainstream video and audio providers have made their players accessible. When deciding on a site that will host a video or audio, their accessibility features need to be compared beforehand. This makes it much quicker and easier to make our content accessible.

There are other considerations, however, as the video needs to be designed with accessibility in mind – an accessible player will not resolve issues such as the lack of audio description (a spoken commentary that explains what is happening on screen if the viewer cannot see). This needs to be included in the video when it is created and included in the transcript.

CHECKLIST 24K: CHECKING VIDEO AND AUDIO DOCUMENT ACCESSIBILITY

Make sure to also consider Checklist 24 for general advice on digital accessibility.

☐ Check before you choose a podcast or video host that it provides an option to post or create a transcript and closed captions or subtitles – some popular sites have neither these features nor an option to link to a transcript hosted elsewhere.

☐ Make sure it is possible to use the video or audio player with keystrokes as well as with the mouse (for example, you can press the space bar to start or pause play).

☐ When uploading the video or audio, select the features that enable closed captions and a transcript.

☐ Set the language of the audio or video when you upload it so the transcript and subtitles will be displayed in the right character set and auto-generated in the right language.

☐ Provide a transcript. If you do not already have a transcript, then a quick way to create one is to upload the audio or video onto a site like YouTube or Vimeo that auto-transcribes spoken words, and wait for the site to auto-generate a transcript. The quality of auto-generated transcripts can be very poor, however (see, for example, Parton, 2016; Besner, 2019), so in order to provide meaningful transcripts they have to be manually checked and corrected.

Printed materials

Access issues related to printed materials are discussed in Chapter 5 (Checklist 13 summarises the key actions). We need to check that printed materials have been set up to be accessible, and then ask for feedback on this in the pilot.

Piloting

Piloting checks several different aspects of the research. As well as testing the recruitment strategy, data collection setting, sample and method, it can give an understanding of how the research might affect participants, which is particularly useful for sensitive topics. If more than one person is collecting data, a pilot study can check that the method is being applied consistently.

The piloting process can also be a useful way to build teamworking skills in a research team and to ensure that the practical challenges of data collection are well understood (Morrison et al, 2016). Finally, if data analysis begins with data obtained in the pilot phase of the study, it can also be used to check the analysis techniques.

VIGNETTE

Nish is Deaf, and British Sign Language is his first language. He is participating in a pilot for a research agency's survey on attitudes towards political parties. Nish takes the survey and uses the feedback field to inform the agency of two problems with the survey and its response options. One issue is that the survey includes a range of demographic questions, among them a question for the respondent's first language, but the list of response options does not include any sign languages at all. In another part of the survey, participants are asked about their responses to a short video of a politician's speech, but there is no transcript of the speech in the video, and the video is not captioned either.

Piloting is an important phase of a research project. Findings can be used to refine the research question, sample and other aspects of the study if they are not functioning as planned. Piloting does not guarantee that the data collection process will be completely problem-free, but it's an important quality control measure that helps to pick up issues in advance, when it is easier to find solutions. For qualitative studies, piloting can add credibility and dependability to the completed research (Malmqvist et al, 2019).

Including pilot data in the main study

One of the distinctions between qualitative and quantitative approaches to piloting is different practices regarding whether data collected from pilot samples are used. In a quantitative study, the pilot sample may not be large enough to reliably identify data collection issues that will affect the whole sample. If significant changes to a questionnaire are made in response, it may not be possible to compare the two datasets; for that reason, data may be collected for piloting purposes and not used.

Separating out pilot data may be less of an issue for qualitative research where it is more common for question wording and focus to be adjusted during data collection, based on developing knowledge about the topic (van Teijlingen and Hundley, 2001). For sensitive subjects there are questions about whether there is an ethical responsibility to participants to use the data that they have made an effort to provide. In a qualitative study, where there is a smaller number of participants and they may be hard to reach, the practicalities and time constraints of recruitment may mean it is not practical to collect data that do not form part of the findings (Morrison et al, 2016).

A potential approach to questionnaire development is to identify topics and approaches through qualitative interviews, using open questions to see where the answers go, which can then be used to develop closed questions (Bryman, 2012).

Evaluation criteria

Before we begin, it is useful to set some criteria to keep track of what needs to be checked to help in identifying what might need to change. They could include:

- Whether participants received and opened bulk emails inviting them to participate, for example whether an online questionnaire link is interpreted as spam by the recipients' email clients and therefore they don't see our request for participation.
- Whether participants could easily get to the research setting and whether it was appropriate (easy to access, peaceful, private).
- The length of time it took to complete the data collection process.
- The point at which participants start to lose focus or drop out.
- The flow of a questionnaire and the sequence of questions – do they make sense?
- The questions that were skipped, not answered or were unclear and needed clarification.
- Which questions, if any, made participants feel uncomfortable or they were unwilling to answer.
- In which places focus group or interview guidance for interviewers needs to be improved based on the clarifying or follow-up questions asked by participants.

The research protocol should be used as planned, and feedback should be elicited during data collection, or immediately afterwards.

Alternative versions of the data collection method need to be included as well, for example the paper version of the questionnaire (with a stamped return envelope if necessary).

Potential solutions to piloting issues

It may be difficult to know whether disabled people are included in the pilot sample, even if we are requesting demographic data. To be sure of this, consider using professional advisers, or specifically recruiting disabled people to the pilot. If possible, conduct some observational user testing, a usability research method that involves in-person observation or recording a participant while they are testing the pilot (paper or online questionnaire) to identify its strengths and weaknesses (Boynton, 2004).

Check whether pilot participants can identify the point in the questionnaire or interview at which they started to lose interest. If it's an online questionnaire, this may be obvious from the length of time that people take to complete each section or the point at which they drop out.

It is particularly important to test self-completion activities because the researcher is not present to answer questions. Providing an 'information' link or tooltip gives context-sensitive help for participants to get clarification on online questions if needed.

Questions that are skipped or not answered can be addressed by using skip logic so users are taken directly to the next set of questions based on their responses. If we do this, we need to check it is equally clear on paper copies of a research questionnaire if users don't have to answer all the questions.

If people are losing interest or are tired, we need to review the length of the questionnaire or interview; ensure the most important questions are placed early on, and check if anything can be missed out. In an interview or focus group, this might be an appropriate point to have a break.

For questions that make people uncomfortable, greater context can be given to this topic in the introduction, participant information sheet or in the tooltip text, explaining why this question is important. An observer or interviewer could explore the reasons for this with them or ask for feedback.

Crucially, report what was learned from the pilot study, and what was changed, in research papers; this is an aspect of accountability. It also means that, where the findings can't be used, the work is still acknowledged.

Summary

In this chapter we explored the principles of digital accessibility and described some practical techniques for making content more accessible in a range of different apps that can be used for research data collection. We also looked at how to test and pilot research, and made some suggestions for resolving access issues.

In Chapter 8, we look at accessibility issues related to mixed methods and a range of different data collection methods.

Notes

[1]   Although not zero, since online infrastructure has a carbon footprint too. In a lengthy analysis, Ong et al (2012) estimate the cost of a videoconference at about 7 per cent of the cost of a comparable meeting that requires domestic and international travel. However, even where much less travel is involved, videoconferencing will still come out better in terms of energy consumption.

[2]   Where parts of a study are conducted in more than language, the issue of semantic equivalency arises. Do the instructions have the same meaning for all participants? And are participants' responses therefore comparable? This is why established testing batteries or scales are usually validated separately for each language they are used in. As sign languages are natural languages, these issues of translatability and equivalence apply here, too.

[3]   Available at: www.iso.org/standard/64599.html

[4]   See https://accessible-pdf.info/en/

Further reading

Burns, E. (2010) 'Developing email interview practices in qualitative research', *Sociological Research Online*, 15(4), 24–35.
Explores the practice of using email for interviews and how it differs from other qualitative methods of data collection.

Hendershot, G.E. (2004) 'Innovative Approaches to Interviewing People with Disabilities', in Proceedings of Statistics Canada Symposium 2004: Innovative Methods for Surveying Difficult-to-reach Populations, Statistics Canada. Available at: www5.statcan.gc.ca/bsolc/olc-cel/olc-cel?lang=eng&catno=11-522-X20040018742
A discussion of how the use of structured online interviews can increase participation from disabled people.

Nikivincze, I. and Ancis, J. (2018) 'Accessible but not usable: Improving practices for surveying people with disabilities.' Available at: www.resna.org/sites/default/files/conference/2018/pdf_versions/cac/Nikivincze.pdf

A succinct and helpful summary of accessibility issues that may arise during the implementation of survey research, and what we can do about them.

WebAIM (Web Accessibility In Mind) Available at: https://webaim.org
A site with a wealth of useful and well-written information about digital accessibility, including step-by-step instructions and a free accessibility tester.

Wilson, E., Campain, R., Moore, M., Hagiliassis, N., et al (2013) 'An accessible survey method: Increasing the participation of people with a disability in large sample social research', *Telecommunications Journal of Australia*, 63(2).
Useful strategies to help increase participation in (particularly online) surveys.

References

Andrews, L., Bennett, R.R. and Drennan, J. (2011) 'Capturing affective experiences using the SMS Experience Sampling (SMS-ES) method', *International Journal of Market Research*, 53(4), 479–506.

Besner, L. (2019) 'When is a caption close enough?', *The Atlantic*, 9 August. Available at: www.theatlantic.com/health/archive/2019/08/youtube-captions/595831

Bigham, J.P., Brady, E.L., Gleason, C., Guo, A. and Shamma, D.A. (2016) 'An Uninteresting Tour through Why Our Research Papers Aren't Accessible', in Proceedings of the 2016 CHI Conference, Extended Abstracts on Human Factors in Computing Systems, May, pp 621–31.

Boynton, P.M. (2004) 'Administering, analysing, and reporting your questionnaire', *BMJ*, 328(7452), 1372–5.

Brace, I. (2018) *Questionnaire Design: How to Plan, Structure and Write Survey Material for Effective Market Research*, London: Kogan Page Publishers.

Bryman, A. (2012) *Social Research Methods*, Oxford: Oxford University Press.

ConnectHear (2020) 'Knowledge base: Strategies for Deaf and Hard of Hearing Communication.' Available at: http://connect-hear.com/

Cumming, T.M., Strnadová, I., Knox, M. and Parmenter, T. (2014) 'Mobile technology in inclusive research: Tools of empowerment', *Disability & Society*, 29(7), 999–1012.

Drümmer, O. and Chang, B. (2014) 'PDF/UA in a nutshell', PDF Association, 16 June. Available at: www.pdfa.org/pdfua-in-a-nutshell

DWP (Department for Work and Pensions)/ODI (Office for Disability Issues) (2018) 'Accessible communication formats', 13 December. Available at: www.gov.uk/government/publications/inclusive-communication/accessible-communication-formats

Egan, J., Chenoweth, L. and McAuliffe, D. (2006) 'Email-facilitated qualitative interviews with traumatic brain injury survivors: A new and accessible method', *Brain Injury*, 20(12), 1283–94.

Gillespie-Lynch, K., Kapp, S.K., Shane-Simpson, C., Smith, D.S. and Hutman, T. (2014) 'Intersections between the autism spectrum and the internet: Perceived benefits and preferred functions of computer-mediated communication', *Intellectual and Developmental Disabilities*, 52(6), 456–69.

Goegan, L.D., Radil, A.I. and Daniels, L.M. (2018) 'Accessibility in questionnaire research: Integrating universal design to increase the participation of individuals with learning disabilities', *Learning Disabilities: A Contemporary Journal*, 16(2), 177–90.

Gottliebson, D., Layton, N. and Wilson, E. (2010) 'Comparative effectiveness report: Online survey tools', *Disability and Rehabilitation: Assistive Technology*, 5(6), 401–10. Available at: http://dx.doi.org/10.3109/17483101003793404

Icheku, V. and Arowobusoye, N. (2015) 'Evaluation of a service intervention to improve uptake of breast cancer screening in a London Borough with many hard to reach communities', *Universal Journal of Public Health*, 3(2), 92–102.

Irvine, A., Drew, P. and Sainsbury, R. (2013) '"Am I not answering your questions properly?" Clarification, adequacy and responsiveness in semi-structured telephone and face-to-face interviews', *Qualitative Research*, 13(1), 87–106.

Ison, N.L. (2009) 'Having their say: Email interviews for research data collection with people who have verbal communication impairment', *International Journal of Social Research Methodology*, 12(2), 161–72.

Kaufmann, K. and Peil, C. (2020) 'The mobile instant messaging interview (MIMI): Using WhatsApp to enhance self-reporting and explore media usage in situ', *Mobile Media & Communication*, 8(2), 229–46.

Kosinski, M., Stillwell, D. and Graepel, T. (2013) 'Private traits and attributes are predictable from digital records of human behavior', *Proceedings of the National Academy of Sciences*, 110(15), 5802–5.

Kroll, T. (2011) 'Designing mixed methods studies in health-related research with people with disabilities', *International Journal of Multiple Research Approaches*, 5(1), 64–75.

Malmqvist, J., Hellberg, K., Möllås, G., Rose, R. and Shevlin, M. (2019) 'Conducting the pilot study: A neglected part of the research process? Methodological findings supporting the importance of piloting in qualitative research studies', *International Journal of Qualitative Methods*, 18, 1609406919878341.

Markham, A.N. (2013) 'Fieldwork in social media: What would Malinowski do?', *Qualitative Communication Research*, 2(4), 434–46.

McCoyd, J.L.M. and Kerson, T.S. (2006) 'Conducting intensive interviews using email: A serendipitous comparative opportunity', *Qualitative Social Work*, 5(3), 389e406.

Morrison, J., Clement, T., Nestel, D. and Brown, J. (2016) '"Underdiscussed, underused and underreported": Pilot work in team-based qualitative research', *Qualitative Research Journal*, 16(4).

Nikivincze, I. and Ancis, J. (2018) 'Accessible but not usable: Improving practices for surveying people with disabilities.' Available at: www.resna.org/sites/default/files/conference/2018/pdf_versions/cac/Nikivincze.pdf

Nović, S. (2020) 'Why "Dinner Table Syndrome" is getting worse for deaf people', BBC Equality Matters, 1 October. Available at: www.bbc.com/worklife/article/20200922-why-dinner-table-syndrome-is-getting-worse-for-deaf-people

ODEP (Office of Disability Employment Policy, US) (no date) 'Effective interaction: Communicating with and about people with disabilities.' Available at: www.dol.gov/agencies/odep/publications/fact-sheets/effective-interaction-communicating-with-and-about-people-with-disabilities-in-the-workplace

ODI (Office for Disability Issues, UK) (2011) *Involving Disabled People in Social Research*. Available at: www.gov.uk/government/uploads/system/uploads/attachment_data/file/321254/involving-disabled-people-in-social-research.pdf

Ong, D., Moors, T. and Sivaraman, V. (2012) 'Complete Life-Cycle Assessment of the Energy/CO2 Costs of Videoconferencing vs Face-to-Face Meetings', in 2012 IEEE Online Conference on Green Communications (GreenCom), September, pp 50–5.

Parsons, J.A., Baum, S., Johnson, T.P. and Hendershot, G. (2001) 'Inclusion of disabled populations in interview surveys: Reviews and recommendations', *Research in Social Science and Disability*, 2, 167–84.

Parton, B. (2016) 'Video captions for online courses: Do YouTube's auto-generated captions meet deaf students' needs?', *Journal of Open, Flexible, and Distance Learning*, 20(1), 8–18.

Rooke, B. (2013) 'Four pillars of internet research ethics with Web 2.0', *Journal of Academic Ethics*, 11(4), 265–8.

SignWriting (2020) 'Sign languages are written languages!' Available at: www.signwriting.org

Tolonen, H., Aistrich, A. and Borodulin, K. (2014) 'Increasing health examination survey participation rates by SMS reminders and flexible examination times', *Scandinavian Journal of Public Health*, 42(7), 712–17.

Tsatsou, P. (2020) 'Is digital inclusion fighting disability stigma? Opportunities, barriers, and recommendations', *Disability & Society*, 1–27.

van Doorn, N. (2013) 'Assembling the affective field: How smartphone technology impacts ethnographic research practice', *Qualitative Inquiry*, 19(5), 385–96.

van Teijlingen, E.R. and Hundley, V. (2001) 'The importance of pilot studies', *Social Research Update*, Issue 35, Department of Sociology, University of Surrey.

8

Mixed media, triangulation and mixed methods

In this chapter we explore the reasons why researchers use more than one data collection method in their research, and the potential benefits this can have for including disabled participants. We look at the use of triangulation, mixed methods and mixed media, and then go on to discuss the accessibility issues linked with a range of individual research methods

Triangulation[1] refers to an approach that strategically uses more than one method, theory or researcher to collect and analyse data. The intended outcome is to derive a more consistent answer by validating the findings using more than one source. It can also mean analysing the same data with different methods, via 'triangulation of data analysis techniques' (Lauri, 2011). It can be used as an analysis strategy, where different members of the research team conduct analysis independently and then compare their findings, a tactic known as intercoder reliability (in qualitative research) or interrater reliability (in quantitative research) (O'Connor and Joffe, 2020). Crucially, triangulation is used to examine the same underlying concept or variable through different means:

> The logic of triangulation is based on the premise that no single method ever adequately solves the problem of rival explanations. Because each method reveals different aspects of empirical reality, multiple methods of data collection and analysis provide more grist for the research mill. (Patton, 1999, p 1192)

However, it is not a given that the different approaches lead to consistent answers. Mathison (1988, p 15) argues that:

> [i]n practice, triangulation as a strategy provides a rich and complex picture of some social phenomenon being studied, but rarely does it provide a clear path to a singular view of what is the case. I suggest that triangulation as a strategy

provides evidence for the researcher to make sense of some social phenomenon, but that the triangulation strategy does not, in and of itself, do this.

In fact, Mathison points out, convergence is but one of the possible outcomes of a triangulation approach, with inconsistency and contradiction being the other two possible outcomes that the researcher is required to resolve.

Mixed methods, on the other hand, usually refers to a mixture of quantitative and qualitative methods, such as, for example, the classical combination of interviews and a questionnaire. Often, mixed methods are used in a sequence where the first step is of a more exploratory nature, and the second step focuses on one of the issues, themes or variables identified in the exploratory phase. In recent years, a new approach of **braiding** has also emerged, where 'multiple methods are simultaneously employed across distinct research phases, with equal significance and attention given to each method in all phases' (Watson, 2020, p 68).

Last, we have used the term **mixed media** (somewhat facetiously) to refer to the use of different communication media in the process of conducting either qualitative or quantitative research, that is, combining the online version of a questionnaire with a paper version, or a face-to-face interview with one conducted via email. This is not without risk, but we will discuss later how we might be able to mitigate those risks.

The three approaches introduced all offer an opportunity to help us make it easier for people to participate, if one or more of the offered alternatives are less suitable because of, for example, sensory limitations and mobility issues, or practical issues such as time or availability of transport. Participants who for various reasons can't participate in focus groups may be willing to participate in interviews or complete questionnaires; people who would struggle with verbal tasks may be willing to produce images or photos (discussed later). Where different groups of participants as well as different methods are involved, the way in which information and understanding overlap and diverge between the two groups can produce a richer understanding of the problem that is being researched (Alhusein et al, 2018).

Risk and mitigation

From an inclusion and accessibility point of view, it would be ideal to offer several options in which individuals can participate in our study – some by questionnaire, some by interview, some by focus group, each to their own preferences, abilities and requirements. Such a choice could empower participants and give them agency. But empowerment and choice carry a substantial risk: random allocation to conditions is one of the cornerstones of quantitative research, even in social science research (see, for example, Oakley et al, 2003). Allowing participants to self-select into conditions could introduce bias into the study and the results (Bethlehem, 2010), although, with careful adjustments, the extent of the bias can be reduced (see, for example Shadish et al, 2008). That said, bias is more likely if self-selection is based on variables that are relevant for the research question, for example if we look into helpfulness and assume that the participants who are less helpful self-select into the conditions that require the least effort on their side, such as doing an online questionnaire. That said, of course, such assumptions might be wrong, and self-selection may reflect access needs rather than individual preference or underlying personality trait.

This does not mean it's impossible to approach a topic from a range of different perspectives and with a range of different methods as part of its core design. For example, we might be interested in different leadership styles for intercultural teams. We could use a focus group to establish desired leadership traits; interviews to identify themes relating to successful leadership; and questionnaires to more systematically compare perceptions from within different cultures. This way, the different methods would complement each other and contribute to a more holistic view of the issue at hand, and the range of methods would mean that we could recruit from a wider and more diverse number of potential participants. Olkin (2004) makes a similar point in the context of researching with people with different disabilities:

> A clear distinction should be made here between changes to methods and format versus changes to the research questions. If researchers ultimately want to be able to make some statement across disabilities, ie across the different methods employed with different disability groups, there has to be a unifying undercurrent to the methods. *That undercurrent is the research questions.* (Olkin, 2004, p 338; emphasis added)

Alternatively, it is possible to offer different versions of the same instrument provided we take care to establish and/or test for equivalence before using the data, particularly in a quantitative context. For example, we could offer participants a written/phone/online version of a questionnaire and treat this as different conditions of a variable, for example the variable *medium of participation* with the values *written*, *phone* and *online*. There is evidence that in some cases this can be done with the results of the different versions being comparable, such as a study showing equivalence between the web- and paper-based versions of a measure on transformational leadership (Cole et al, 2006), or face-to-face and online research with people with multiple sclerosis (Synnot et al, 2014).

But this measurement equivalence is not a given and cannot be assumed (see, for example, Ripat and Colatruglio, 2016, on finding different patterns of answers when using both face-to-face and online approaches). Using different versions requires careful planning and testing, and it would be advisable to test during the pilot whether the different conditions yield similar data (on the importance of pilot studies, see also Kezar, 2000; van Teijlingen and Hundley, 2002). Because pilots are usually run at a much smaller scale than the main study, testing here can probably only be done through scanning the data and checking for contradictions or, more preferably, substantial overlap. With larger datasets we can employ statistical analyses after data collection and check whether the data collected through the different media are significantly different; what we are looking for is, in essence, whether there is an effect of medium of data collection. Conditions that do not differ significantly from each other can be collapsed into one dataset. Conditions that do differ from each other need to either be analysed separately, or the effect of the medium controlled for, for example by using an analysis of covariance.

We have previously stressed the iterative nature of research, along with the self-correcting process of conducting a pre-study or a pilot. In this context, Arfken and Balon (2011, p 326) suggest a further reason to 'incorporate a sub study with minimal data collection within the larger study to characterise people who did not agree to the full study. Qualitative interviews with the target population may suggest reasons why some people refused to participate in a specific study.' This, too, can be interpreted as a form of triangulation.

> ## CHECKLIST 25: DEVELOPING A RATIONALE FOR TRIANGULATION
>
> ❏ Think about the different facets of the research question. Do they all have to be examined with the same method, or can some elements be split off into separate studies?
>
> ❏ Can the same concept or variable be measured through different approaches?
>
> ❏ Can the same measurement instrument be offered in different modes?
>
> ❏ Can triangulation be achieved in other ways? For example, can different members of the research team code independently and then cross-check their work?

In previous chapters we have discussed some of the ways in which individual research methods can be made more accessible, distinguishing between face-to-face and remote research, and focusing on the methods most frequently used, such as:

- Questionnaires or surveys (online or paper) (covered in Chapter 7).
- Interviews (covered in Chapter 6).
- Focus groups (also covered in Chapter 6).

In this chapter we want to look at additional approaches that we might use to complement our research methods and which accessibility issues we need to consider. In this context, we will be looking at experiments, observation or ethnography and the use of secondary data as overall approaches, as well as a range of individual methods such as photography and visual material, diary studies and participatory mapping.

However, while some of these methods are more accessible to some groups of participants than others, we should be wary of making assumptions: wherever possible, the choice of method – and, with it, the agency – should rest with the participant.

VIGNETTE

Kira lives in a rural area with poor internet connectivity. She is 69 and suffers from rheumatoid arthritis. Kira works as a cleaner to supplement her low pension. A neighbour has passed on a leaflet to participate in research on growing up in Australia in the 1960s. Kira would like to participate, but the leaflet only gives a link to an online questionnaire. Kira has no internet at home, and the only reliable internet can be found at the nearest library. She doesn't like taking public transport any more than absolutely necessary because it usually exacerbates her arthritis, and she doesn't want to sit at a public computer telling strangers on the internet about her childhood.

Experiment

How it works

The hallmark of an experiment is the combination of a controlled environment and random allocation of participants to conditions. Very, very broadly speaking, if we randomly allocate participants to either an experimental or control group, by providing both groups with the same environment, we are increasing the probability that any differences between groups of participants are due primarily to the variables we changed or manipulated. But for some variables a random allocation isn't possible – we can't[2] randomly allocate participants to either the smoking or non-smoking group because people already are either smokers or non-smokers. In a quasi-experiment, the second requirement is relaxed, which allows for the formation of groups based on existing properties or traits that cannot be experimentally manipulated. This can be mitigated to some extent by the research design and the statistical analyses used, but there remains a fundamental limitation on the range and validity of conclusions we can draw from these kinds of studies.

Accessibility issues

Because the controlled environment is such a key element, conducting an experiment in circumstances other than a face-to-face setting becomes a challenge. Of course, there are computer-based instruments or online tests such as the Implicit Association Test (IAT)[3] that are self-contained and easy to take at home. But there remains the methodological issue of having little to no control over environmental factors such as distraction, use of resources and so on, even though some research suggests that respondents are capable of managing distractions to their benefit (Zwarun and Hall, 2014). This emphasis on control of the environment makes them less suitable for accessible research. Some of these issues, like timing, can be controlled through the use of tools, but not all can be remedied. If control of external factors is paramount to the success of the experiment, this usually requires a laboratory setting – in other words, face-to-face research.

VIGNETTE

Adebayo is a programmer with a hearing impairment. He saw a banner ad asking minority ethnic programmers to participate in a research study on the perception of self-employed programmers within the industry. The study website offers different versions of interviews: email, video interview, in person or by phone. Adebayo uses a hearing aid that would allow him to use the phone, but he finds these calls quite exhausting because, although the hearing aid does amplify the volume of sounds, it takes a lot of energy to distinguish between background noise and dialogue. Adebayo therefore instead prefers to be interviewed by email.

Observation or ethnography

How it works

The methods discussed so far have all require a sort of active participation – participants have to take a certain amount of time out to actively engage in the research, time that takes them away from their usual routine or activities. Observation and ethnography differ in that regard as the researcher acts as an observer and puts themselves in a situation that participants are already in, while critically observing and reflecting on their own position. Although, as Chiseri-Strater observed, '[a]ll researchers are positioned' (2020, p 115), the ethnographer's position is a unique one because, '[f]or ethnographers, writing about how we are positioned is part of the data' (2020, p 116) and reflexivity forms a key part of the approach (Salzman, 2002).

Accessibility issues

On the one hand, this may mean that the participants have already adjusted the environment to an extent that it is less disabling. However, a lack of accommodations potentially raises ethical and methodological issues for an ethnographer who is in a position to offer accommodations – particularly if a power differential exists between the researcher and participants. It is important to consider how barriers to access in the research setting may have affected the sample. Ethnography need not be conducted face-to-face; it can also be conducted asynchronously, from a distance, for example by asking participants to collect digital data using a mobile phone that are then shared with the researcher (Rebernik et al, 2020). While this approach may also introduce barriers (see Chapter 7), it may give access to locations that a researcher cannot reach (Gregory, 2020).

Wherever researchers come into close contact with participants, we need to consider potentially immunocompromised participants, and there is more detail on this in Chapter 5 (in particular, see Checklist 15).

Use of archival data or secondary data

Finally, using archival or secondary data has almost no immediate issues since no direct participation is involved, nor does the researcher have to be in close contact with participants. This makes it a great method to combine with others, although it is not entirely without issues – in Chapter 3 we looked at the issues with using secondary data and relying on the accessibility of previous data collections.

The following sections look at ways in which creative research methods can be used to engage participants. They briefly describe the methods, focusing on the accessibility issues related to the different ways in which they can be used, rather than providing a general in-depth discussion of the uses, benefits and limitations of these data collection tools.

Arts-based methods can be useful for a range of situations (Kara, 2015), including working with people whose first language is not English, exploring sensitive topics and working with people with cognitive or communication impairments.

Photography and visual material

How it works

There are several different ways to use photos and other types of visual material in research using methods such as photo elicitation and photovoice (the methodological issues involved are discussed extensively in Pauwels, 2010). This method can include any form of visual material: provided by the participant, provided by the researcher, taken specifically for the research project or sourced in other ways, and either hard copy or digital. It can involve some of the following methods (Kara, 2015):

- Digital storytelling
- Film making
- Photography
- Map making

In photo elicitation (Harper, 2002), photos or other visual images are used as an elicitation tool to support another data collection method such as an interview or focus group. Photos are used to encourage the participant to reflect so they can talk in more depth and tell their own stories.

VIGNETTE

Thalia is a city historian and is compiling an oral history of the city in the 1950s–1960s. She is working with people who grew up in this city and spent their childhood and young adulthood there. Initially, she used existing photos of the city around that time as an aid to jog people's memories and to get them talking. For the most recent sessions, she has begun to complement this by including sound recordings from the time, and also provides a thorough verbal description of the scene depicted in the photo, which is helpful for participants with poor vision.

While elicitation can use photos provided by the researcher or participation, photovoice is an emancipatory method that enables participants to create a visual representation of their life or their experience that highlights social issues and concerns, either individually or in the wider community. It has been used successfully with participants who are considered to be vulnerable, such as children and young people (Luttrell, 2010), and people with learning difficulties or difficulties with verbal communication (Aldridge, 2007; Manning, 2010). However, there are additional ethical issues related to the use of images in research, data security and storage, consent, identifiability and ethical anonymising of images, particularly where images identify minors or adults whose consent status is unclear (Wiles et al, 2008).

Accessibility issues

One of the strengths of visual methods is that they can provide the researcher with access to physical spaces, times and experiences they would not be able to access themselves, enabling a better understanding of the participants' experience. For example, it can give access to the workplace in a way that is unobtrusive (Akkerman et al, 2014). Another advantage is that it puts participants in control of taking and interpreting the images for the researcher, which can be empowering (Mannay, 2010).

Using visual-based content as an elicitation tool may not work well for people with low vision, although it depends on the person and the way adjustments are made during the session (Arcilla, 2011). Depending on the approach, it may be possible to substitute other art forms (such as music) or tangible objects that enable the participant to talk about the research topic from their own experience. Photographic methods have also been adapted for use with people who use augmentative and alternative communication devices (AACs) (Dee-Price et al, 2020). However, some researchers stress the importance of including participants in the analysis, since what participants say about them in the data collection sessions may differ from the interpretation placed on them by researchers (Cluley et al, 2020).

Arts-based methods can take many forms, and are particularly useful for elicitation. For example, model making has been used to elicit thoughts and feelings about mental health (Dalton, 2020), performance poetry to explore young people's feelings about living with a disability (Hodges et al, 2014), and theatre, to explore identities (Raynor, 2019).

Diary studies

How it works

In a diary study, the researcher asks participants to note down their responses to research questions at regular intervals. It is a longitudinal method that can be either qualitative or quantitative, and is useful for understanding more about behaviour, experiences or time-based states such as mood changes or how long activities take. Participants used to use paper diaries, which was labour-intensive for both participant and researcher, and required reasonable literacy skills. Technology can now offer alternatives to this.

VIGNETTE

Ngarra is the father of a 12-week-old son, Minjarra. When his wife and child were still at the hospital, they were approached by a researcher who was interested in the ways in which new parents manage the change of identity that comes with the birth of a child. Ngarra was told that the research would take the form of a diary study, which concerned him greatly as he has severe dyslexia and does not like writing text for others. However, to his great relief, the format of the study is an audio diary: participants are asked to record their thoughts and comments via WhatsApp voice messages, which also allows them to take photos complementing their diary entry. This means Ngarra does not have to write entries and can instead speak them, and it's also much faster and easier to do.

There are numerous options for diary research software apps, which normally come at a cost, and are more or less useful depending on how complex and interactive the study needs to be. However, if there is no budget, then other tools can be repurposed to collect diary data: blogs, email, web forms, voice recordings or video recordings are all available to most people who have access to a computer or smartphone. Some people may prefer to use a conventional diary.

Accessibility issues

Although (as mentioned in Chapter 3) it is preferable not to over-recruit to a study, attrition is such a common problem in diary studies, where participants drop out of the study part-way through or don't complete every aspect of the data collection that is needed, that it is important to over-recruit in order to ensure an adequate sample at completion. Participation can be improved through a well-designed and easy-to-use data collection method that is piloted (Kenyon, 2006).

Moderation helps to ensure effectiveness. When diary entries are available to the research team as they are created (rather than in one batch at the end of the data collection period, as in a paper diary), we can monitor progress. It will become clear early on whether the study will produce an adequate sample of data. Researchers can see which participants are not contributing and find out why, and check whether entries are being completed on time, or that participants are following instructions. Participants can then be contacted with reminders and encouragement, or to discuss the process.

Methods that don't involve using text (such as enabling participants to provide data as images, audio or video) can be useful for people with low literacy or fatigue. For participants with memory and attention issues, a lower-effort option to make contributions could also be useful, alongside regular reminders, and this could help improve completion rates (Palen and Salzman, 2002).

Participatory mapping

How it works

Mapping exercises are a way for participants to describe and illustrate features of the space around them, and often complement another form of data collection such as an interview or focus group. The map could show geographical space, but equally it could refer to a social network and the relative locations of people and organisations within it, to emotional proximity, to interpersonal relationships, and to relationships between concepts (Kara, 2015, Chapter 5). Maps could be elicited individually or in groups, and on paper, digitally, or as an interview conducted while moving around a space. The participant creates a map to represent their understanding, and then explains or describes it to the researcher (Emmel, 2008).

Accessibility issues

Drawing methods can work well for people whose verbal communication skills are not strong (Kramer-Roy, 2015). Participants with manual dexterity issues or low vision may need a helper to create a drawn map on their behalf based on their instructions. Where we instruct participants to use colours to indicate meaning, people with colour blindness need to be able to distinguish between them so they can accurately complete the exercise. Printed materials need to be at a legible font size. Also consider that if people are drawing out a map or moving around sticky notes on a large sheet of paper, either on a table or on a wall, some participants may not be able to stand, stretch or bend. Providing mapping or drawing software on a tablet may make this more accessible.

Summary

In this chapter, we looked at the use of triangulation and mixed methods as they are applied both in qualitative and quantitative research. We then discussed how these techniques are used in practice, describing methods that are often used alongside questionnaires, surveys, interviews and focus groups, and the accessibility issues that may arise from the use of creative methods.

In Chapter 9, the final chapter, we look at ways to increase research impact by making impact and research engagement activities more accessible.

Notes
1 The term has its origin in a technique used in surveying, where it describes the process of using known distances and angles between two locations to establish the distance to a third, not-yet-measured, location.
2 Within the constraints of ethics and/or physics.
3 See https://implicit.harvard.edu/implicit/takeatest.html

Further reading
NCVO Knowhow, 'Participatory methods.' Available at: https://knowhow.ncvo.org.uk/organisation/impact/measuring-your-impact/participatory-methods
A brief summary of different types of creative methods that can work to engage people, which could inspire you to explore further.

Hammersley, M. (2008) 'Troubles with triangulation', in M.M Bergman (ed) *Advances in Mixed Methods Research*, London: SAGE Publications Ltd, pp 22–36.
Discussing different types of triangulation and their implications.

Ison, N.L. (2009) 'Having their say: Email interviews for research data collection with people who have verbal communication impairment', *International Journal of Social Research Methodology*, 12(2), 161–72.
Discussing benefits and disadvantages of the use of email interviews.

Olsen, W. (2004) 'Triangulation in social research: Qualitative and quantitative methods can really be mixed', *Developments in Sociology*, 20, 103–18.

Providing an argument for the use of triangulation.

Petit-McClure, S.H. and Stinson, C. (2019) 'Disrupting dis/abilization: A critical exploration of research methods to combat white supremacy and ableism in education', *Intersections: Critical Issues in Education*, 3(2), 4.
An argument to expand the definition and conduct of research.

Watson, A. (2020) 'Methods braiding: A technique for arts-based and mixed-methods research', *Sociological Research Online*, 25(1), 66–83.
An introduction to methods braiding as a type of mixed method.

References

Akkerman, A., Janssen, C.G., Kef, S. and Meininger, H.P. (2014) 'Perspectives of employees with intellectual disabilities on themes relevant to their job satisfaction. An explorative study using photovoice', *Journal of Applied Research in Intellectual Disabilities*, 27(6), 542–54.

Aldridge, J. (2007) 'Picture this: The use of participatory photographic research methods with people with learning disabilities', *Disability & Society*, 22(1), 1–17.

Alhusein, N., Macaden, L., Smith, A., Stoddart, K.M., et al (2018) '"Has she seen me?" A multiple methods study of the pharmaceutical care needs of older people with sensory impairment in Scotland', *BMJ Open*, 8(8), e023198.

Arcilla, A. (2011) 'Inclusion in visual workshop activities: Reflections from a blind participant.' Available at: www.eenet.org.uk/enabling-education-review/enabling-education-review-1/eer-1/1-9/

Arfken, C.L. and Balon, R. (2011) 'Declining participation in research studies', *Psychotherapy and Psychosomatics*, 80(6), 325–8.

Bethlehem, J. (2010) 'Selection bias in web surveys', *International Statistical Review*, 78(2), 161–88.

Chiseri-Strater, E. (2020) 'Turning in upon ourselves: Positionality, subjectivity in case study and ethnographic research', in P. Mortensen and G. Kirsch (eds) *Ethics and Representation in Qualitative Studies of Literacy*, Urbana, IL: National Council of Teachers of English, pp 115–33.

Cluley, V., Pilnick, A. and Fyson, R. (2020) 'Improving the inclusivity and credibility of visual research: Interpretive engagement as a route to including the voices of people with learning disabilities in analysis', *Visual Studies*, 1–13.

Cole, M.S., Bedeian, A.G. and Feild, H.S. (2006) 'The measurement equivalence of web-based and paper-and-pencil measures of transformational leadership: A multinational test', *Organizational Research Methods*. Available at: https://doi.org/10.1177/1094428106287434

Dalton, J. (2020) 'Model making as a research method', *Studies in the Education of Adults*, 52(1), 35–48.

Dee-Price, B.J.M., Hallahan, L., Nelson Bryen, D. and Watson, J.M. (2020) 'Every voice counts: Exploring communication accessible research methods', *Disability & Society*, 36(2): 240–64.

Emmel, N. (2008) *Participatory Mapping: An Innovative Sociological Method*, Real Life Methods, Toolkit #03. Available at: http://eprints.ncrm.ac.uk/540/2/2008-07-toolkit-participatory-map.pdf

Gregory, K. (2020) 'The video camera spoiled my ethnography: A critical approach', *International Journal of Qualitative Methods*, 19, 1609406920963761.

Harper, D. (2002) 'Talking about pictures: A case for photo elicitation', *Visual Studies*, 17(1), 13–26.

Hodges, C.E., Fenge, L. and Cutts, W. (2014) 'Challenging perceptions of disability through performance poetry methods: The "Seen but Seldom Heard" project', *Disability & Society*, 29(7), 1090–103.

Kara, H. (2015) *Creative Research Methods in the Social Sciences: A Practical Guide*, Bristol: Policy Press.

Kenyon, S. (2006) 'The "accessibility diary": Discussing a new methodological approach to understand the impact of internet use upon personal travel and activity participation', *Journal of Transport Geography*, 14(2), 123–34.

Kezar, A. (2000) 'The importance of pilot studies: Beginning the hermeneutic circle', *Research in Higher Education*, 41(3), 385–400.

Kramer-Roy, D. (2015) 'Using participatory and creative methods to facilitate emancipatory research with people facing multiple disadvantage: A role for health and care professionals', *Disability & Society*, 30(8), 1207–24.

Lauri, M.A. (2011) 'Triangulation of data analysis techniques', *Papers on Social Representations*, 20(2), 34.1–34.15.

Luttrell, W. (2010) '"A camera is a big responsibility": A lens for analysing children's visual voices', *Visual Studies*, 25(3), 224–37.

Mannay, D. (2010) 'Making the familiar strange: Can visual research methods render the familiar setting more perceptible?', *Qualitative Research*, 10(1), 91–111.

Manning, C. (2010) '"My memory's back!" Inclusive learning disability research using ethics, oral history and digital storytelling', *British Journal of Learning Disabilities*, 38(3), 160–7.

Mathison, S. (1988) 'Why triangulate?', *Educational Researcher*, 17(2), 13–17.

Oakley, A., Strange, V., Toroyan, T., Wiggins, M., Roberts, I. and Stephenson, J. (2003) 'Using random allocation to evaluate social interventions: Three recent UK examples', *The Annals of the American Academy of Political and Social Science*, 589(1), 170–89.

O'Connor, C. and Joffe, H. (2020) 'Intercoder reliability in qualitative research: Debates and practical guidelines', *International Journal of Qualitative Methods*, 19, 1609406919899220.

Olkin, R. (2004) 'Making research accessible to participants with disabilities', *Journal of Multicultural Counseling and Development*, 32, 332–43.

Palen, L. and Salzman, M. (2002) 'Voice-mail Diary Studies for Naturalistic Data Capture under Mobile Conditions', in Proceedings of the 2002 ACM Conference on Computer-supported Cooperative Work, November, pp 87–95.

Patton, M.Q. (1999) 'Enhancing the quality and credibility of qualitative analysis', *Health Services Research*, 34(5 Pt 2), 1189–208.

Pauwels, L. (2010) 'Visual sociology reframed: An analytical synthesis and discussion of visual methods in social and cultural research', *Sociological Methods & Research*, 38(4), 545–81.

Raynor, R. (2019) 'Speaking, feeling, mattering: Theatre as method and model for practice-based, collaborative, research', *Progress in Human Geography*, 43(4), 691–710.

Rebernik, N., Favero, P. and Bahillo, A. (2020) 'Using digital tools and ethnography for rethinking disability inclusive city design: Exploring material and immaterial dialogues', *Disability & Society*, 1–26.

Ripat, J. and Colatruglio, A. (2016) 'Exploring winter community participation among wheelchair users: An online focus group', *Occupational Therapy in Health Care*, 30(1), 95–106.

Salzman, P.C. (2002) 'On reflexivity', *American Anthropologist*, 104(3), 805–11.

Shadish, W.R., Clark, M.H. and Steiner, P.M. (2008) 'Can nonrandomized experiments yield accurate answers? A randomized experiment comparing random and nonrandom assignments', *Journal of the American Statistical Association*. Available at: https://doi.org/10.1198/016214508000000733

Synnot, A., Hill, S., Summers, M. and Taylor, M. (2014) 'Comparing face-to-face and online qualitative research with people with multiple sclerosis', *Qualitative Health Research*, 24(3), 431–8.

van Teijlingen, E. and Hundley, V. (2002) 'The importance of pilot studies', *Nursing Standard*, 16(40), 33.

Watson, A. (2020) 'Methods braiding: A technique for arts-based and mixed-methods research', *Sociological Research Online*, 25(1), 66–83.

Wiles, R., Prosser, J., Bagnoli, A., Clark, A., et al (2008) *Visual Ethics: Ethical Issues in Visual Research*, Review Paper, Southampton: National Centre for Research Methods.

Zwarun, L. and Hall, A. (2014) 'What's going on? Age, distraction, and multitasking during online survey taking', *Computers in Human Behavior*. Available at: https://doi.org/10.1016/j.chb.2014.09.041

9

Writing up, publication and impact

This chapter outlines how to write up and disseminate research findings and research resources. We discuss how to develop and disseminate information such as research data in a more accessible format, whether through conferences, publication as books or journal articles, or through public outreach in other formats.

Why should we talk about our research to the public?

In many ways, this chapter braids together the various strands of themes discussed so far. In Chapter 3 we mentioned that lack of transparency and lack of obvious benefit are some of the factors negatively influencing participants' willingness to participate in research, and we suggested making research findings available to participants once the study has been completed. But we need to look not only at our current but also potential future participants: making findings available to the public, that is, not only through the usual academic channels, can help to make the research process more transparent and improve trust in the institution. In a sense, accessibility is about making research findings easy to find, and easy to understand, and we will talk about some of the ways in which that can be done. But we also talk about accessibility in the sense mostly used in this book. If we are making our research and our findings available, what is the best way to present the information so that as many people as possible can access it? In this context, we refer back to Chapters 6 and 7.

Accountability

Accountability describes the researcher's responsibilities to their employer, research funders and stakeholders, as well as to research participants. It means that research must be conducted, delivered and disseminated according to professional standards and best practice. Accountability is seen as an aspect of ethical conduct. And there is another ethical dimension. Where research findings inform decision-making and policy, people may have to live with the direct and immediate consequences (see, for example, the plastic straw ban mentioned in Chapter 1). This makes it all the more important to communicate with participants throughout the process, not just during the recruitment phase and after the research has concluded.

The idea of accountability to research participants originated as part of an emancipatory approach to research (Barnes, 2002). In this model, research takes place for the benefit of disabled people according to their views of what is important. The purpose of emancipatory research is to bring about change through research that is led by members of a disadvantaged group, for example by having an advisory group of members of that group attached to the project. The research provides evidence of policy and practice-based changes that are needed. Advising on research dissemination with the public is often part of the role of a group like this.

Developing and sharing research findings with participants is an important feature of accountability; it is seen as an acknowledgement of the effort involved in taking part in research. There is an ethical dimension to research participation, particularly for sensitive research, as the changes that can be made as a result are used to justify the potential risks of participation. It is important to keep promises that have been made to participants about what will happen after they have taken part, particularly about sharing the findings with them.

Effective communication means academic research findings and recommendations need to be presented in ways that are relevant and accessible to people who are not academics and researchers. Producing research outputs that are both accessible and appropriate for a non-academic audience used to be considered a marginal activity, making it difficult to justify the time and effort involved in working on them (Goodley and Moore, 2000). The priorities, information needs and interests of people taking part in research (and their representative groups) can be very different from the requirements of academic research funders and publishers. Because of this, there is a perceived tension for researchers in producing work to the format required by funders but in a way that is understandable and inclusive for a lay audience, particularly given the research funders are in a position of relative power. In recent years, research impact has been introduced as a quality measure that needs to be evidenced; effort is focused not only on publishing but also on translating research findings into practical, measurable outcomes.

We are aware that many academic researchers are under immense pressure to produce published work in journals deemed to be of a high enough quality, while research outside academia has its own set of requirements and restrictions. Additionally, while impact is often referred to and required as a result of disseminating findings – and often has to be planned and budgeted for in the context of funding applications – the definition of impact is often quite narrow and may not include the kind of outreach work we are describing. For many researchers, an existing high workload may present a barrier to doing what might be seen as additional work. We argue that the ability to meet the access needs of participants and other audiences should not depend on the skills and time available to individual researchers: it is fundamental to ethical research practice as well as research communication, and, for that reason, more support should be available. For senior colleagues and those in a more privileged position, this is an opportunity to use the power afforded to them by the system to improve conditions and to implement and change policies, for example by participating in policy development workshops, contributing to policy briefings or briefings to public sector organisations, thereby affirming the value of the participants' work and promises made to them.

Conferences

Conferences are interesting in the context of accessible research from two perspectives. First, they are one of the established means of making research accessible (that is, available) to an interested audience. And second, because they are a means to make research available, conferences themselves need to be accessible (that is, barrier-free). In this way, organising an accessible conference pulls together different strands of previous chapters.

Like recruiting participants, attendants of the conference should be recruited through a variety of media, which starts by reaching out through different channels (see Chapter 7). The availability of accommodations, and what the accommodations are, needs to be clearly communicated. There should be at least one designated accessibility liaison contact conference participants can approach in advance, during and after the conference, with any questions or feedback.

CHECKLIST 26: CONFERENCE PLANNING

☐ Identify the accommodations that can be offered, and share them alongside the conference advertising and call for papers.

☐ Alongside this, ask attendees for access requirements well in advance:

○ Is a sign language interpreter needed?

○ Does the attendee require material in Braille or other accessible formats?

○ Are there any dietary restrictions or allergies?

○ Is anyone attending with a carer or personal assistant, and what needs do they have?

○ Is anyone attending with a guide or support dog, and what needs to they have?

☐ Make sure conference flyers, posters and websites are accessible (see also Chapters 6 and 7).

☐ Provide the contact details of at least one accessibility liaison contact.

☐ Tell participants and presenters to avoid strong fragrances such as perfumes, to be considerate towards attendants with allergies or sensitivities.

For accommodations and conference venue, the guiding principle is that everyone should be able to use them. In other words, the main conference accommodation needs to be accessible; there must not be a case where most participants can use the main (and close) accommodation and disabled participants have to use a different hotel (one of nine principles for accessible conferences devised by the Nordic Centre for Welfare and Social Issues, 2016). Similarly, conference premises and presentation rooms must be accessible for all (see also Chapter 6).

VIGNETTE

Natasha has severe asthma that is often triggered by heavy fragrances. She tends to avoid public transport as it often gets crowded and means she can't avoid being exposed to people's perfumes. She used to go to conferences much more often but had to cut down substantially because they no longer felt like a safe environment for her. With some trepidation she attends this year's main conference in her field, but she's delighted to find out that the organising team has taken a more comprehensive approach to accessibility this year. Not only does the conference programme explicitly state that all presentations are taking place in properly ventilated rooms with open windows but all attendees are also asked to avoid wearing heavy perfume or fragrances; attendees who do so anyway may be asked to leave the presentation so as to ensure a safe environment for everyone.

CHECKLIST 27: CONFERENCE FACILITIES

☐ Premises need to be accessible by public transport, with little additional walking required.

☐ Accessible parking should be available close to the premises.

☐ Make sure that all walkways and paths are accessible so disabled attendees don't have to enter through a different door to non-disabled attendees.

☐ Doorways need to be wide enough to allow for both manual and powered wheelchairs.

☐ All rooms used for presentations, breakout or rest should be accessible, including wide doorways, low to no bevels on the door frame, and without having to use stairs.

☐ Stairs need to have visible step boundaries and handrails.

☐ Lifts have to be wide enough to allow for both manual and powered wheelchairs.

☐ Check that the venue operates or allows a closed loop system to be operated.

☐ Rooms need to be lit with non-glare light.

☐ Offer quiet, not-too-brightly lit rooms with an uncluttered interior (this includes fabric and, for example, wallpaper) for people to relax and calm down in an environment suitable for people with sensory processing disorders.

☐ Ensure that venue staff as well as conference staff and volunteers are trained to address the requirements of participants with a disability or an impairment, and that they do not interfere with accessibility provisions, such as blocking off accessibility equipment, turning equipment off or blocking disabled car parking spaces or drop kerbs.

In Chapter 6 we talked about creating and providing accessible material, and this is also important for any material such as the schedule or the collection of abstracts that is distributed during a conference.

CHECKLIST 28: CONFERENCE SCHEDULE

☐ Include comprehensive accessibility information on the conference programme and website.

☐ Ask presenters to provide abstracts in PDF format, and distribute them in an accessible format (see also Chapter 7).

☐ Brief presenters that they need to provide presentations in an accessible format, and provide them with sufficient information to do so (Mallett et al, 2007; see also, for example, Lattner, 2016, for creating accessible visualisations that can help understanding).

☐ Allow for sufficient breaks between individual sessions.

☐ Allow for enough time for participants to switch rooms.

☐ Include contact information for the accessibility liaison contact(s), as well as information on available accommodations on the schedule.

Not only the rooms but also the presentations need to be accessible, for the audience and presenters alike. For presenters, make sure that everyone can communicate as equals – this means avoiding bar stool-like chairs, or making presenters stand for the entire presentation. If presenters are seated at tables, make sure they can accommodate wheelchairs.

CHECKLIST 29: CONFERENCE, ON THE DAY

☐ Make sure there are no loose cables in the presentation room that can constitute trip hazards; if they have to be situated where people have to step over them, make sure to highlight them appropriately and/or provide means of safely crossing them (such as taping them down or using wheelchair-friendly cable protectors) so that they don't obstruct the path for wheelchair users or other attendants with mobility issues.

☐ Make sure that all presenters can participate on equal terms (another principle from the Nordic Centre for Welfare and Social Issues, 2016).

☐ Ensure that sign language interpreters are present; for conferences with a multi-lingual audience, you may have to provide translation into more than one sign language.

☐ If you have to dim the light or darken the room, leave a spotlight on the presenter and/or the sign language interpreter.

☐ Announce any substantial changes of light ('We're now going to turn on the big light system'), if there's a chance of stroboscopic light or if there are going to be sudden loud noises. The use of strobing lights must comply with local health and safety laws and guidelines to minimise the risk of triggering photosensitive seizures.

☐ Have roving microphones ready so all audience members can participate in a discussion.

☐ Remind the audience to properly stash bags and coats so that they are not trip hazards.

Having a designated accessibility liaison contact present and available during the conference can be extremely helpful to provide assurance that the issue of accessibility is taken seriously. Immediate feedback from conference participants improves the chance of solving problems at the time, and not just learning of them after the conference, although getting feedback is important to improve planning and performance for the next conference. Feedback should therefore be actively elicited (through an accessible medium) both during and after the conference.

Of course, researchers aren't always the conference organiser – sometimes they are attending or presenting. If we cannot attend a conference or event in person, but are presenting, there are ways to make our content more accessible, for example, by sharing the slides in advance (either in native format or in PDF format). As mentioned before, some video conferencing tools (Zoom, Skype, GoToMeeting) auto-generate subtitles live, and will generate a transcript, although auto-generated subtitles can be poor quality. A professional captioner should be employed to produce reliably accurate live captions and a transcript.

Journals

Journal submission guidelines are often quite specific, but, for all that detail, outside disability studies, accessibility is not a core part of the requirements journals make of authors; in addition, there is not much in terms of design and layout that is under our control. What we can do is focus on the parts that we can control, such as providing accessible graphics in a suitable colour scheme, and providing alternative formats.

Open access is another issue related to making research findings accessible that does not apply specifically to disabled people but to non-academic audiences for the work who do not have access to an academic library. That said, some academic papers are inherently inaccessible to some people because of their length and the language used (Garbutt, 2009). To make research accessible, think about how we can repurpose what we have written, for example by creating a lay summary (Tancock, 2020) of the research abstract for potential interested lay people, which might be presented as a video or animation as well as in writing. This is often required in health research funding bids and is now also an option for some journals.

CHECKLIST 30: JOURNAL ARTICLE PUBLISHING

☐ Where possible, give preference to journals that explicitly consider accessibility of manuscripts and publications (including open access options).

☐ Make sure to use accessible colour schemes for your graphs and images, and don't use colour alone to communicate meaning.

☐ Provide alt-text descriptions in the captions for your figures.

We can also contribute to normalising talking about accessibility in research methods by explicitly talking about steps we took to make our methods accessible – and describing the potential methodological consequences of aspects that weren't accessible. Last, we need to acknowledge the contribution made by members of the public, stakeholders and research partners, and describe how they helped.

VIGNETTE

Lee has previously interviewed a number of experienced teachers on their impression of generational change between students. He is now writing up his findings in a paper for publication. In his methods section, he takes care to note that he specifically reached out to the Disabled Teachers Network to increase the chance for disabled teachers to be included in the sample. He reports that he offered to conduct interviews in a range of different modes, and reports that this was very well received by participants.

CHECKLIST 31: JOURNAL ARTICLES' CONTENT

☐ Discuss the measures you have taken to make participation possible for as many people as possible.

☐ Describe whether your material was accessible and how accessible it was.

☐ Where it wasn't possible, describe the implications in terms of representativeness or validity of findings.

Books

Particularly for academic researchers, monographs or book chapters form one of the main ways in which research findings are communicated and disseminated. Although we have less control over the form in which our manuscript is published, there are some measures we can take. In the last few years, it has become easier for people with visual impairments to get access to books in accessible formats as many countries have signed up to the Marrakesh Treaty, an international agreement initiated by the World Intellectual Property Organization (WIPO) that stipulates exceptions to a range of copyright regulations. This has been in force in Australia since 2016, the US and EU since 2019, and New Zealand joined in 2020.

There are also industry standards covering accessible publishing. One of those standards is the DAISY (Digital Accessible Information System);[1] this is a technical standard aimed at publishers, which provides a set of specifications to make digital books and publications accessible. The DAISY website has a range of resources for publishers and content creators; more information is available from the Accessible Book Consortium (ABC)[2] (2016), which offers best practice guidelines for publishers. Another standard is the electronic publication (EPUB) standard, the industry standard for eBooks, which allows for reading text on a device. This standard in itself is not necessarily accessible; however, the World Wide Web Consortium (W3C) has provided guidelines for the EPUB standard that help do just that. For self-publishing authors who are using the EPUB format, the ABC (2011) offers a general guide, and a more specific guide is available on making visual elements of a manuscript accessible in either the DAISY or EPUB3 format (Diagram Center, 2013).

Last, for educators who want to make their text accessible, a free guide on making a textbook accessible is available from BCcampus (Coolidge et al, 2018).

CHECKLIST 32: BOOKS

☐ Ask your publisher to follow W3C EPUB Accessibility 1.0 guidelines.

☐ As an author, communicate information by more than just colour (for example, don't use green and red to communicate right or wrong; also use ticks and crosses).

☐ Provide descriptive alternative text for images and graphics for your manuscript.

☐ Refer to tables and figures by name ('Figure 2') rather than placement ('figure above'), and cross-reference by section rather than page, as putting texts into an accessible format may change pagination.

☐ When collaborating with others on a manuscript, use symbols or text to indicate required changes rather than colour; reference manuscript passages by text fragments rather than pages (both suggestions from Gies et al, 2016).

Research-informed teaching

For researchers who also teach, integrating research findings into teaching is one way of engaging with an audience who are not well-informed about research: 'research-informed teaching' is highly valued because it helps ensure that students are up to date with the latest theories, approaches and practices in the topic. As teachers, we also have a great opportunity to normalise thinking about accessible research methods and the advantages of making sure as many people as possible can participate.

Impact

Impact describes the contribution that research makes to its field and to wider society. UK Research and Innovation (UKRI) and the Economic and Social Research Council (ESRC) (2020) distinguish between two broad categories of research impact:

- **Academic impact** is the contribution that research makes to knowledge and to the academic community. This could be to increase understanding of aspects of social life, develop and apply new methods or theoretical perspectives, apply theory to new areas or develop and apply new theories or methodologies to interdisciplinary work.
- **Economic** and **societal impact** is the contribution that research makes to society. It could include a change to policy or practice that has a positive impact on research participants, research partners or stakeholder organisations involved in your project, or which has wider benefits to individuals and social groups at national or international levels.

How does accessibility fit into this?

The ability to demonstrate impact is essential, especially for applied research that is intended to improve outcomes for patients or service users. The government body that directs UK research funding, UKRI, offers funding guidance jointly with the ESRC for researchers, which says:

> A proposal which demonstrates a high-quality approach to enable social science impact will include explicit awareness

of principles and practices of knowledge exchange – including the application of principles and practices of co-production – as opposed to dissemination. (UKRI/ ESRC, 2020)

A similar approach is taken in other countries. For example, the Health Research Council (HRC) of New Zealand defines impact as 'not created by researchers alone; but rather, requires communication, relationships and actions that connect academic research to people from organisations beyond academia' (Ministry of Health NZ, 2017). Translating health and social research findings into policy and practice is one of the funding body's four strategic priorities.

In other words, it is not enough to publish research in academic journals and present at academic conferences, which can tend towards one-way communication in specialised settings. Researchers need to actively engage with the communities they are researching with, listen to what they have to say, and extend their communication and knowledge exchange to the wider community, policy-makers and practitioners.

This means considering how to communicate with and involve ordinary members of the public who may have personal experience of the topic we are researching but who may not be familiar with academic practice or language. This group of people is likely to be more interested in the practical outcomes of the research than in the conceptual work underlying it, or the methodology. While accessibility is only one feature of a successful knowledge exchange or public engagement programme, accessible research removes a barrier to research participation and communication that is within our control. Planning accessible ways to communicate with and involve lay people and organisations can increase the audience for our work by making it easier for non-academic audiences to quickly grasp the purpose of our research and its implications.

In Australia, the Engagement and Impact Assessment National Report 2018–19 describes how universities were required to evidence specifically how they encouraged the translation of research to impacts beyond academia (ARC, 2018), including knowledge exchange, and it gives some good examples of how some universities achieved this. UKRI/ESRC (2020) specifically refers to the importance of including knowledge exchange activities in the research funding bid, led by senior members of the research team. This could include consulting users during the research planning process and when planning impact activities, including users as co-investigators on the research team, running training and events designed for users as well as professionals and academics, or building working relationships and creating research partnerships with community groups, charities and other stakeholders whose remit is to support or represent users.

Universities are also measured on their performance on knowledge exchange in the UK, using the Knowledge Exchange Framework (KEF) (UKRI/Research England, 2020). This has seven proposed measures, including community and public engagement, research partnerships, and working with the public and third sector.

These activities can both inform the research we are doing, and also increase its reach within the communities it touches on: involving members of the public in creating a dissemination plan has been shown to increase awareness (Hayes et al, 2012). Public understanding and support of research can increase support for any recommended policy and practice changes, which could potentially provide another source of research impact.

Who are the audiences for research outputs?

It is useful to begin by identifying our key audiences; this will vary depending on the type of project that we are doing, but it could include the following:

- **Academic beneficiaries:** researchers in specific disciplines, researchers in the UK or other countries, the specific research areas where the research will add to knowledge.
- **Economic and social beneficiaries:** this could include related practitioners, policy-makers, government bodies, patient support groups and charities, non-governmental organisations, public sector organisations, campaigning groups and the commercial sector.

Once we have identified who our audiences are, it is then easier to consider whether and how they could be included in the research, what communication needs they have, and the best way to reach them.

The plan for impact needs to cover who is impacted by the research and a measure of how it affects them. The research might explore a relatively niche topic, meaning that a small number of people are immediately affected by the implementation of the findings. However, the findings could have a significant impact if they change practice or policy. There may also be transferability potential: implications for related populations or research fields.

Here, influencing stakeholders and service users or patients is a useful way to apply pressure on policy-makers to consider research evidence to change their approach, particularly in health research. To achieve this, it's necessary to identify potential ways to translate findings into direct health benefits for the impacted population. More broadly, this could also be done in the form of stakeholder meetings; this requires identifying who the stakeholders are and what their primary interests are, and finding ways to engage them that make the best use of their skills and knowledge.

Develop networks and working partnerships

Creating partnerships and relationships, or making use of existing working relationships and networks, is a meaningful way to involve non-academic partners and users in our research in ways that help to develop impact. In the UK, NIHR Involve is a national body that can also help us find lay people to get involved in research as needed – as well as advertising for participants, they publicise opportunities for people to become research partners.

Other ways of achieving impact could take the form of liaising with professional associations to share research findings – whether via blog, interview, podcast or guest lecture. Communicating research to practitioners could also happen through project briefings for practitioners, practitioner training or articles in publications in practitioner journals. All of these mean carefully adapting the language to an interested lay audience.

Most people who get involved in research as lay participants have existing time commitments such as employment or caring responsibilities. They may not be available during the working day or be able to attend day-long meetings in person. It is important to plan out the time commitment involved and the kind of involvement that is expected, so that partners are able to manage it around their existing schedule.

These are some issues to consider when working with non-academic research partners (Hayes et al, 2012):

CHECKLIST 33: RESEARCH IMPACT

☐ Be clear about which aspects of the project can be influenced by partners and which cannot, so efforts are focused on the areas where people can make a difference.

☐ Be clear on the time commitment that you are looking for, what you need from people and how often you will need to be in touch with each other.

☐ Check if anyone has specific access needs and ask permission to ensure their needs are known to those members of the project team who work with partners and arrange meetings and events.

☐ Ensure expenses payment arrangements are clear in advance and expenses are paid quickly. Consider whether you can pay some expenses on behalf of partners, for example buying rail tickets in advance.

☐ Check which method people prefer to use to communicate, and bear in mind that not everyone has email or access to a printer; ensure that people who don't use technology can still be involved.

☐ Give explanations of technical jargon and terminology, and provide documents in plain language, as concisely as possible.

☐ Appreciate that people in work may need to book meeting dates months in advance and the time is likely to come out of their annual leave allowance, so the time you have together needs to be used as effectively as possible. People who need to attend with a carer or supporter will also need to ensure this person's time is booked in advance and all their expenses are covered, and it may be difficult to make changes at short notice.

☐ Allow enough time to read documents, and enough time to comment on them if needed.

Using social media for research

Social media is a powerful communication tool and there are now some good general guides on how to use social media to publicise academic research and engage different audiences (see, for example, Carrigan, 2019). However, using its accessibility features (Jenkinson, 2017; RNIB, 2020) means our messages can reach more people. Table 1 provides an overview of accessibility measures to consider for individual types of social media.

CHECKLIST 34: SOCIAL MEDIA FOR RESEARCH IMPACT

☐ Learn and make use of the accessibility features of the tools you are using.

☐ Use concise, plain language.

☐ Avoid academic jargon.

☐ Use a URL (Uniform Resource Locator) shortener to save limited space in messages.

☐ Edit auto-generated alternative text to make sure it makes sense, and gives the right context to the image.

☐ Use scheduling tools to post to Twitter and Facebook at times of day when your audiences are using them (avoid posting anything important on a Friday, and, unless there's a big news development, there is no need to post over the weekend).

☐ As well as using your own social media accounts, coordinate post sharing and retweets with your department or research centre, your institution, your research funder and your research partners. Using accessibility features means the content is accessible even when it's shared.

Table 1: Overview of social media accessibility

Activity	Accessibility measures to consider
Blogs	• The simplest way to achieve this is to choose an accessible blog provider and an accessible visual theme (WordPress is one good option but there are others; check the accessibility statements of providers as they should give details)
	• Use image descriptions
Facebook	• Keep posts short and use a link to a longer article if necessary. People often only read the visible text and don't open the post to see more, so, if the post needs to be long, put the most compelling information first. Put hashtags at the end of the image caption or link title
	• Use image descriptions
Instagram	• Instagram is designed to share photos and infographics. It will create custom description text and this can be checked and edited
	• Use hashtags in 'camel case', that is, capitalise the first letter of every separate word. It's easier to read and will read out correctly on a screen reader
	• Indicate the beginning of an exhaustive block of hashtags so that users of screen readers know that no further text content is forthcoming, for example with #HashtagsIncoming
LinkedIn	• Use image descriptions
	• Enable captions for videos, and provide a caption file (or a transcript)
Podcasts	• Provide a link to a transcription in guest podcasts or on your own blog, and ask the guest blog host to include the link when they post the podcast
Twitter	• Turn on 'alternative text' so you can add image descriptions
	• Use hashtags in 'camel case' (every separate word has an initial capital letter) and put them at the end of posts
	• Write a really concise research summary that will fit into one tweet and use the hashtag #1TweetResearch
YouTube	• Add a transcript if you have one; if not, upload the video and set it to private, enable transcription and set the language. When the auto-transcriber has completed, check and edit the transcript, and make it public
	• Consider audio-describing video where needed
	• YouTube can open your research out to an international audience. It is frequently used for abstracts and other types of research communication; some journals have started offering the option of video abstracts as a more accessible way to reach an audience than the standard academic text format
	• Journal author interviews are another way of reaching a non-academic audience. Free animation tools can be used to create video; they offer a visual way to present information that works well for some audiences

Conventional media

One of the difficulties of using conventional media is that we are not in control of the way our messages are delivered or presented. However, they still have a wide reach and are a good way of sharing information about the project. There are some options for the following types of communications:

- Press releases or briefings to the media
- Reviews
- Magazine and journal articles such as *The Conversation*
- Local radio

Even if the media is not presented in an accessible format, it can be reshared on a blog or social media site, where accessibility features can be added and a context provided. For example, rather than sharing a photo of a news article or review, provide the text or a link.

Journalists may want to know details about our participants if they are looking for a human story to present to their readers. This could be problematic, particularly if it is a sensitive topic (Kara, 2015, Chapter 9). Before an interview, take special care to remove or alter identifying details, including details of the participant's name, ethnicity, location and family circumstances.

Public engagement

This section gives some ideas for ways to communicate research findings to the general public through public engagement activities, accompanied by suggestions for accessibility. For any kind of public engagement activity, we will need to publish a first point of contact (both phone and email) who can respond to queries.

Engagement partners

One way to engage with the public is to try and foster local connections to institutions and organisations that either work to engage with citizens or to whom our research might be relevant (patient advocacy associations, Citizens Advice, local school boards and so on).

There are also several fascinating initiatives aimed at engaging citizens as active contributors in so-called 'citizen science projects', for example:

- Citizen Science (US): www.citizenscience.gov/#
- Citizen Science (EU): https://eu-citizen.science
- Citizen Science: www.citizenscience.org (US national association for citizen science initiatives, with links to associations in other countries)
- SciStarter: https://scistarter.org/citizen-science (US-based website offering opportunities for people to take part in research as citizen scientists)
- Zooniverse: www.zooniverse.org (a platform for linking citizen scientists with academic research projects in arts and social science as well as science subjects)
- Australian Citizen Science Association: https://citizenscience.org.au (provides a project finder for people to take part)
- SciFabric: https://scifabric.com/projects

While most of these citizen science projects are primarily (although not exclusively) located in the natural sciences, there are some that look specifically at social science, for example the London Prosperity Board (https://londonprosperityboard.org/citizen-scientists).

Other options include podcasts, blogs or YouTube channels whose owners or authors focus on introducing their audience to new and current research, or talk about current affairs – or even just an abstract of the findings. If there is no account that fits our very specific audience, there is always the option to create one ourselves.

CHECKLIST 35: PUBLIC ENGAGEMENT

☐ Connect with local channels and associations to whom research might be relevant, for example, Chamber of Commerce, school boards, advisory panels, local councils, neighbourhood associations etc.

☐ Consider specifically reaching out to marginalised communities to talk about your research and research findings, particularly when it has relevance for their experience.

☐ When you talk about your research, also mention how you made it (more) accessible.

Whichever channel we use, make sure that the information provided is accessible to as many people as possible. These suggestions are based on the guiding principles of Universal Design (UD) listed in Chapter 2: ensure that what we are doing can be accessed in different ways, is as simple and intuitive to use as possible, and communicates using different formats. So, for example, while a blind person may not be able to see the photographs in an exhibition, there are other ways to enable them to access the meaning of each visual image and the overall exhibition (see Table 2).

Table 2: Accessibility implications of public engagement activities

Medium	Accessibility measures to consider
Artwork	There are at least two ways to consider the accessibility of artwork: as a co-creation with participants, and as an accessible object or multi-sensory experience that people can engage with in multiple ways (Boydell et al, 2012)
	Co-created artwork can be a way to communicate participants' feelings and experience. For example, the Hidden Voices project (Collin and Clayton, 2018) used focus groups of mothers of girls with threatened fertility to create a multi-layered quilt. Each layer is separate and can be handled and the quilt is displayed in a context telling the story of how it was made. This is used to raise awareness, both with family support groups and as part of a bigger exhibition
Case studies	Telling a story can work well to help people understand the participants' circumstances and perspective and explain their choices. Using case studies based on participant experiences can be a good way to do this
	For example, a Children's Society report (Royston and Siddique, 2020) on the impact of expensive school uniforms on low-income families used quotes from parents and schoolchildren to bring the statistical findings to life. The National Maternity and Perinatal Audit (NMPA, 2019) used cases to show how hospital trusts used the Audit's 2017 findings to improve the safety of birth for women and newborns. The Office for National Statistics (ONS) has a set of case studies to illustrate how different groups, such as the Church of England (ONS, 2016), use census data to allocate funding and grants

(continued)

Table 2: Accessibility implications of public engagement activities (continued)

Medium	Accessibility measures to consider
Exhibition	There is some excellent advice on making art exhibitions accessible (Shape, 2020) and the section on conferences earlier in this chapter also covers accessible events, but there are a few summary points to consider: • As well as providing an accessible venue, ensure that the artwork is displayed in an accessible way, for example that display cases, picture labels, signage and videos can be viewed at wheelchair height and labels are in a sans-serif font that is large enough to read easily • An audio-described tour of the exhibition, which discusses the visual materials and gives directions to any interactive exhibits, can make it more accessible to people with visual impairments • Ensure the person managing enquiries knows about the accessibility of the event or knows who to ask
Theatre	Drama can be used both as an elicitation tool to generate research findings, and also to communicate research findings in an engaging way (Keen and Todres, 2007). The way that performances are usually presented has not always reflected the needs of some groups of disabled people (Richardson and Thompson, 2018). Moves towards 'relaxed performance' make drama performances accessible to a more diverse audience, as they are flexible regarding the normally strict rules about seating, talking and engagement between the performers and the audience (Rice and Besse, 2020) Farcas (2017) gives a useful summary of every aspect of running inclusive theatre
Comics or graphic novels	Graphic novels or comic strips can be a great way to convey research findings – see for example Katie Vigurs's research on student debt (Priego, 2016) It is possible to make this kind of visual material digitally accessible (Sethfors, 2018); one current solution is to create a tagged PDF file of the comic, using optical character recognition to recreate the text, so it can be used with a screen reader
Local non-academic events	Many organisations are looking for short, informal talks or presentations, such as Pint of Science, Bright Club, the Women's Institute, and secular societies. While you are not in control of the venue or the equipment available you can ensure that your presentation, language and handouts are accessible

VIGNETTE

5318008 is a scented sculpture, inspired by theme of 'infection', celebrating the immune-boosting properties of bifidobacteria, shared by the mother in breast milk for babies. It can be touched, and it releases a sweet smell that evokes human breast milk. There is an accompanying audio description. It is on permanent display at the Wellcome Collection, in a gallery designed to be accessible for all (Marks, 2019).

CHECKLIST 36: ENGAGEMENT STRATEGY

- ☐ Plan an impact and engagement strategy at the beginning of the project that identifies how you are going to measure impact for each strand of work that you do.

- ☐ In your research proposal, budget for the cost of user consultation processes.

- ☐ Take advice from your institution on marketing, promotion and ways to achieve and measure impact.

- ☐ Consider whether the researchers have any training needs, for example disability awareness, technology and research methods.

- ☐ If you are including an advisory group, identify the kind of people you would like to invite, your existing links with them and a budget for their travel and related expenses.

- ☐ Include travel and expenses for participants in research project costs.

- ☐ Identify knowledge exchange activities and budget for them.

- ☐ Track your public engagement activities so you have a record of what you have done.

- ☐ In publications, acknowledge the contribution made by partners and members of the public.

Support for impact and public engagement activities

These organisations give further information about how to run impact-related or public engagement activities, and to suggest ideas. Although they are based in the UK, the techniques and suggestions can be adapted for other countries.

- Involve, a national charity supporting public involvement and public engagement work: www.involve.org.uk
- National Co-ordinating Centre for Public Engagement (NCCPE): www.publicengagement.ac.uk
- UK Research and Innovation (UKRI) Public Engagement: www.ukri.org/public-engagement

Summary

In this chapter, we looked at communicating research findings as an aspect of accountability to participants. We examined the growing trend towards including the public in engagement activities, not just academics, and the way that accessibility can enhance that process, potentially giving the work more impact. We looked very briefly at some of the accessibility implications of different communications media, and gave sources of further information to take these ideas forward.

Accessibility: necessary, not optional

We began this book by making the case for accessible research so that the views and experiences of disabled people could be included in research that is not focused on disability. By now, we hope that we have made a convincing case, not just for its necessity, but also its feasibility. At every stage of the process, accessibility can and should be considered in an act of active accessibility. This will take effort, and it will take time. Too often accessibility is an afterthought; it's considered esoteric, burdensome or simply unnecessary. We hope we have shown that none of this is true. Accessibility is relevant throughout the entire process of research, supported by many institutions, sources and tools, and it's absolutely vital to conducting ethical research. The more accessible our research, the more people we can reach. And if we ask more people, we get better answers.

Notes

[1] Available at: https://daisy.org
[2] Available at: www.accessiblebooksconsortium.org/portal/en/index.html

Further reading
Hayes, H., Buckland, S. and Tarpey, M. (2012) *INVOLVE: Briefing Notes for Researchers: Public Involvement in NHS, Public Health and Social Care Research*, NHS–NIHR (National Institute for Health Research). A good summary of all aspects of public involvement in research with guidance on what researchers need to consider at each stage.

Marlin, M.L. (2017) 'Accessibility at American Library Conferences', Paper presented at IFLA WLIC 2017, Wrocław, Poland, Libraries. Solidarity, Society in Session 72 – Library Services to People with Special Needs with Library serving persons with print disabilities. Available at: http://library.ifla.org/1821/1/072-marlin-en.pdf
An account of the historical accessibility concerns at American Library Association conferences, and the measures recommended by the Association's Accessibility taskforce.

UKRI (UK Research and Innovation)/ESRC (Economic and Social Research Council) (2020) 'Demonstrating support for impact in your research proposal.' Available at: https://esrc.ukri.org/research/impact-toolkit/developing-pathways-to-impact
Useful guidance on what funding bodies look for in research funding applications.

References
ABC (Accessible Books Consortium) (2011) *Accessible Publishing Best Practice Guidelines for Publishers*. Available at: www.accessiblebooksconsortium.org/publishing/en/accessible_best_practice_guidelines_for_publishers.html
ABC (2016) *Charter for Accessible Publishing*. Available at: www.accessiblebooksconsortium.org/portal/en/charter.html
ARC (Australian Research Council) (2018) *Engagement and Impact Assessment*, 2018–19, National Report. Available at: www.arc.gov.au/engagement-and-impact-assessment
Barnes, C. (2002) '"Emancipatory disability research": Project or process?', *Journal of Research in Special Educational Needs*, 2(1).
Boydell, K., Gladstone, B.M., Volpe, T., Allemang, B. and Stasiulis, E. (2012) 'The production and dissemination of knowledge: A scoping review of arts-based health research', *Forum Qualitative Sozialforschung/Forum: Qualitative Social Research*, 13(1).
Carrigan, M. (2019) *Social Media for Academics*, London: SAGE Publications Ltd.

Collin, J. and Clayton, A. (2018) 'Hidden voice: How to give voice to mothers of daughters with Turner syndrome', King's Cultural Community. Available at: www.kcl.ac.uk/cultural/projects/2016/ecr-hidden-voice

Coolidge, A., Doner, S., Robertson, T. and Gray, J. (2018) *Accessibility Toolkit* (2nd edn). Available at: https://opentextbc.ca/accessibilitytoolkit

Diagram Center (2013) *Accessible Image Sample Book*. Available at http://diagramcenter.wpengine.com/samplebook/index.xhtml

Farcas, S.B. (2017) *Disability and Theatre: A Practical Manual for Inclusion in the Arts*, London: Taylor & Francis.

Garbutt, R. (2009) 'Is there a place within academic journals for articles presented in an accessible format?', *Disability & Society*, 24(3), 357–71.

Gies, T., Boucherie, S., Narup, T., Wise, A. and Giudice, N.A. (2016) 'What goes unseen in accessible publishing: Good practice and remaining gaps', *European Science Editing*, 42(3), 66–9.

Goodley, D. and Moore, M. (2000) 'Doing disability research: Activist lives and the academy', *Disability & Society*, 15(6), 861–82.

Hayes, H., Buckland, S. and Tarpey, M. (2012) *INVOLVE: Briefing Notes for Researchers: Public Involvement in NHS, Public Health and Social Care Research*, NHS–NIHR (National Institute for Health Research).

Jenkinson, P. (2017) 'Social media accessibility and inclusion is a crucial consideration', *Access*, 31(3), 34–6.

Kara, H. (2015) *Creative Research Methods in the Social Sciences: A Practical Guide*, Bristol: Policy Press.

Keen, S. and Todres, L. (2007) 'Strategies for disseminating qualitative research findings: Three exemplars', *Forum: Qualitative Social Research*, 8(3), Article 17.

Lattner, K. (2016) 'Visualizations as Part of Accessible Conferences', in Proceedings of the 7th International Conference on Software Development and Technologies for Enhancing Accessibility and Fighting Info-exclusion, December, pp 182–7.

Mallett, R., Runswick-Cole, K. and Collingbourne, T. (2007) 'Guide for accessible research dissemination: Presenting research for everyone', *Disability & Society*, 22(2), 205–7.

Marks, T. (2019) '5318008.' Available at www.avmcuriosities.com/#/5318008

Ministry of Health (NZ) (2017) *New Zealand Health Research Strategy 2017–2027*. Available at: www.health.govt.nz/publication/new-zealand-health-research-strategy-2017-2027

NMPA (National Maternity and Perinatal Audit) (2019) *Clinical Report 2019*. Available at: https://maternityaudit.org.uk/FilesUploaded/NMPA%20Clinical%20Report%202019.pdf

Nordic Centre for Welfare and Social Issues (2016) 'Meetings for all', Disability Issues, 12 December. Available at: https://nordicwelfare.org/en/publikationer/meetings-for-all

ONS (Office for National Statistics) (2016) 'Case study: The Church of England', 26 January. Available at: www.ons.gov.uk/census/2011census/2011censusbenefits/howothersusecensusdata/thirdsectorandcommunitygroups/casestudythechurchofengland

Priego, E. (2016) 'Comics as research, comics for impact: The case of higher fees, higher debts', *The Comics Grid: Journal of Comics Scholarship*, 6, 16.

Rice, C. and Besse, K. (2020) 'How a radical form of accessibility is pushing the boundaries of theatre performance', *The Conversation*, 7 January. Available at https://theconversation.com/how-a-radical-form-of-accessibility-is-pushing-the-boundaries-of-theatre-performance-125797

Richardson, M. and Thompson, D. (2018) 'Deaf people and the theatrical public sphere', *Scottish Journal of Performance*, 5(2).

RNIB (2020) 'Making your social media accessible', 20 March. Available at: www.rnib.org.uk/rnibconnect/technology/making-your-social-media-accessible

Royston, S. and Siddique, A. (2020) *The Wrong Blazer 2020*, The Children's Society, March. Available at: www.childrenssociety.org.uk/what-we-do/resources-and-publications/the-wrong-blazer-report-2020

Sethfors, H. (2018) 'Accessible comics.' Available at: https://axesslab.com/accessible-comics

Shape (2020) 'How to put on an accessible exhibition.' Available at: www.shapearts.org.uk/news/accessible-curating

Tancock, C. (2020) 'In a nutshell: How to write a lay summary', Elsevier, 30 November. Available at: www.elsevier.com/connect/authors-update/in-a-nutshell-how-to-write-a-lay-summary

UKRI (UK Research and Innovation)/ESRC (Economic and Social Research Council) (2020) 'What is impact?' Available at: https://esrc.ukri.org/research/impact-toolkit/what-is-impact

UKRI/Research England (2020) 'Knowledge exchange framework (KEF).' Available at: https://re.ukri.org/knowledge-exchange/knowledge-exchange-framework

APPENDIX 1

Associations for people with disabilities based on profession or personal interest

We have collected a (by no means exhaustive) list of associations explicitly promoting the professional networking of disabled people to help you reach out to disabled professionals or special interest groups.

Where organisations are marked with ★ this indicates that in our judgement, and from what we can glean from their websites, they are primarily or exclusively run *by* disabled people; a missing ★ indicates either that this is a charity run *for* disabled people or that not enough information was available to make a determination.

Some professions have their own network of disabled members, although, if a profession does not appear in the list, this does not mean there are no resources.

There are often individual chapters or sections of an organisation, such as the Lawyers with Disabilities Division of the Law Society (UK) (www.lawsociety.org.uk/support-services/practice-management/diversity-inclusion/lawyers-with-disabilities-division). Note, however, that some may only be visible to those who are already members of the parent organisation.

Disabled parenting

- ★Disabled Parenting Project (US): https://disabledparenting.com
- Disability, Pregnancy & Parenthood (UK): https://disabledparentsnetwork.org.uk
- ★Family Network on Disabilities (US): https://fndusa.org

Teachers

- ★Disabled Teachers' Network (UK): https://disabledteachersnetwork.weebly.com/about.html

The arts

- *Deaf and Disabled People in TV:
  www.facebook.com/groups/1693347897634099
- *Disabled Writers (UK): https://disabledwriters.com
- Society for Disabled Artists (UK): www.societyfordisabledartists.org
- *Mouth and Foot Painting Artists (Ireland): www.mfpa.ie
- *FWD-Doc – documentary filmmakers with disabilities:
  www.fwd-doc.org/
- Tangled Art and Disability (Canada): https://tangledarts.org
- *The Deaf, Disability & Mad Arts Alliance of Canada (Canada):
  https://ddmaac.weebly.com

Healthcare professionals

- *Disabled Doctors Network (UK):
  www.disableddoctorsnetwork.com
- *Society for Healthcare Professionals with Disabilities (UK):
  www.disabilitysociety.org

General professionals and entrepreneurs

- *Association of Disabled Professionals (UK):
  www.adp.org.uk/about.php
- Disabled Entrepreneurs (UK): www.disabledentrepreneurs.co.uk
- PurpleSpace network hub (International): www.purplespace.org

Students

- In the UK, most universities have a local students with disabilities
  network (DSN), but at the point of writing there was no single
  umbrella organisation available as a point of contact.
- For the US, www.dreamcollegedisability.org/campus-clubs-and-
  organizations.html provides a list of campus-based organisations
  relating to disability and D/deafness.

APPENDIX 2

Disability-focused charities and organisations

In this appendix you find a selection of disability-focused charities you can contact for further information and guidance.

Organisations marked with ★ indicate that, in our judgement, and from what we can glean from their websites, they are primarily or exclusively run by disabled people; a missing ★ indicates either that this is a charity run for disabled people or that not enough information was available to make a determination.

UK

- ★Action for Deafness: www.actionfordeafness.org.uk
- ★Asian Disability Network: https://www.asiandisabilitynetwork.com
- ★Asian People's Disability Alliance (APDA): https://apda.org.uk
- ★Black Disabled People's Organisation, PO Box 1051, London, HA0 9HG, 07963 117 730, bdpauk@aol.com
- British Deaf Association: www.bda.org.uk
- ★Deaf Rainbow UK: http://deaflgbtiqa.org.uk
- ★Disability Rights UK: www.disabilityrightsuk.org
- ★Inclusion Scotland, Disabled People's Organisation: www.inclusionscotland.org
- Mind (Mental health): www.mind.org.uk
- National Association of Disabled Staff Networks: www.nadsn-uk.org
- ★OBAC (Organisation of Blind Africans & Caribbeans): www.obac.org.uk
- ★Regard (Disabled LGBTQ): http://regard.org.uk
- ★Royal National institute of Blind People (RNIB):[1] www.rnib.org.uk
- Scope (Disability equality charity): www.scope.org.uk
- ★Sisters of Frida (Disabled Women): www.sisofrida.org
- ★Spinal Injuries Association: www.spinal.co.uk

Ireland

- ★ABLEize: www.ableize.com
- Disability Federation of Ireland:
  www.disability-federation.ie/about/overview.html

USA

- ★Autistic Self-Advocacy Network: https://autisticadvocacy.org
- ★College Diabetes Network:
  https://collegediabetesnetwork.org/find-a-chapter
- ★Eye to Eye National, organisation run by and for people with learning and attention issues: https://eyetoeyenational.org
- National Disability Rights Network: www.ndrn.org
- National Wheelchair Basketball Association (NWBA): www.nwba.org
- Native American Disability Law Center:
  www.nativedisabilitylaw.org/resources
- US Access Board, independent federal agency: www.access-board.gov

Australia

- ★Australian Federation of Disability Organisations (AFDO):
  www.afdo.org.au
- Australian Network on Disability (AND): www.and.org.au
- ★First Peoples Disability Network Australia: https://fpdn.org.au
- ★Blind Citizens Australia (BCA): www.bca.org.au
- ★Deaf Australia: https://deafaustralia.org.au
- Deafblind Australia (DBA): www.deafblind.org.au
- Deafness Forum of Australia: www.deafnessforum.org.au
- Disability Advocacy Network Australia (DANA): www.dana.org.au
- National Disability Services (NDS): www.nds.org.au
- ★National Ethnic Disability Alliance (NEDA): www.neda.org.au
- ★People With Disability Australia (PWDA): https://pwd.org.au
- ★Physical Disability Australia: www.pda.org.au
- ★Women With Disabilities Australia (WWDA):
  https://wwda.org.au

Canada

- British Columbia Aboriginal Network on Disability Society (BCANDS): www.bcands.bc.ca

- ★Council of Canadians with Disabilities (CCD): www.ccdonline.ca/en
- ★Disabled Women's Network (DAWN) of Canada: www.dawncanada.net
- Little People of Canada: www.littlepeopleofcanada.com
- Multiple Sclerosis (MS) Society of Canada: https://mssociety.ca

New Zealand

- ★Disabled Persons Assembly NZ: www.dpa.org.nz
- Life Unlimited: www.lifeunlimited.net.nz
- New Zealand Disability Support Network (NZDSN): https://nzdsn.org.nz
- Whakapi Hauora Charitable Trust: www.whakapaihauora.maori. nz/information/maori-disability-support-services-i-6.html

Other international organisations

- Disability Council International (DisabCouncil): https://disabilitycouncilinternational.org
- ★Disabled Peoples' International (DPI): www.dpi.org
- ★International Disability Alliance: www.internationaldisabilityalliance.org
- ★European Disability Forum (EDF): www.edf-feph.org
- ★Inclusion International: https://inclusion-international.org
- International Disability and Development Consortium (IDDC): www.iddcconsortium.net

Note

[1] Run *with* disabled people, although it does not appear to be run primarily *by* disabled people.

APPENDIX 3

Checking accessibility yourself

Most academic projects are either managed on a sub-site of their own institution, where the site design is covered by legislation on making public service content accessible, or on a service such as WordPress, where much of the way the design is presented is managed on your behalf.

If you know little about the technical aspects of web accessibility and don't want to or don't have the time to learn, these are the two simplest options for research project site hosting. You will still need to ensure that content presented on the site is accessible (for example, that images have alternative text) by following the suggestions given in Chapters 7, 8 and 9.

Checklists

If you are running your own website, you will need to check that the pages, as well as the content, are accessible. A summary is available at: https://webaim.org/standards/wcag/checklist

You will need to comply with the guidelines and conformance level that your funder or institution recommends (WCAG 2.0, WCAG 2.1). Check if your institution offers tools; the better tools cost money, and they may be able to give free or discounted access.

Software tools checking aspects of web accessibility

Accessibility Viewer, checks compliance with W3C Web Content Accessibility Guidelines (WCAG) 2.0, Section 508, and US federal procurement standards:
https://developer.paciellogroup.com/resources/aviewer
Accessibility Checker, checks compliance with W3C Web Content Accessibility Guidelines (WCAG) 2.0, W3C Web Content Accessibility Guidelines (WCAG) 1.0, Section 508, US federal procurement standards, BITV, Italian accessibility legislation, Stanca Act and German government standards:
https://achecker.ca/checker/index.php

HTML CodeSniffer, checks compliance with Web Content Accessibility Guidelines (WCAG) 2.0, and the web-related components of the US Section 508 legislation. Paste your HTML code in to have it checked; also offers bookmarklet, that is, browser extensions: http://squizlabs.github.io/HTML_CodeSniffer

JavaScript Bookmarklets for Accessibility Testing, checks compliance with W3C Web Content Accessibility Guidelines (WCAG) 2.0, Section 508, and US federal procurement standard: http://pauljadam.com/bookmarklets

Checking colour contrast

A quick and dirty way to check whether colour combinations are easy to read is to print out the document (or a screenshot of the document) in black and white, and see whether it is still easy to read. Custom tools use an algorithm to calculate whether the contrast has reached minimum acceptable levels.

- WebAim Contrast Checker: http://webaim.org/resources/contrastchecker
- Colour Contrast Analyser: www.paciellogroup.com/resources/contrastanalyser

Browser extensions

Axe extension for Chrome browser, Web Content Accessibility Guidelines (WCAG) 2.0 and Section 508 accessibility: https://chrome.google.com/webstore/detail/axe/lhdoppojpmngadmnindnejefpokejbdd

PDF checker

CommonLook PDF Accessibility, for testing and adjusting PDF documents for accessibility (commercial software, but demo can be requested): https://commonlook.com/accessibility-software/commonlook-pdf-globalaccess

Screen readers

Screen readers may offer insight into how your website or content is interpreted.

- Job Access With Speech (JAWS): http://webaim.org/articles/jaws, JAWS Screen Reading Software: www.freedomscientific.com/downloads/jaws/jaws-downloads.asp
- Non-Visual Desk Access (NVDA): http://webaim.org/articles/nvda
- VoiceOver: http://webaim.org/articles/voiceover

Using a screen reader as a sighted person does not mimic the experience of a person with low vision, but it may help show how screen readers deliver content. Increasing numbers of dyslexic people are also using screen readers as a way to access text content without having to read it, which considerably enlarges the audience.

Standards

As mentioned in this book, most governments have a legal requirement for buildings and services to be accessible, and the interpretation of what this means refers to guidelines and standards. Although standards in many English-speaking countries are broadly similar, there are different national and international standards bodies that develop standards for accessible digital content, the most well known of which is the Web Accessibility Initiative (WAI), which produces the Web Content Accessibility Guidelines (WCAG), giving standards of digital accessibility. Some governments refer back to the WAI standards as a requirement for their own digital content, although others have developed their own.

The Accessible **Canada** Act passed into law in 2019, and Accessibility Standards Canada is the standards-making body that translates this into practice. WCAG 2.0 is currently the accepted standard for digital content: https://accessible.canada.ca

Ireland's National Disability Authority maintains the Irish National IT Accessibility Guidelines: http://universaldesign.ie/Technology-ICT/Irish-National-IT-Accessibility-Guidelines

The **New Zealand** government has produced its own guidance, the New Zealand Web Accessibility Standard 1.1: www.digital.govt.nz/standards-and-guidance/design-and-ux/accessibility

As well as referring to WAI, the **UK** government applies additional standards to public sector bodies, arguing that they should operate to a higher access standard than other organisations because everyone has to use them: www.gov.uk/guidance/accessibility-requirements-for-public-sector-websites-and-apps

The **EU** Web Accessibility Directive (2016) aimed to harmonise legislation on accessibility across member states, and the European Accessibility Act sets out how this should be implemented. The EU is developing its own set of standards: https://ec.europa.eu/social/main.jsp?catId=1485&langId=en

The **International Organization for Standardization** (ISO) released a set of digital accessibility standards in 2019: ISO 30071-1 Code of practice for creating accessible ICT products and services: www.iso.org/news/ref2351.html

Web Content Accessibility Guidelines (WCAG) 2.1 are summarised in: www.w3.org/WAI/standards-guidelines/wcag/glance

APPENDIX 4

Text relay services

Text relay services offer text-to-speech and speech-to-text services for d/Deaf, hard-of-hearing or speech-impaired users. They can relay a text message or talk to a sign language interpreter via video; this message is then forwarded as a voice message. Alternatively, other users can relay a voice message that is being either forwarded as a text message or translated into the equivalent sign language.

UK

Text Relay Service: this service is currently only provided through BT, and regulated through Ofcom:

- When calling from a regular phone to someone using textphone: 18002
- When calling from a textphone: 18001.

Ireland

- Irish Text Relay Service requires downloading an app: www.itrs.ie

Australia

National Relay Service:

- Voice Relay number: 1300 555 727
- TTY number: 133 677
- SMS relay number: 0423 677 767.

Canada

- Video Relay Service: https://srvcanadavrs.ca/en
- A Message Relay Service can be accessed by TTY users via the number 7-1-1; other users may access the service via 1-800-855-0511.

USA

Telecommunications Relay Service:

- ASCII (American Standard Code for Information Interchange), relays typed text: (800) 877-8339 TTY
- VCO (Voice Carry Over), relays spoken text: (877) 877-6280
- Speech-to-Speech, revoices and relays spoken text from people with speech disabilities: (877) 877-8982
- Voice, relays spoken text from hearing users: (866) 377-8642
- TeleBraille, relays text in Braille: (866) 893-8340.

New Zealand

New Zealand Relay:

- Hearing Carry Over/Voice Carry Over/Voice to Text-Relay: 0800 4711 711
- Speech-to-Speech: 0800 8715 715
- Video Relay Service:
  - Deaf callers: Skype usernames nzvis01, nzvis02, nzvis03, nzvis04, nzvis05
  - Hearing callers: 08004 877877.

APPENDIX 5

Tagging languages in a document

This appendix gives a short explanation on how to mark whole documents or specific sections of a document as being in a particular language. Doing so helps other applications (screen readers, text-to-voice apps and so on) to more accurately read the structure and content of the document.

PDF: setting the language for an entire document

- Navigate to <u>File</u>, then <u>Properties ...</u>, and then select the <u>Advanced</u> tab.
- In the <u>Reading Options</u> section, you can then select a language in the <u>Language</u> picklist.

PDF: tagging a section of a document as a different language

This is only available in Adobe Acrobat Pro.

- To be able to tag individual sections, you first need to show the <u>Tag</u> pane. To do so, navigate to <u>View</u>, then <u>Show/Hide</u>, then <u>Navigation Panes</u>, and then select <u>Tags</u>.
- Navigate to the regular view of the document (close the thumbnail view if it is open).
- Select the text you want to tag and click the <u>Tag</u> icon (it looks like a shopping label). Right-click on the highlighted text and select <u>Find Tag from Selection</u>.
- Right-click and select <u>Properties ...</u>
- In the <u>Tag</u> tab, select the correct language from the <u>Language</u> picklist.

Word: setting the language for an entire document

- Navigate to <u>File</u>, then <u>Options</u> and select the <u>Language</u> tab.
- You can set the document language under <u>Set Proofing Language</u>.

Word: tagging a section of a document as a different language

- Select the text you want to tag.
- Navigate to the <u>Review</u> tab at the top of the document.
- Click the <u>Language</u> button, select <u>Language</u> and then <u>Set Proofing Language</u>.

APPENDIX 6

Encrypting documents

General IT safety advice

- If you send a password-protected file, send the password in a separate email or by text; sending both together defeats the purpose of the password.
- Pick good passwords. Avoid 'Password', '123456', 'abcdefg' and so on. At a bare minimum, change the default password set on devices you own or use, and try not to reuse existing passwords.
- Keep track of your passwords, but preferably not on a Post-it Note on your desk.
- There are excellent apps that suggest strong passwords and that can help you keep track of your passwords.
- The steps listed below are a first, simple approach to protecting documents, but they don't necessarily provide strong protection. Your IT department will likely be very happy to advise you on further measures you can take to protect you and your participants' data.

Encrypting Microsoft Office documents (for example Word, Excel, PowerPoint)

- Navigate to File, then the Information tab.
- Click the button Protect Document.
- Select the Option Encrypt with Password and enter the password you want to use. Make a note of that password in a safe place!

Encrypting PDF documents

- Navigate to File, then to Properties ...
- Select the Security tab.
- In the Document Security section, go to the picklist Security Method and change it to Password Security.
- This opens the Password Security – Settings tab.

- Select <u>Require a password to open the document</u> and enter the password. The progress bar will indicate the strength of the chosen password. Make a note of that password in a safe place!

Index

Index

recruitment (continued)
checklist 52
communication of accessibility
92–4, 103
communication of purpose and
benefit of research 102–3
confidentiality and anonymity 106
dealing with mistakes 95–6
diverse channels 43, 94–5
expert knowledge 96
immunocompromised participants
104–5, 106
microaggressions 95
payment 105
reviewing the process 107–8
routes of communication 97
see also sampling
reference/advisory groups 56–7, 76,
184, 204
reflexivity 26, 47–8, 53–5, 75–6, 171
relational model 22
reliability (sampling) 78
representativeness 9, 39, 78–9
research (general)
ethics 26–8
impact of research 184–5, 193–7
participation 7–12
quality of 73–5
summary of approaches 28–30
Universal Design (UD) 31–3
with or on disabled people 25–6
see also accessible research design;
dissemination of research
see also individual research methods
research design *see* accessible research
design
research impact *see* impact of research
research-informed teaching 193
research question 40–3
research relationship 25–6, 28, 47–8,
56
researcher
attitudes of 49–51
disabled 91
reflexivity 26, 47–8, 53–5

relationship with participants 25–6,
28, 47–8, 56
safety of 123–4
resonance of research 75
respondent validation 57, 73, 76
Reynolds, J.M. 58
risk 167–8
Ritz, S.F. 13
Royal National Institute of Blind
People (RNIB) 99

S

sample size 46–7
sampling 69–88
and bias 1, 79, 80–6
issues with 71–2
mitigation strategies 86–7
non-probability sampling 83–6
probability sampling 79–82, 85
and qualitative methods 69–77
and quantitative methods 78–87
representativeness 9, 39, 78–9
sample size 46–7
Scharff, D.P. 46
screen readers 98, 143, 154, 199,
216–17
secondary data 53, 172
security of data 106, 150–1, 223–4
semantic coding 141
Shields, N. 74
sign language 23–4, 127, 131, 132,
149, 157, 189, 219
simple random sampling 80
Skloot, R. 46
SMS for data collection 147–8
snowball sampling 70, 71, 83
social media, dissemination of research
198–9
social model 4–5, 21–2, 32
stereotypes 50, 58
stigma 21, 23, 33, 50, 55, 95
stimulus materials 135
Story, M.F. 32
stratified sampling 70, 82